ITALIAN DESIGN

ITALIAN DESIGN

1870 TO THE PRESENT

PENNY SPARKE

THAMES AND HUDSON

PICTURE CREDITS

First published in the UK in 1988 by
Thames and Hudson Ltd, London

ISBN 0–500–23531–7

This book was designed and produced by
JOHN CALMANN AND KING LTD, LONDON

Designed by Newell and Sorrell Design Ltd and Matthew Ward
Picture Research by Julia Engelhardt
Typeset by Fakenham Photosetting Ltd, Norfolk
Printed in Italy by Graphicom SrL

To the memory of my father

ACKNOWLEDGMENTS

In preparing this book I would like to thank staff and students at the Royal College of Art, London, who have helped me develop many of my thoughts about Italian design over the last few years; to John Styles and Jonathan Zeitlin for introducing me to ideas about the complex nature of Italian industry; to numerous friends in Italy – among them Ettore Sottsass, Michele De Lucchi and George Sowden – who have helped enormously over the years; to Julia Engelhardt for finding such exceptional illustrations; to Jane Havell for patient editing; and to John and Molly for putting up with me while the book was being written.

Penny Sparke

Half-title: "ET Personal 55" electronic typewriter, designed by Mario Bellini and manufactured by Olivetti in 1987.
Frontispiece: "Andrea" chaise longue in wood, tubular steel, fibreglass and sheepskin, designed by Andrea Branzi and manufactured by Memphis in 1987.

INTRODUCTION
7

INTRODUCTION

If other countries have had a theory of design, Italy has had a philosophy of design, maybe even an ideology.

Umberto Eco, 1986[1]

Twentieth-century Italian design is only one facet of the cultural, political, social and economic story of modern Italy. The stylish, mass-produced pieces of furniture, decorative household goods, electrical appliances, office equipment, cars and, latterly, designer clothes and accessories that have earned Italy such a key position in the world of contemporary material culture are, in essence, a mirror of that country's bid for modernity and of its struggle, through this century, to establish itself as one of the modern industrial nations.

In achieving this ambition Italy has evolved a unique approach towards the practice, the aesthetic and the theory of design which depends, only minimally, upon models borrowed from elsewhere. As one of Italy's leading critics and theorists of design, Gillo Dorfles, explained in 1986: "Here we have experienced the development of our own objects industrially made to native Italian design and therefore more original and more imaginative than those of other industrialized countries."[2] Unlike Japan, for instance, which learned its lessons about design through years of careful imitation, Italy was, from the outset, more determined to discover a new formula for its particular marriage between art and industry.

It owes this achievement to a number of factors, among them the support of such powerful and far-sighted industrial patrons as the Olivetti company; Italy's deep-seated need to

Left: "Selene" side chair, designed by Vico Magistretti and produced by Artemide in 1966. Magistretti began work on this elegant, all-plastic chair in 1961. At first he conceived it in reinforced polyester but this was changed in favour of ABS plastic. Its curved forms, designed with the problems of fabrication and strength in mind, helped establish a new Italian aesthetic for plastic goods.

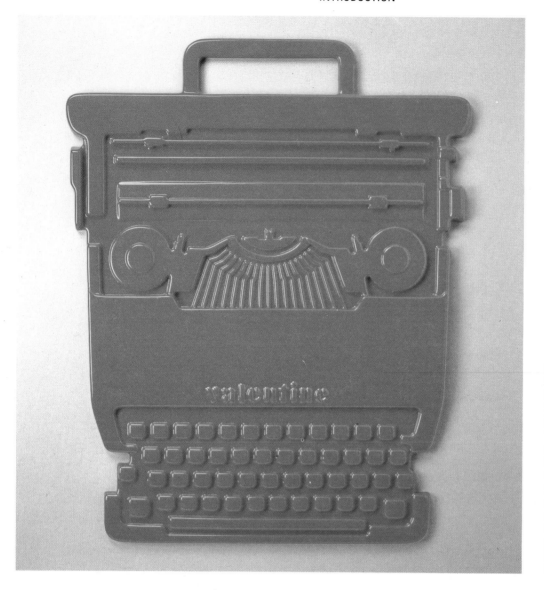

Left: Bas relief moulding of the "Valentine" typewriter, designed by Ettore Sottsass for Olivetti in 1969. The Olivetti company has been a constant force in twentieth-century design, sponsoring innovative products as well as integrating design with all its activities, from publicity material to homes for its workforce. A number of leading Italian designers, including Marcello Nizzoli and Mario Bellini as well as Sottsass, have been closely associated with the company and have received much support from it. Their creations have established Olivetti designs among Italy's most memorable icons.

Right: Mirror, entitled "(For Girls) Looking at Yourself like a Temple Prostitute", designed by Ettore Sottsass for an exhibition at the Blum Helman gallery, New York, in 1987. Following his experimental projects for the Memphis group exhibitions of the early 1980s, Sottsass went on to design a range of domestic objects that exploited the monumental and textural qualities of marble. This piece juxtaposes that ancient material with startling pastel colours, thus providing a link between the culture of the past and the culture of the present.

ally design with the dramatic transformations in its political scene (and the sustained debate about the ideological meaning in design which this brought with it); the special nature of Italian industrialization, which has respected craft traditions while implementing new systems of mass production; and the creative geniuses of the small cluster of Italian architect-designers whose names have become synonymous with the concept of modern Italian design.

It is this last factor, however, which is the most significant in highlighting the special contribution of Italy to the general story of modern design in this century. While, on one level, everything that is made and used in Italy has (as in any other country) been designed, whether in a modern or in a traditional idiom, and can therefore justifiably be called "Italian design", the more specific, and more generally understood, definition of the concept – and the one with which this book is

primarily concerned – relates to what the writer and critic Umberto Eco has called "identified design". This is best understood by contrasting it with the other two types of design he also isolates and which he dubs "anonymous" and "non-conscious", examples of which include coffee-machines and farmers' tools respectively. "Identified design", defined by Eco, is, in contrast to these other two categories, "design which is the outcome of an expressed theory and of a practice in which the object aims to exemplify explicitly its author's theory". He cites the work of the car designer, Battista Pininfarina, as an example of this phenomenon.

Eco places the emphasis firmly on the self-conscious intentions of the "author" or "designer". His thesis is derived from the so-called "auteur" theory, evolved within the context of film criticism, which distinguishes between the self-conscious "high culture" film and the more spontaneous

"mass culture" film which expresses, unselfconsciously, the values and aspirations of mass society as a whole. The evolution in Italy of a selfconscious "high culture" design movement, which coexists alongside design within the more banal production and consumption of goods, is what has earned Italy its special place within the world of contemporary material culture. Inevitably, however, "identified", "anonymous" and "non-conscious" types of design have not evolved completely independently of each other, and there are many overlaps between them.

Other characteristics also differentiate this special concept of Italian design from the broader definition of the term, however, which Eco has neglected to point out. These relate, primarily, to its ideological function as a purveyor of Italian nationalistic values and its important role within the international economy. Not only does it depend upon a sophisticated, theoretical framework, and a number of thinking protagonists, it also has a special economic role to play within the world as a whole. In fact the modern Italian design movement originated in, and is still today largely restricted to, the wealthy industrial cities of the north, particularly Milan and Turin. It came into its own, in the years after 1945, as part of Italy's need to penetrate new, foreign markets, and to become established as a viable economic, industrial and cultural power within the modern industrialized world. As such, while modern Italian design owed its origins to specifically Italian conditions, and displayed visual traits that have been described as particularly "Italian" in character (Italy's rich artistic heritage is frequently mentioned in this context), its effects were greater outside Italy. Its special role was to provide a national image within the context of international trade and culture. Thus most modern Italian design was (except in the very early stages of its evolution) "design for export", and as such its influence on the greater part of Italian society was, and is, minimal. From the early 1960s onwards its impact was felt most strongly in the wealthy quarters of London, Paris, New York and Tokyo. Thus, while the production of Italian design is inextricably linked to the economic, social and cultural context of modern Italy, its consumption is not.

Below: Stainless steel cooking equipment made by Lagostina in simple, elegant, yet highly utilitarian forms – although of contemporary manufacture, they have remained essentially unchanged since the years between the wars. They represent an important aspect of Italian design in this century: "anonymous", rather than selfconscious and individualized. Countless pieces of metal household goods – *oggetti casalinghi* – have retained their forms in this way for several decades.

However, this definition of Italian design, while providing the focus for this account, does not explain Italy's extraordinary success in evolving such stunning forms for its objects, and in encouraging the emergence of a post-war generation of "super-star" designers. It is clearly not enough to suggest, as many have, that Italy's past achievements in the areas of architecture and the decorative arts account for its contemporary successes in the world of industrial design, although this rich cultural heritage may well be a contributory factor. And it does not explain the industrial and commercial successes of contemporary Italy which are intrinsic parts of the phenomenon that provides the focus for this study. Ironically, while Italy has a highly refined industrial design culture,

it does not have an industrial design educational system worth speaking of. Nearly all the members of the group of designers who began practising as independent designers of interiors and industrial goods immediately following the Second World War were trained as architects before the war. Graduates, for the most part, of the polytechnics of Milan and Turin, which had become two of the most powerful centres of architectural training in these years, they emerged from the war to find a dearth of architectural projects and the possibility of earning a living only from the wealthy northern clients who commissioned them to design the interiors of their private dwellings. Thus interior design, along with exhibition design, which was growing in strength as a means by which

Above: "Cumano" tables, designed by Achille Castiglioni and manufactured by Zanotta in 1979. The little metal garden tables, inspired by an anonymous nineteenth-century example, folded flat and could be hung on the wall for storage. Available in striking colours, they turned a "ready-made" artefact into a "designer object".

Italy could show the rest of the world where its creative talents lay, played an important role, allowing the architects to establish themselves in independent professional practices and providing an outlet for their as yet untested skills.

The real breakthrough, however, came with the growing desire of the consumer goods manufacturers – some already established, others newly formed – to modernize their products; they turned to the architects as the obvious people to do this for them. Strong relationships developed from these initial liaisons and quite quickly the architects were transformed into "designers for industry", acquiring their training for this position very speedily on the factory floor and in the boardroom. The relatively small scale of most Italian manufacturing concerns permitted the designers easy access to all stages of production and they were in direct communication with the management, often the members of the family which owned the company in question.

The emphasis on "styling" over technological sophistication, as the way Italian goods were promoted abroad, meant that the designers needed to have only a rudimentary knowledge of the technical aspects of the manufacturing process. Trained, as they mostly were, within the tradition of architectural Rationalism (the Italian equivalent of the Modern Movement in architecture and design), they were, however, enthusiastic about the use of new materials and adept at finding new forms to suit them.

Above: Mario Bellini's "Il Colonnato" table, manufactured by Cassina in 1977. The structure of this "classical" design, with its three marble columns and top, depends entirely on the weight of the material employed. It is available in square or round versions; in 1980 a smaller coffee-table was added to the range.

tended beyond the process of visualization into the production and marketing of goods. In the Italian industrial design movement the production processes often dictated the forms of the finished products.

Most of the architects who moved into this new arena retained their professional independence, continuing to work from small offices in Milan and Turin, and many of them took on consultancy work from a number of companies simultaneously. As the reputation of Italy as a manufacturer of sophisticated modern products continued to grow in the postwar decades, so the names of designers became increasingly well known, and by the 1980s a cluster of "super-star" designers – a handful of them now in their sixties, and a few more in their forties and fifties – had achieved widespread renown and had come to be much in demand worldwide. They earned their reputations not only by means of the design labels to which their names were attached, but also through the sophisticated network of design promotional activities – mainly exhibitions, awards and publications – which had grown up in Italy in the years since 1945, and which helped enormously to propagate the reputations of both Italian design and designers.

The continued close links between manufacturing industry and design in Italy since the Second World War has meant that the culture of design that emerged in that country has been associated with a particular range of products. These have been emphasized to the detriment of other possible areas of design which have been largely underdeveloped. Thus while in the pre-war years there were signs that graphic design – posters, packaging, book design and typography – was part of the emerging modern design movement in Italy, this faded from view after the war, and the emphasis swung instead in two different directions: on the one hand, towards the products of the revitalized traditional applied art industries, which aimed their goods at the domestic arena; and, on the other, towards the products of the new industries – electrical appliances, cars and office equipment. Design in Italy, in the present-day sense, became increasingly associated with three-dimensional products, most of them aimed at the domestic context. Given the architectural backgrounds of

The companies, keen to provide an exclusive, highly sophisticated image for their goods on the export markets, not only used the designers to evolve new forms for their products, and to help them rationalize their production systems, but also attached their names to their goods, in imitation of the current practice in fashion design, as a means of individualizing their mass-manufactured products and of injecting a form of "added value" into them. Quite quickly the old-fashioned concept of "applied art", a traditional practice in the decorative art industries – ceramics, glass and metalwork – that implied the addition of an aesthetic surface, or a decorative form, on to a product, was replaced by the much more integrated concept of "industrial design", which ex-

Above: Advertisement for Campari by Marcello Nizzoli, 1926. Nizzoli's early career in graphic design provided him with an opportunity of assimilating European avant-garde artistic ideas. The striking use of perspective in this *tableau vivant* proved highly effective in a commercial context. From this background in two-dimensional art Nizzoli became one of Olivetti's most prominent product designers.

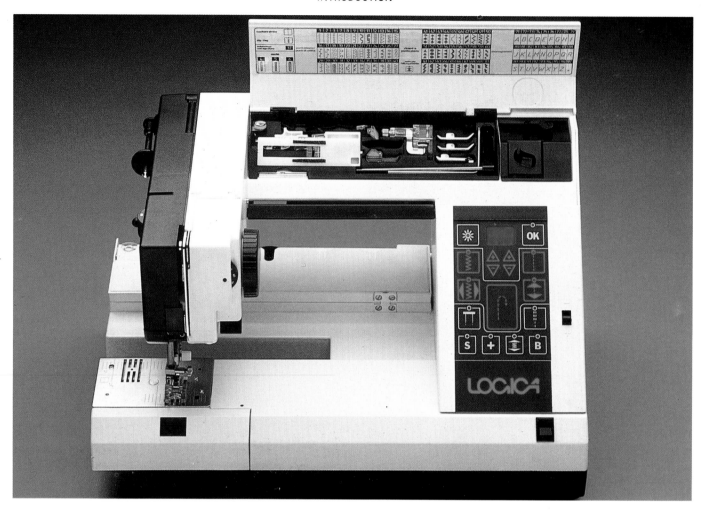

Above: "Logica" sewing machine designed by Giorgio Giugiaro for Necchi, 1982. Best known for his automobile designs, Giugiaro also ventured into product design in the 1980s. The sharp contours of this high-tech sewing machine, which boasted electronic programming, represented a move away from the more sculptural aesthetic of earlier decades. Giugiaro wanted to improve the machine's ease of operation rather than turn it into "art".

most of the designers involved, and the particular strengths within Italian manufacturing industry at this time, this was an inevitable formula and one that was sustained throughout the post-war period. Single projects – architecture and interiors – and two-dimensional design areas, such as graphics and textiles, failed to move into the centre of the picture, in spite of a flurry of activity in the latter area in the 1950s. In addition, those areas of the traditional decorative arts that did not respond to the new technological stimuli also played a decreasingly important role as the post-war years progressed. Furniture, on the other hand, went from strength to strength, its designers grasping with enthusiasm the possibilities offered by the new materials, plastics in particular; by the 1980s it had become one of the most vital symbols of the modern Italian design movement. Meanwhile fashion design, a relative latecomer to the scene, emerged in the 1970s to become a key area in that and the subsequent decade. It

Left: Drawing for the "Sinvola" table lamp by Michele De Lucchi for Studio Alchymia in 1980. The "knitting needle" lamp consciously employed imagery from the 1950s, not for nostalgic reasons, but as a reflection of the contemporary "banal" environment.

Below: Bathroom equipment designed by Achille Castiglioni and manufactured by Ideal Standard in 1971. A skilful manipulation of abstract forms provided an elegant solution to the problem of making such utilitarian objects look both functional and attractive.

found its strength in the emergence of the concept of ready-to-wear clothing, which joined the earlier emphasis on the more exclusive haute-couture movement. Also, along with furniture, the production of fashion garments and accessories (the latter a traditional area of craft production in a country that has long been known for its high-quality leather goods – shoes and handbags in particular) was ideally suited to the small-scale design-led industries from which Italy derived its economic strength.

This special definition of design, along with the forces that sustain it and the product emphases outlined above, determine the main content of this study of modern Italian design. The story of Italian design in this century – the years up to 1939 being essentially formative in nature – is not, therefore, merely the aesthetic tale that it might seem at first sight. It is a much more complex matter, requiring a general discussion of the transformations of the Italian economy and of the

Below: "Marille" pasta, designed by Giorgio Giugiaro for Voiello in 1983. Taking designer culture into the area of food, Giugiaro created a shape that resisted being broken while boiling and that trapped and retained the maximum amount of sauce.

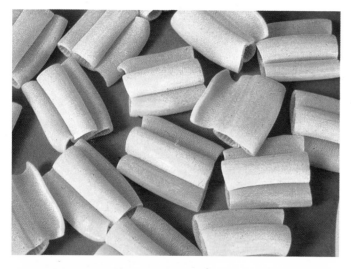

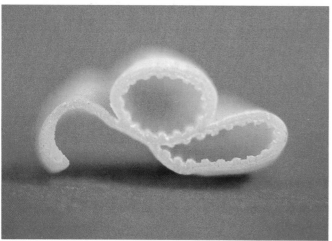

political status quo, as well as a more detailed examination of the life stories of individual designers and their attitudes towards their work. Ultimately, perhaps, the most important factor within the particular picture of modern Italian design to emerge in this study is the continued level of debate that has, since the ideological discussions of the 1930s, underpinned design activity in Italy, provided much of the energy behind it and richness within it, and made it an important aspect of contemporary Italian culture as a whole.

In spite of the disillusionment experienced by many designers in the late 1960s and 1970s, who became aware of the possibility that the laws of politics and the economy might be at odds with their idealism, the idea has survived that modern design and democracy go hand in hand: in the early 1980s it was still the main motivating force behind many of the new design manifestations. This sense of commitment has been linked to the progress of Italian design since 1945, re-emerging like a leitmotif through the years.

There is a feeling today, however, that the level of debate is disappearing and that design idealism is increasingly being replaced by a more pragmatic approach. As many historians of modern Italy have been at pains to point out, the country has been in a state of permanent crisis since 1945: design seems to have flourished as a symptom of that unstable state of affairs. But in the late 1980s the forty-year period of crisis and cultural growth that followed the end of the war has drawn to a close. This is confirmed, perhaps, by the fact that the final "Vespa" motor-scooter – that potent symbol of post-Fascist democracy and hope for the future of post-war Italian society, designed in 1946 and in production for forty years – came off the Piaggio lines in 1987. Now seems a good moment, therefore, to look back at that period and to assess its meaning and its importance in the world of contemporary design and culture.

Below: "Vespa" motor-scooters leave the Piaggio factory in 1949. Designed by Corradino D'Ascanio, whose previous experience had been in helicopter design, the "Vespa" was launched in 1946. With its streamlined body-shell it provided a highly novel and aggressively modern addition to the post-war landscape in Italy, and quickly became a potent symbol of a new democratic lifestyle. It remained in continuous production until 1987.

CHAPTER 4

1870–1914

TOWARDS A MODERN ITALY

INDUSTRY AND
THE NEW NATION-STATE

The fusion of art and industry came late to Italy, compared with Great Britain, Germany and the USA. In spite of its rich artistic heritage, which crossed the barriers that so frequently separate the fine from the applied arts, Italy was backward in developing an industrial culture that could benefit from its sophisticated artistic achievements.

One reason for this tardiness lay in the relative economic disarray of the new nation-state that emerged in the early 1860s. The prolonged efforts of the *risorgimento* – the movement towards unification – had led to the emergence of a country that was, in theory at least, ruled by a central government, but which had a long way to go in order to be able to compete economically, technologically, and industrially with its European neighbours.

In the last decades of the nineteenth century Italy depended for survival upon its agriculture. In 1871, the year following the occupation of Rome which completed the process of unification, 60 per cent of the Italian workforce worked on the land and the majority of the population was, inevitably, a rural one. Most of the industry that existed at that time was domestic in nature; clothing, furniture and many other small goods were manufactured, and food was processed, at home. The few urban artisans who existed tended to work on a casual basis, retaining a small plot of land in the country. The building trade began to expand at

Left: Artist's impression of the Ansaldo steelworks in Genoa around the turn of the century. Along with Breda and Fiat, Ansaldo was one of the largest manufacturers in Italy and a major source of employment for immigrants from the south. The metal industries, steel in particular, were among Italy's key concerns whose "centralized" production was vital to the country's programme of industrial expansion.

Far right: Italy in 1850, before unification, when it was ruled by a number of different masters. Until 1814 Napoleon had held sway over the entire country; then the Austrians controlled most of northern Italy and the Bourbons the south, while Rome was in the hands of the Papacy. In 1861, King Victor Emmanuel II of Piedmont and Sardinia came to rule most of the peninsula and the kingdom of Italy began to achieve unity for the first time.

Right: Ploughing with oxen in Lombardy in the early 1900s. While the urban centres of northern Italy were subject to rapid industrialization in the first decade of the century, the south of the country, and the rural areas of the north, remained primarily agricultural. Not until after the Second World War did the balance shift in favour of industry as the occupation of the majority of working Italians.

Above: A little girl spins in the streets of Prato at the turn of the century. Most of Italy's traditional industries at this time were organized on an artisanal, small-scale, family-run basis, particularly in the applied arts – ceramics, glass, textiles. Mechanization was soon to influence textiles, however, and production of silk, cotton and wool developed rapidly in the vicinity of Como.

this time to accommodate the construction boom of the 1880s and provided a lucrative form of casual labour for workers who moved seasonally between the town and the country. Textile manufacturing, namely, the production of silk, cotton and woollen fabrics, was a workshop industry employing large numbers of women and children. A decade later cotton production was to become increasingly mechanized but silk manufacture went into decline.

In spite of the dominant role of agriculture Italy could boast an industrial tradition, as those goods that fell within the "applied art" sector had had a long and healthy lifespan on Italian soil. Ceramics, glass and furniture had long been manufactured in Italy, albeit on a highly regional, and craft-workshop, basis: for several centuries local manufacturers had supplied both the peasantry and the aristocracy with these goods. However, the skilled labour necessary for such production came under threat with the abolition of the guild system in the last decades of the nineteenth century.

One of Italy's present-day industrial strengths lies in the fact that, in many areas of production, the evolution from workshop to factory was never fully completed. This was particularly true in the applied arts where regionalism, hand work and small-scale operations prevailed into the twentieth

Above: Artist's impression of the Ansaldo steelworks in about 1900. Ansaldo's steel went mainly into the rapidly expanding ship-building industry, and the company was responsible for major achievements in naval engineering.

century. The last decades of the nineteenth century were characterized, however, by a great degree of specialization and cooperation, and a national market began to emerge alongside local ones.

However, in addition to the workshop and traditional applied arts industries, by the 1880s there were signs that Italy was becoming increasingly aware of the need to develop "new industries" in imitation of those that featured strongly within the "industrial revolutions" of Europe and the USA. Keen both to compete with these countries and to show a commitment to progress, the Italian government poured funds into the development of a new power source, electricity, and into the engineering and metal industries. Concentrated in the north of Italy, in the industrial triangle which covered Piedmont, Lombardy and Liguria, iron- and steel-making developed steadily through the 1880s, and the manufacture of objects of transportation, principally railway stock and ships, grew rapidly as a result. Funded by the state, which had primarily military ends in sight, the Italian railway system developed swiftly, with large companies such as Tosi (formed in 1882) and Breda (formed in 1886) taking the lead. The Terni Iron and Steel works (also formed in 1886) concentrated on producing ships for the Italian navy.

The mini-boom of the 1880s was followed by a darker economic period – 1887–95 – during which no further progress was made in the new industries. From the mid-1890s, however, up until the outbreak of the First World War, Italy experienced a minor industrial revolution, which has been described as a "mini economic miracle". Industrially, economically and culturally the Italian nation made an impact on the international scene for the first time and progressed rapidly in the attempt to align itself with the other great European powers.

During this time the new industries began to come into their own, although the First World War was to provide the first really substantial stimulus for the Italian engineering industries. The most significant industry to develop in these years was automobile manufacturing, while another of the greatest leaps forward was achieved by the development of hydro-electric power, which facilitated improved factory production. The government played an important role in this period, nationalizing the railways in 1905 and subsidizing a number of electric companies. Banks also played a vital role, investing in many of the new industries. Mechanization and modernization also affected the traditional industries, and in fact the bulk of industrial workers were occupied in the production of textiles, furniture, ceramics and glass.

DESIGN AND INDUSTRY

Where design was concerned an enormous gulf divided the approach towards the products of the traditional industries on the one hand, and those of the new, engineering-based industries on the other. While the former clung to the concept of "applied art" and were dominated, stylistically, by references to the past and the co-existence of different idioms, the latter embraced a new, simplified, unselfconscious "machine aesthetic" – the result of economic and technical expediency rather than an established aesthetic language that conformed to the fashionable taste of the day. The new products – trains, typewriters – remained, as yet, outside the sphere of status symbolism and were not subject to the same

degree of visual elaboration as those goods that constituted the "culture of consumption".

The role of design in Italian production was vital in this period of economic growth. It served to persuade the new middle-class market, with its new-found wealth, to consume status objects for their homes, while at the same time it provided a means by which Italy could identify and promote its national unity and strength, and compete with other countries in the international market. Through the development of its design, Italy was able to demonstrate the level of its technological expertise and its commitment to progress and modernity.

Exports were vital to Italy as the country had to import most of its primary materials, and the use of design as a means by which Italian manufacturers could promote their goods to both a home and a foreign market was nowhere more evident than at the numerous trade exhibitions which took place in these years. These exhibitions also chronicled the changes in Italy's manufacturing capability and in its international standing. This can be observed by comparing the exhibits at the National Exhibition of Milan of 1881 with those at the

Turin International Exhibition of 1902. As the names indicate, the latter event represented Italy's entrance into an international context, whereas the earlier exhibition had taken place at a relatively early stage in the country's own national unification, a fact that was reflected in its contents. The products in the 1881 exhibition – predominantly applied arts – were characterized by a use of styles from the past, in particular by the re-emergence of Baroque and Rococo forms of applied decoration, which reflected nationalistic pre-occupations. The Turin exhibition represented a high point of internationalism, with Italy showing its own version of Art Nouveau – a particularly floral variant, named the "Stile Liberty" after the London shop which specialized in it.

In 1911, the year of a major Italian industrial exhibition held in Turin, the Olivetti company showed its "M1" typewriter, a simple black, undecorated object. This demonstrated not only that Italy was beginning to compete in the area of the decorative arts but also that a new Italian industrial aesthetic, which acknowledged the new artistic consciousness associated with the idea of the "machine age", was beginning to emerge.

Far left: The Galleria Vittorio Emmanuele, Milan, in about 1900. Highly decorated in a grandiose, neo-Classical style, the glass-covered arcade became a popular venue for shopping, meeting and eating. Freed from the Austrian empire, Milan, with its strong banking traditions and proximity to the new manufacturing centres, was fast becoming one of the wealthiest urban centres in the newly unified Italy. People from the rural south flocked there, keen to participate in its growing affluence.

Left: The ceramics hall at the National Exhibition of Milan held in 1881; among the exhibitors were the firms of Farina, Richard Ginori, Rubbiani and Sequi. The objects displayed were all highly decorative and exhibited the characteristic historicism and eclecticism of the period.

Left: Silk manufacture at Gustavo Daverio, Milan, 1887. Compared to the smaller cottage industries that predominated at this time, this silk workshop was geared to large-scale production. But silk manufacture did not survive into the twentieth century as a key industry; cotton and wool proved much more successful.

DESIGN, CULTURE AND SOCIETY

While manufacturers saw the appearance of their products primarily as a matter of commercial exigency, a critical debate also developed in Italy in the second half of the nineteenth century around the question of art and industry – a debate that strongly influenced Italian technical education at this time. Camillo Boito was among the major protagonists and he argued energetically, like Henry Cole in England before him, for an alliance between the worlds of art and technology. His ideas were fed directly into the syllabuses of Italian technical schools – which, with the demise of the apprenticeship system, were taking on the responsibility of training engineers for the new industries. The role of the polytechnics was also becoming important (Milan Polytechnic was established in 1863): they helped close the gap between science and technology and provided recruits for the new industries, in particular members of the top management. On the other side of the coin the group of philosophers who clustered around Benedetto Croce, the leading Italian intellectual of the period, favoured an approach towards artistic practice which drew it as far as possible into the world of pure spirituality and away from what they considered the tainted world of industry and commerce. This antagonism to industry, shared by many leading members of the Italian aristocracy, helped to keep one face of Italian culture firmly rooted in the past.

While industrial development was changing the face of Italy, major social changes were also occurring that contributed to the story of design in these years – at least where goods aimed at the home market were concerned. Most significant were expanding urbanization; the growth in population; the drift of agricultural workers towards the north to make up the urban workforce, and the growing influence of the new middle-class sector of the population as a market force. Many goods were produced which were aimed directly at this wealthy social group, and new distribution systems were organized to cope with the ensuing growth in consumerism. This was the era, for instance, of the department store. Following the French example of large stores such as the Bon Marché, shops like Alle Citta d'Italia in Milan helped to cater for the increased demand for household goods. Some shops specialized in kitchen utensils alone, selling metal goods such as coffee-machines to the new status-conscious bourgeois clientele.

Another social factor which influenced the nature of consumption and the design of certain artefacts was the growth of leisure activities among the middle- and working-class population. Pastimes such as Alpine walking and cycling, hitherto exclusively aristocratic, grew increasingly popular, and the demand for bicycles, for instance, expanded dramatically as a result.

THE APPLIED ARTS AND DESIGN

As the role of design in the applied, or decorative, arts had a long history in Italy, it is not surprising that it continued to play a part in production and consumption. The emergence of national distribution systems was evident in the area of furniture. The wood-working, workshop-based furniture industry, which grew up in Brianza, catered mostly for the new urban middle-class market. It provided a third level of furniture manufacture in Italy, existing alongside, on the one

hand, the production of regionally manufactured rustic furniture, which met the needs of the peasant population particularly in southern Italy and, on the other, the production of high-class cabinet-made furniture, which was highly skilled and largely urban-based and which catered exclusively for the fashion-conscious aristocracy. This particular form of furniture manufacture continued into this period, providing exclusive models which were subsequently often emulated by companies producing cheaper goods, often with the assistance of some machinery.

The best-known cabinet-makers or *ebanisti* of the day included Eugenio Quarti, Vittorio Valabrega, Carlo Zen, Carlo Bugatti, Giovanni Buffa and Gaetano Moretti, whose work moved from the historicist, emulative styles (mainly derived from seventeenth-century examples) of the 1870s and 1880s into the much more original and aggressively modern *stile floreale* (floral style) of the 1900s. It was at the Turin exhibition of 1902 that their work was seen by an international audience for the first time. The furniture of

Carlo Bugatti, inspired by African culture – a direct result of contemporary Italian colonial activity – was particularly original and impressive. Collectively the work on exhibition represented a response to modernity and to the growing internationalism of Italian culture.

The furniture pieces produced at Brianza were, in sharp contrast, much less exclusive in nature and considerably less radical in design. Catering for a much less daring clientele, they continued to conform to conventional aesthetic formulae. A firm like Poltrona Frau, for example, began at this time to produce upholstered easy chairs, a furniture item which originated in England and subsequently became a favourite of the Italian bourgeois market. There was a high degree of specialization and cooperation within the suburban workshops: Cesare Cassina, who founded the Cassina company in the 1920s, commented later that during his childhood he had worked in Meda (a suburb of Milan) for his uncle Gilberto who owned a small firm producing only work-tables with interior quilting. While some firms produced only beds, or

Page 26: One of a pair of chairs, in wood and vellum, designed by the cabinet-maker Carlo Bugatti in about 1900. Much simpler than many of his pieces, it showed a closer affinity with the familiar curved forms of the Italian Art Nouveau movement, "Stile Liberty".

Page 27: Table with drawers by Carlo Bugatti, about 1898. This eccentric piece of furniture was part of a range produced in the 1880s and 1890s inspired by the Egyptian style. Bugatti employed unusual materials – among them painted vellum, brass, copper and inlaid wood – to create a unique, highly decorative and exclusive idiom.

Right: Artist's impression of the opening of the Turin Exhibition, from the weekly *La Tribuna della Domenica* of 1902; Raimondo D'Aranco's rotunda, in the fashionable "Stile Liberty", was one of its most dramatic buildings. The exhibition demonstrated Italy's level of awareness of international high style in architecture and the applied arts at a time of increasing affluence. Innovative exhibits included work by the Glasgow designer Charles Rennie Mackintosh, shown in Italy for the first time.

Far right: Glass-blowing at the Salviati workshop, Venice, in 1880. Salviati was among the leading glass manufacturers, producing items in a range of eclectic styles. Later it moved into a larger scale of production, catering for markets in London and Paris where there was a growing demand for traditional Italian glass.

sideboards or wardrobes, others simply applied decoration to the surfaces of furniture items. This specialization of skills meant that firms had to work quite closely with each other.

The new level of furniture production was mechanized to a degree but did not show a full-scale commitment to either mass production or standardization. The furniture items produced by the Brianza manufacturers were neither fully standardized nor entirely individualized: components were rearranged to give an impression of variation and applied decoration was used in such a way as to create an illusion of uniqueness, a common compromise where economy and individualism were both involved. Machinery, powered by water or steam, was used where necessary, but hand work remained common practice. The special nature of this intermediate kind of production, prevalent in the applied arts as a whole at this time, provided the broad context within which the concept of Italian design was to emerge. Halfway between craft and mass production, it utilized design as a means of both rationalizing production methods and making its goods artistic and individual. The industries that conformed to this model produced goods that were neither totally exclusive nor manufactured at the cheapest possible price. Concerned as they were with enhancing the social status of their customers, these manufacturers emphasized product appearance, and the retention of much skilled labour within production meant that a level of "quality" was maintained in the products concerned. It was to be some decades, however, before the dominant taste of this middle-class market would abandon traditional values and show a commitment to the "modern" idiom.

Ceramics and glass manufacture also underwent a number of changes at the end of the nineteenth century. As in furniture manufacture, established practice contrasted expensive, exclusive, highly decorated ware, aimed at the nobility and the wealthy, with the simpler pieces manufactured for rural life. Once again, in these years, a new, compromise model of manufacturing was introduced which was increasingly geared to factory production, but still retained a strong element of hand work. The ceramics firms which made the strongest impact, both at home and abroad, were those of Giulio and Richard Ginori, both of which

undertook a degree of rationalization in the organization of their production facilities. Inevitably, where product style was concerned, the famous French companies – Sèvres and Limoges – set the pace and the Italians simply followed their example, employing large numbers of modellers and decorators to work on their highly elaborate goods.

The Italian glass industry had by now already earned an impressive international reputation. Based in Venice and the neighbouring island, Murano, the glass manufacturers had long catered for the wealthy who sought decorative items for their ornate homes. In the 1881 Milan exhibition a number of Venetian companies displayed neo-Rococo mirrors and candelabras which they were producing, increasingly, for the Italian middle-class market. A few decades later, once lighting with electricity had become fairly widespread, and the Art Nouveau style had become the most fashionable idiom of the day, Murano glass manufacturers moved into the production of small, glass-covered, decorative side-lights. Few other concessions were made to the modern age by this industry until much later on, however, and the majority of Venetian and Murano glass items continued to be manufactured in historical styles by traditional methods.

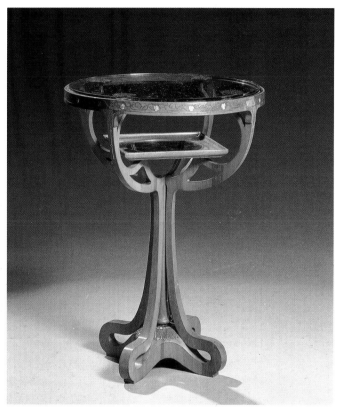

The Italian version of Art Nouveau, "Stile Liberty" was called after the London store that specialized in items in such a style. In Italy, the idiom had particularly florid and baroque characteristics and remained the preserve of the wealthy. It reached its height at the Turin International Exhibition of 1902, at which the architect Raimondo D'Aranco designed a rotunda and the cabinet-maker Carlo Bugatti created a suite of rooms in a highly organic idiom. "Stile Liberty" contained a number of national traits, often referring to Italian architecture from the past. The Palazzo Castiglioni of 1901–3 (left) retained a high degree of Classicism, while other buildings were heavily neo-Baroque in character.

The small table (above right), dating from 1890, was the work of Eugenio Quarti, one of the period's most important cabinet-makers, along with Carlo Zen, Vittorio Valabrega and Carlo Bugatti. They tended to combine exclusivity and traditional, hand-made quality with the new Liberty style. The vase (above) designed by Galileo Chini, artistic director of L'Arte della Ceramica, in about 1900, had typical conventionalized floral forms. The decorative arts were traditionally slow to grasp the opportunities of mechanization, but new ranges were soon developed as markets for luxury goods expanded. The design of glassware succumbed easily to the new vogue, with the examples of the French masters Lalique and Gallé offering models; the examples shown (below) date from about 1900. Much traditional glass, however, continued to be made.

THE "NEW PRODUCTS" AND DESIGN

The process of electrification had wide implications for the story of Italian design in these years. Electrical engineering was one of the key areas of technological strength in Italy after 1870. Milan was one of the earliest cities in the world to have electric street lighting (1876) and as early as 1892 electric trams were introduced into that city. Several electrical companies – the Societa Alta Italia, Edison (the Italian company was formed in 1884) and Negri among them – were given government subsidies and it was not long before a number of electrical products for the home were being manufactured in Italy. Electrical appliance design in Italy was strongly influenced by German examples, which led the way internationally.

While the growth of the electrical industry helped speed up the process of modernization that took place in Italian industry after 1900, as well as leading to the introduction of a number of new consumer products, the design of many of the goods that depended on the new technology was most crucially influenced by the advances that took place in the manufacture of iron and steel. The effects were felt almost immediately in the area of transportation – trains, boats, aeroplanes, cars, bicycles and motor-cycles; in domestic appliances, and in the production of small items of mechanized equipment for the home and office, such as typewriters and coffee-machines. Other related developments included metal furniture, metal jewellery and small components for items such as umbrellas. After 1900 all these areas of manufacturing were increasingly modified by industrial ration-

Right and below: The Olivetti "M1" typewriter, designed by Camillo Olivetti and exhibited at the Turin International Exhibition in 1911. It owed much to American models such as the Underwood, which Olivetti had seen in the USA. Although it was not technologically an innovative machine, it displayed a level of visual integration unusual at the time which gave it a special appeal.

alization and product standardization – innovations that could not themselves have been effected without parallel advances in the technology of steel manufacturing. After 1900 a number of Italian manufacturing industries which depended upon steel production and were not geared to military production, among them the typewriter, automobile and bicycle industries, benefited directly from government subsidies.

After 1896 the industrial emphasis in Italy shifted perceptibly from the traditional to the new industries and a number of companies emerged that became important to the Italian economy and took the concept of modernization to heart. This was reflected not merely in their progressive manufacturing methods but also in the appearance of their products, which emphasized their commitment to the new century.

The Olivetti typewriter company was established by Camillo Olivetti in 1908 amidst an atmosphere of extreme optimism. Camillo had visited the USA to observe American manufacturing techniques at first hand, an experience that proved crucial not only in exposing him to examples of industrial rationalization but also in showing him what products manufactured by the new producers of mechanical goods looked like. Thus the main foreign influence on the goods manufactured by the new Italian industries was a transatlantic one, unlike that of Europe on the decorative arts. Olivetti is said to have based the design of his first typewriter upon the Underwood model which he saw in the

USA. Whatever the derivation of this simple, standardized black machine, relieved only by the logo which adorned its surface, it became the Model "T" Ford of typewriters and played an important role in helping Italian industry move towards the formulation of a new industrial aesthetic.

While Olivetti was a significant new Italian company inasmuch as it looked forward to the new century rather than back to the safer traditions of the Italian past, it was, none the less, nowhere near as vital to the economy at this time as the automotive industry, which helped put Italy on the worldwide industrial map for the first time. Design played an important role in efforts to achieve this.

Car manufacturing in Italy provided the first large-scale instance of the new, engineering-based industries that aimed their products at the open market rather than at commerce, the military or the government. As in most other European countries, at first the car was enjoyed only by the very wealthy who saw it as an object of sport rather than a necessity of everyday life. Thus the models produced by the new companies – among them Fiat, established in 1899 in Turin by a group of ex-cavalry officers; Lancia, set up in 1905; and Alfa Romeo, established in 1910 – were essentially luxury items and they bore all the expected visual trappings, boasting, for example, such details as richly upholstered seating finished with braid.

The roots of Italian car manufacturing lay, as in a number of other countries, in the railway workshops and the craft

Right: The drivers and conductresses of the first electric tram in Milan, manufactured by the Breda Carminati and Toselli works. Milan was among the first European urban centres to introduce electric trams, in 1893.

Below: The Alfa Romeo 40–60 HP chassis was built by Castagna for Count Ricotti in 1913. With a top speed of 133 km per hour, it was one of the first aerodynamic, rear-engined, "tear-drop" automobile designs in the world. No further designs of such a progressive nature emerged again in Italy until the early 1920s.

traditions of coach-building. Names such as Castagna and Alessio represented the most stylish of the companies that moved from the latter area into car body design. Many of the most successful coachworks were clustered in and around Turin so it is not surprising to find that same city hosting the emerging car industry at the turn of the century. Of the seventy-one car firms existing in Italy in 1907, thirty-two were located in Turin. The recession of that year led to the collapse of many of the small manufacturers but in 1911 there were six and a half thousand car workers in Turin. This did not mean the end of craft traditions, however, as the new Italian motor-car mass producers retained strong links with the smaller, craft-based coach-builders. Alfa Romeo used Castagna, for example, to style a number of its car bodies and interiors.

One striking exception to the general rule of the production

of luxury cars was the example of the Fiat "Zero". In 1912 Giovanni Agnelli, the head of Fiat, travelled, as Camillo Olivetti had before him, to the USA with the specific purpose of studying American mass manufacturing techniques, in particular those in operation at the Ford factory. Designed by the engineer Carlo Cavalli, and styled by the coach-builder Giovanni Farina, the Fiat "Zero" was conceived and developed between 1912 and 1915 as the first Italian utility car aimed specifically at the new middle-class market. Mass production along Fordist lines was not fully achieved for this model, however: this development had to wait until the post-war years. Prior to 1914, Italian car manufacturing remained, like its European counterparts, essentially small-scale: in 1912, for instance, the Milan-based company, Alfa Romeo, produced only two hundred cars. Significantly, however, with the Fiat "Zero" the seed for change had been

Below: A Bianchi bicycle of 1885, before the invention of pneumatic rubber tyres which were later manufactured by Pirelli. The single, diagonal piece of tubular steel providing the main structural support was a forerunner of the familiar triangulated form of the 1890s.

Bicycles became enormously popular at the turn of the century, attracting consumers from a wide social spectrum and providing a new means of transport – for both work and leisure – for many people who previously had had very limited mobility.

sown, in concept at least, and the way was prepared for the mass-produced Italian utility car.

The bicycle was another engineered metal product which succeeded in becoming extremely popular among the new consumers. Formed in 1894, the Touring Club Italiano had twenty thousand members by 1900. This expansion of interest in cycling took it out of the hands of the aristocracy once and for all and a number of manufacturers were quick to cater for the demand, among them Bianchi and Pinetti e Stucchi (the latter moved from cookers to this new product). In 1892 Giovanni Battista Pirelli opened his rubber business in Milan and the rubber-wheeled bicycle became a possibility. By 1913 there were about seventy bicycle factories in Italy.

Another Italian industrial strength was motor-cycle production. A number of bicycle manufacturers were quick to exploit the growing demand for this new product. The first models, which looked like nothing more than mechanized bicycles, appeared in the first decade of this century. They gradually became more sophisticated, acquiring metal motor-housings and wider wheels.

The real harbingers of the new Italian industrial aesthetic, however, were goods such as agricultural machinery, ships, locomotives, trams, aeroplanes and a wide range of items destined for military use – these were not produced for consumption on the open market and could not, therefore, be classified as "status objects" in any way. Their unselfconscious forms were achieved by technological and economic expediency alone, by the eyes and hands of skilled engineers. By 1914 Italy could boast an impressive array of such goods, and during the war steps were taken to rationalize and standardize the production of many of them.

This page: A prototype Fiat "Zero" of 1911, Italy's answer to the "Model T" Ford. With a torpedo-shaped body designed by the Farina coachworks for mass production along standardized lines, it was planned for large-scale manufacture at a low cost. Due to Fiat's need to switch to military production, however, the car was never made in great numbers.

Right: Lorry chassis at Fiat just before the First World War, when the company diversified its interests and significantly increased its production. The reorganization that took place along more rational, efficient lines enabled a high production rate to continue after 1918.

TOWARDS MODERNITY

The years leading up to 1914 lack consolidation where the idea of modern design is concerned. While the applied arts tended to ape the past in order to fulfil the status requirements of the new middle-class consumers (with the exception of those luxury items that emerged under the banner of Art Nouveau), the goods produced by the new industries merely reflected the inevitable joint requirements of production and utility.

What did emerge from this period, however, was a set of conditions – economic, industrial, technological and cultural – that encouraged a new alignment of the hitherto disparate worlds of art and industry in the context of the "modern age". This was nowhere more evident, in theory at least, than in the words and work of members of the Futurist group which set out, in the second decade of this century, to develop cultural forms appropriate to the age of the machine. An emphasis upon speed, the fragmentation of images, the dynamism of line, and the excitement of living in the new, mechanical age, underpinned all their work. Primarily a fine art and literary movement, Futurism also produced the visionary architectural projects of Antonin Sant'Elia and Mario Chiattone in addition to the furniture and textile designs of Giacomo Balla. But these projects remained locked within the context of high cultural, rather than everyday, production, more in tune with fantasy than reality.

While the Futurists hailed the new technological age, however, the spirit they communicated was one of extreme individualism. In sharp contrast with the collective ideals of the Arts and Crafts Movement, which originated in Great Britain and strongly influenced the formulation of Modernism in Germany, Scandinavia and the USA, the Italian vision of the future developed from a different picture of society and its relationship with material culture. The sensibility that gave rise to the "romantic nationalism" that characterized the Futurists' work and ideas, and that was at its strongest in those of the poet D'Annunzio, led directly into Fascism, the political movement which was to dominate the post-First World War period of Italian history and culture. It was, as we shall see, in these later years that the concept of modern Italian design was finally born.

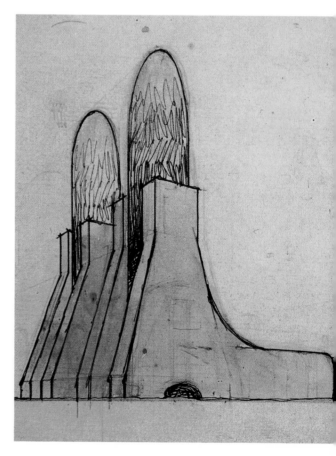

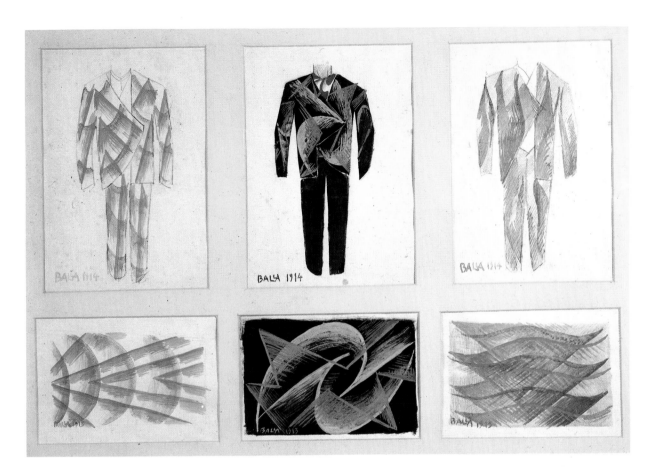

FUTURISM

The Italian Futurist painters, architects and designers added a new dimension to the fragmented forms of French Cubism – that of speed. According to the movement's acknowledged leader, Tomasso Marinetti, Futurism set out to express the dynamism of the modern age as demonstrated by the new machines, such as the automobile. It found its watershed in the years of the First World War when the excitement of modernity clashed head on with the grimmer realities of the age.

Where the visual arts were concerned, the majority of the Futurist protagonists were painters and sculptors, but the architectural visions of Antonio Sant'Elia and Mario Chiattone also captured the mood of the moment. Chiattone's sketches for a group of concert pavilions (left) date from 1914 and he also made designs for other, future, urban environments (far left and above left). Sant'Elia's building (above far left) is taken from his city of the future, also of 1914. Both envisaged an environment dominated by the flow of the new objects of transportation and by the accelerated movement of people living in a mechanized city.

Futurist designs for the decorative arts were few in number in the pre-war years. A notable example, however, were designs for clothing by the painter Giacomo Balla of 1914 (above). They represented the movement's desire for a complete renewal of the environment and borrowed their imagery from the work of the fine artists.

In the 1920s the mood of Futurism became linked with the growing influence of Fascism in Italy and members of the group were associated with that political stance. As a major cultural movement, Futurism failed to survive, but ceramics and interior designs did appear in the inter-war years.

1915–1939
"PROTO-DESIGN": TRADITION AND MODERNITY

The years between the two world wars were marked in Italy by a deep-seated ambivalence towards the "modern age". While one face of industry and culture sought energetically to embrace modern practices and styles, another, closely linked to the traditional aspects of Italian life, strove to retain links with the past, in an attempt to define the essence of "Italianness".

The "Annitrenta" exhibition, held in Milan in 1983, described the 1930s in Italy as a decade of "proto-design". While there are obvious problems of historical method in this essentially retrospective categorization, the inter-war period was undoubtedly a time during which much of the framework for the post-war Italian design movement was established. A modernized Italian industry emerged and a number of experiments in modern design were undertaken, albeit on a small scale and with little or no impact outside Italy.

At the same time, however, this was also a period during which much production remained both regional and small-scale in nature, and in which many objects retained their traditional appearances. As G.D.H. Cole explained:

There are large-scale capitalist enterprises in Italy, notably in the motor-trade and other branches of light engineering; and it is significant that Italy's greatest industrialist, Pirelli, has been throughout Mussolini's principal economic adviser. But large-scale industry occupies a relatively small place in the national life; and there are still many trades carried on by means of very

Left: The "Victory" Salon at the Sixth Triennale in 1936, a key exhibit designed by Marco Nizzoli, with the architects Giancarlo Palanti and Eduardo Persico, with a sculpture by Lucio Fontana. A minimal, dramatically lit environment with a marble floor, columns and images of heroes from the classical past, it conveyed a strong mood of neo-Classicism, albeit transformed into a modern idiom by the reduction to essentials.

small-scale enterprises. Such types of industry cannot be easily planned, for they depend largely on local markets and produce very varied goods.[1]

Where design is concerned, the concept of variety is central to this period. Fiat, Olivetti and the other large-scale operations were committed to the idea of product standardization and the development of modern forms to match their production techniques. They translated the concept of mass production, defined along Fordist lines, into Italian terms. Meanwhile, furniture-makers in Brianza and elsewhere continued to manufacture their goods either individually or in small batches, and in mostly traditional styles. The period was characterized by differing levels of production, and varied approaches to design. On the whole the newer, technologically progressive industries with new products to sell tended to embrace the concept of modern design with enthusiasm, while many of the older industries clung firmly to their traditions for fear of losing existing markets or offending potential new middle-class consumers.

POLITICS AND ITALIAN INDUSTRY

The strongest inter-war influence on the economics of manufacturing, as well as on the cultural life of Italy, was politics. The sudden shift from Liberalism to Fascism in the 1920s brought with it a change in emphasis from encouragement of foreign trading to a commitment to autarchy, and from an atmosphere of free enterprise to one of increased state control. By the end of the 1930s Italy continued to trade only with its empire, so that production for public consumption had given way to manufacturing for exclusively imperialistic and militaristic ends. The large-scale new industries – shipbuilding, transportation, chemicals – which had spin-offs in the areas of imperial expansion or war, flourished. (Even Olivetti entered into the production of machine-guns as well as typewriters for a short time.) Italy had to become increasingly self-sufficient, and to this end the State supported many of the small-scale artisanal firms which produced goods for the members of their local communities. With no foreign goods coming into the country this became essential rather than merely desirable. While cultural isolation and provincialism characterized Italy in these years, the absence of foreign imports helped it maintain its own indigenous manufacturing structure. The absence of international competition, however, meant that the goods produced were largely unsophisticated and traditional in nature.

The early years of the period set the pattern for what was to come later. While the first boom in the Italian economy had taken place in the early years of the century, the second came during the First World War as a result of the process called "industrial mobilization". Italy entered into what has been

Left: Artist's impression of Il Duce addressing 50,000 workers in Turin in 1939. Benito Mussolini (1883–1945) was leader of the Italian Fascist party from the March on Rome in 1922 to the liberation of Italy by the Allies in 1945. He retained a tight hold on the nation through the twin values of traditionalism and modernity. In his pursuit of the autarchic state he discouraged trade relationships between Italy and other countries.

Left: The Fiat 508C of 1939 is closely linked in this painting by Marco Sironi with the ideology of the Fascist state. Mussolini encouraged modern methods of manufacture while retaining strong links with many cultural traditions, especially the artisanal basis of many small-scale production units.

described as a programme of "production at any cost".[2] As the State was the sole consumer of most of the industrial goods produced – the trucks and lorries manufactured by Fiat, for example – cost was no problem. Huge State subsidies were provided, enabling companies producing steel, vehicles, hydro-electric power, chemicals, rubber and woollen textiles – among them Ilva, Breda, Ansaldo, Fiat, Montecatini and Pirelli – to become very powerful, absorb their competitors and expand dramatically. Fiat, for instance, had only six thousand workers pre-war compared to thirty thousand in 1919.

Inevitably, when hostilities ceased, the loss of the State as a patron created problems for the manufacturers and a post-war crisis ensued. This was one of the factors which allowed the twin forces of nationalism and Fascism to rise up and destroy the old Liberal regime. The inter-war period was characterized by a mood of bellicose nationalism which was personified in the figure of the leader of the Fascist party, Benito Mussolini. He came to rule in 1922 and, by 1926, he had established a totalitarian regime in Italy.

MODERNIZATION AND DESIGN

Mussolini's rule was distinguished by the twin pulls of tradition and modernity, themes which were to become central to Italian culture in this period and, in particular, to the debate about architecture and design. Modernization was expressed most clearly, in the 1920s and 1930s, by the leading industrialists' desire to adopt American mass manufacturing techniques and to rationalize the production process by introducing product standardization, moving assembly lines, interchangeability of parts and a clear division of labour. The Fiat and Olivetti plants reflected this tendency most openly. Both companies built new factories – Fiat's Lingotto building, designed by Giacomo Matte Trucco in concrete and glass with a high-speed test track on the roof, was opened in the early 1920s. Later, in 1939, when Lingotto proved inadequate for the company's expanded production, the Mirafiori plant was opened, based on Ford's River Rouge factory. Luigi Figini and Gino Pollini's factory for Olivetti in Ivrea appeared at the end of the period, in 1940. Ivrea encapsu-

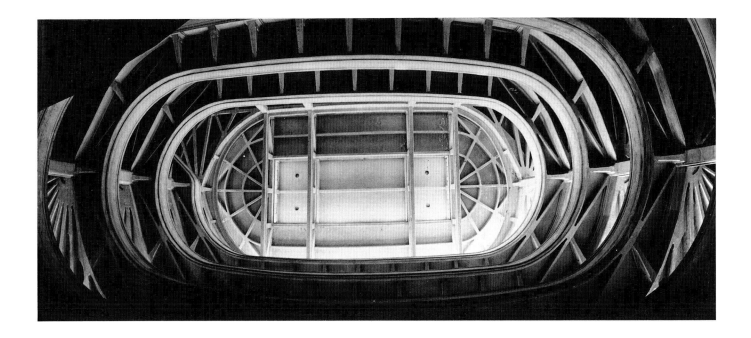

lated Camillo Olivetti's essentially European ideas about providing social and welfare facilities for the workforce but, where modern industrial production was concerned, both Giovanni Agnelli and Camillo Olivetti considered the American manufacturing system the only possible model.

In fact the USA played an important role in defining not only the nature of Italian industrial organization in these years but also the appearance of many of the products that emerged from it. Mechanical and electrical consumer goods and objects of transportation began to be styled in a manner that owed much to the American idiom of streamlining, a modern aesthetic which derived from experiments in aerodynamics and, through its sleek forms, symbolized the dynamism of modern life. The Fiat 1500 of 1935 was a prime example of American styling, realized on Italian soil: its flowing body-lines were clearly indebted to the work of the Chrysler stylists on their "Airflow" model, launched ahead of its time in 1933. Lancia followed suit by bringing in the body-stylist, Pininfarina, to create the form of its "Aprilia" model, which appeared on the market two years later: it was

Above left: Fiat's Lingotto factory in the 1930s. Built in the early 1920s on the lines of Henry Ford's Highland Park factory, it created a strong image of modernity at a time when nationalism and neo-Classicism were the most telling cultural forces in Italy. The test track was built on the factory roof, and the cars were driven to it up a spiral ramp (above).

Left: The Lancia "Aprilia" Coupé of the 1930s, Pininfarina's aerodynamic version of the "Aprilia". He took the idea of streamlining to the point where every line of the body-shell was curved and, in theory at least, air-resistant. While in the USA streamlined cars tended to be big and bulbous, their Italian counterparts were smaller and much more elegant.

Far left: Poster for the Fiat 1500 by Giuseppe Riccobaldi Del Bava, 1935. Its sleek, streamlined forms combine with the architectural ruins in the background to convey the new nationalistic style.

designed like the section of an aeroplane wing with a curve in its windscreen.

If the 1500 was Fiat's answer to American styling, its little "Topolino" reflected Henry Ford's social philosophy. This was a small, standardized, utility car produced cheaply enough to be affordable by a large sector of the population, in imitation of the Model "T" Ford. The chief innovation, introduced by its designer, the engineer Dante Giacosa, was its reduced size. By 1948 a hundred and fifty thousand "Topolinos" had come off Fiat's production lines.

While the Fiat company, with much support from the Italian government, developed into one of the country's leading manufacturers in the inter-war years, diversifying its production into aeroplanes, trucks and buses to meet the State's military requirements, other automobile companies pursued alternative routes. With the help of the coach-builders, both Alfa and Lancia continued to produce expensive, speciality cars for wealthy markets.

In 1930 Pininfarina established his own company with rather different ends in sight. He had had experience in both coach-building, working as an apprentice-designer in the workshop of his brother Giovanni (who, in turn, had worked for one of the great Italian body-makers, Marcello Alessio), and in the mass production industry, working with Fiat on its "Zero" model. In 1921 he visited Detroit and observed Ford's moving assembly line in action but, in his own country, he saw the need for a rather different kind of company that would work in tandem with mass production industry. His interest lay in producing short series and single models, and in designing and developing prototypes which would be picked up by larger-scale manufacturers. Thus, along with a handful of others, Pininfarina sustained the Italian tradition of coach-building by transforming it into a modern practice. Through the work undertaken by his Automobile Body Corporation he succeeded in creating a bridge between the high standards of craftsmanship achieved in coach-building and the aesthetic excellence of the modern Italian body-makers who have earned Italy its high reputation for automobile design in this century. He also provided a link between large-scale automobile production and the more exclusive end of the industry, showing that the aesthetic component was an equally important ingredient in both areas. As he explained:

> I have always believed that inventions ought to benefit a wider public and not remain at the disposal of a privileged few: if the market were expanding, the study of prototypes . . . ought to take advantage of the fact and the construction side ought to be suggesting economical practical solutions.[3]

The collaboration between the body-makers and the car manufacturers remained a constant through this period and beyond, showing how the acceptance of modernity was, in Italy, tempered at all times by the retention of craft skills and the aesthetic values perpetuated by them.

Olivetti was the other large-scale manufacturing company to adopt American production techniques, as well as using the streamlined aesthetic for its mass-produced machines. After graduating as an engineer from the Polytechnic of Turin, Adriano, the son of Olivetti's founder, had gone to the

Right: The interior of the Fiat 519 in the early 1920s, when car interiors reflected the luxury that went with automobile culture. The upholstered seats, padded cushions and carpeted floor indicate a desire for comfort rather than mere utility. With the advent of the little "Topolino" and other cheaper models, car interiors became much less sumptuous.

This page: The Fiat 500, launched in 1936, was known as the "Topolino" – the Mickey Mouse. It was the first truly democratic car to come off an Italian production line. Designed by the engineer Dante Giacosa, it combined compactness with engineering sophistication and a streamlined body. By the end of the decade it had become a familiar sight on Italian roads.

USA in 1925. As a direct result of the production and organization techniques he saw there, he returned to Italy, hired a team of engineers from Turin and set about transforming Olivetti's production system from one founded on piecework to one based on more analytic lines. Production figures rose by 63 per cent between 1926 and 1929; in the latter year thirteen thousand units of one typewriter were manufactured.

For Olivetti, modernization meant not only new forms of organization but also a complete overhauling of the visual image that the company presented to the world. Adriano instigated a programme of visual reform and modernization

Left: Adriano Olivetti (1901–1960), son of Camillo Olivetti, the firm's founder. After a period spent in the USA in the late 1920s, he reorganized the factory along more rational, efficient lines. Later, he brought in a number of key designers – including Marcello Nizzoli and Ettore Sottsass – who were largely responsible for the reputation for design sophistication that the company still enjoys today.

Above: Interior of the Olivetti factory in 1920, when production was still organized on the principle of one worker making every stage of one machine – here, the "M20" typewriter, launched in 1920. Division of labour and assembly lines were introduced in the 1930s.

which embraced the company's graphic design, industrial design and architecture. At this time Germany and the USA led the way not only in the production of office machinery but also in all matters concerning its design; Adriano showed his awareness of German pre-eminence in this field by employing a number of graphic designers who had been trained at the Bauhaus in Weimar, among them Alexander Schawinsky. Other artists and designers who played a part in transforming the two-dimensional image of the Olivetti company included Giovanni Pintori, who was trained at the design school at Monza, the sculptor Constantino Nivola and Leonardo Sinisgalli, an unusual individual who combined the skills of an engineer with those of a poet. The programme they initiated entailed revitalizing Olivetti's graphics by rejecting outmoded realism and replacing it with a much simpler, experimental idiom that combined photography and typography in dramatically innovative compositions.

Because of the relatively high costs involved in retooling, initiatives in the two-dimensional area preceded a radical reworking of the nature and appearance of the products themselves. However, the machines that came off the Olivetti production lines in the years between 1929 and 1939 exhibited a growing awareness of the tenets of the international Modern Movement in architecture and design. The simplicity and functional form of the new machines were in sharp contrast to many of the highly ornate nineteenth-century models. In pursuing this line the Olivetti company helped bring about the transition from applied art to industrial design that was to be fundamental to post-war developments. In effect, Olivetti was one of the first modernized Italian industrial firms to consider the links between the means of production of a new technological product, its appearance and its cultural role in the contemporary environment. Back in 1912, Camillo Olivetti had written, in connection with his design for the "M1" typewriter, that "a typewriter should not be ornate and in questionable taste. It should have an appearance that is serious and elegant at the same time"[4] – these words remained at the heart of the Olivetti industrial design enterprise for many decades.

The "MP1" typewriter, designed by the engineer A. Magnelli and produced in 1932, was among the first of the company's machines to benefit from the new rationalized production techniques. Its simple, engineered form was the result of a systematic arrangement of its components, according to the dictates of both assembly and use, and the applica-

Below: The Olivetti factory at Ivrea, designed by the Rationalist architects Luigi Figini and Gino Pollini and built between 1939 and 1941. The factory, built in steel and glass on a grid structure, was strongly influenced by America and represented Olivetti's aspirations as a progressive organization, both technologically and socially.

tion, for practical as well as visual reasons, of a simple body-shell. The company's name was clearly displayed at the rear of the machine. In a subsequent model – the "Studio 42" machine, designed by Schawinsky and the architects Figini and Pollini – the body-shell was more sophisticated. It concealed more of the machine's working parts and no longer had screws visibly joining it together. Although inspired by American examples, the machine aesthetic evolved by

Far left: Advertisement for Olivetti's "M40" typewriter designed by Alexander Schawinsky in 1934. Trained at the Bauhaus in Germany, Schawinsky was invited to work for the firm by Adriano Olivetti, who had set up a graphic design department. His exciting publicity material introduced a new modern style into Italian graphic design.

Left: Poster for Olivetti's "MP1" typewriter by Schawinsky, 1934; the "new woman" image helped to establish Olivetti as a forward-looking company. Under the leadership of Adriano Olivetti, the company concentrated on projecting a unified corporate image through its posters and two-dimensional material and later, its three-dimensional products as well.

Olivetti designers in these years shunned the showy, streamlined forms of so many contemporary American machines in favour of a more geometric appearance, inspired by European examples.

In 1936 Adriano Olivetti employed Marcello Nizzoli as the chief consultant designer for his office machines. Nizzoli had already proved his abilities as a skilled and forward-thinking graphic and exhibition designer in the modern idiom. He had collaborated, with Eduardo Persico, the editor of the progressive architectural magazine *Casabella*, on the design of one of the exhibits at the 1934 Italian Aeronautical Exhibition in Milan, an event that had proved a dramatic testimony to Italy's commitment to the modern age. Nizzoli's and Persico's display consisted of an open-grid construction of vertical and horizontal steel tubes, shaped on a cross formation, like the fuselage of an aeroplane. Photographic and typographic material was suspended from it.

Nizzoli's entry into the Olivetti company confirmed the firm's commitment to evolving a modern image for the whole of its production, from its publicity material right through to the machines themselves. The only example of Nizzoli's three-dimensional designs for the company to appear in the pre-war years, however, was the "MC45 Summa" calculating machine, a brilliant exercise in body-shell design and composition. Nizzoli's greatest industrial projects were to emerge later, after 1945, when the Olivetti company and its products moved into the international arena.

The application of modern aesthetic principles to the design of mechanical and electrical consumer goods was on the whole, however, limited in the inter-war years to a few isolated objects. These included the Necchi sewing-machine of 1934 (the "BDA" model); a television set, manufactured by the Marelli company in 1938; and a number of radio designs. Into the latter category fell one of the most inventive products of that decade, Livio and Pier Giacomo Castiglioni's little "Phonola" radio which was designed in 1939, but made its impact in 1940 at the Seventh Milan Triennale. Its originality lay not just in its sophisticated, one-piece Bakelite shell and its rejection of the furniture-symbolism traditionally used for radios, but in the way it utilized the language of familiar domestic machinery – in particular that of the telephone – as a means of presenting the public with a new concept, the "radio-machine". As such it set an important precedent for the numerous exciting post-war Italian domestic machines. While the concept of the body-shell and the technology employed were both American in origin, the design concept was wholly original and entirely Italian.

Of course most of the machines encountered by Italians in their homes and offices in the inter-war years were far less far-reaching in their design ambitions. They either echoed American or German models, or simply reflected the economic and technical exigencies of mass production. Objects such as electric cookers, refrigerators and electric irons were still relatively expensive and therefore unavailable to the vast majority of the population who still made do with their kitchen ranges. None the less the all-electric kitchen, imported from across the Atlantic, became an ideal of the period, while telephones represented the height of luxury. For designers the radio was a potent symbol of modernity that offered them an opportunity to evolve a modern style appropriate to the age of the machine and of mass communications. The first Italian radio station had been established in the mid-1920s and by

the mid-1930s radio had become one of the most popular forms of entertainment in Italy. Broadcasting was State-controlled and in 1932 over thirty thousand sets were registered. In 1938 Franco Albini launched a model with a transparent Perspex body which had a speaker and the other mechanical components embedded, visibly, within it. This was as near an interpretation of European Functionalism (the design theory that required that outer form be dictated by inner structure) applied to radio design as could be imagined. However, most of the million sets registered in Italy in that year were nowhere near so audacious in their appearance, indeed the majority favoured some kind of link with traditional furniture pieces.

RATIONALISM

The main protagonists of the modern style in Italy in the 1930s were members of a small group of architects associated with the movement called Rationalism. This was the Italian variant of the international Modern Movement in architecture and design, which had its roots in the experimental work of architects such as Walter Gropius in Germany and Le Corbusier in France. From this fountainhead of ideas emerged a

Above: Radio designed by Luigi Caccia Dominioni and Livio and Pier Giacomo Castiglioni, made by the Phonola company in 1939. With its all-in-one Bakelite shell, it could be hung on a wall or placed on a table. Although it emulated the shape of the telephone, it evolved a new form for a new product that was both novel and acceptable.

Piero Bottoni's "Lira" armchair, designed in the 1930s and produced in the 1980s by the Zanotta company. Bottoni was one of the group of Italian Rationalist architects who tested their skills on the new material, tubular steel. This design, which makes ingenious use of tension wires connecting the back rail to the seat support, is sophisticated both technologically and aesthetically, as well as being highly dramatic to look at.

Italy's version of the European Modern Movement in architecture and design emerged in 1926, in the form of a manifesto written by a group of young architects called Gruppo Sette (Group Seven). Their projects appeared at the Triennale exhibitions in the early 1930s and promised to be highly favoured by the State. Rationalism's inherent internationalism and stylistic radicalism were against it, however, and it was replaced by the more conservative Novecento style. A few monuments to Rationalism remain, but most of its proposals were unrealized.

The Craja bar (far right) was built in the Piazza P. Ferrari, Milan, in 1930 to designs (right) by Luciano Baldessari. In Giuseppe Terragni's Casa del Fascio of 1933 (below right), the boardroom chairs were made of tubular steel in a cantilevered design (below left). The Electric House (below) was designed by Piero Bottoni, with Figini and Pollini, for the Biennale at Monza of 1930; while Gabriele Mucchi's "S5" tubular steel stacking chair (left) was produced by E. Pino in 1934.

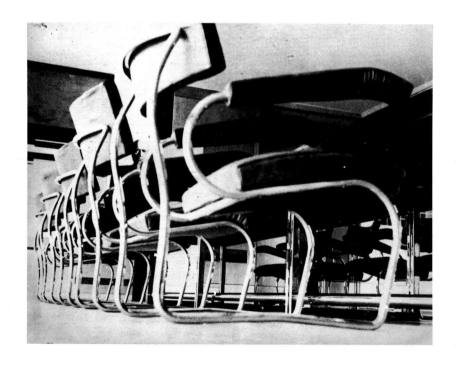

RATIONALISM

Right: Transparent radio, cased between two pieces of clear Perspex, designed by Franco Albini for a competition in 1933. Here Albini was applying the ideas of European Functionalism, which required that the interior of an object should dictate its external appearance. The radio was only a prototype and was never put into production.

Below: Television set manufactured by Magnetti Marelli in 1938. This early design for a domestic set is both modern and traditional: modern in the style of the wooden cabinet, but traditional in that it is still considered to be an item of furniture rather than a piece of equipment. Such a tension between the past and the present characterized many goods from this period.

Below right: Advertisement for domestic electrical appliances dating from 1920. The smaller household appliances – for example, water-heaters and irons – were the first electrical goods to penetrate the Italian home in the inter-war years, but they were restricted to affluent, middle-class households. Publicity material linked them with increased freedom for housewives, and women were, undoubtedly, the main consumers of such goods although they were rarely the wage-earners. The goods themselves were visually very unsophisticated, their technological novelty being enough to make them attractive.

social programme, and an aesthetic formula, which influenced a number of buildings and associated products in the inter-war period.

Much has been written about the achievements of Italian architectural Rationalism which has been emphasized at the expense of the more traditionally oriented architecture and design emerging alongside it. But it remains highly significant, none the less, as a reflection of Italy's internationalist ambitions in this period of intense nationalism, and as one face of the complex relationship between politics and design that developed in Italy between the wars. Ultimately Mussolini favoured the stripped classical style as the appropriate embodiment of his regime, but the simple forms of Rationalism represented for a brief period the revolutionary, socialistic, anti-middle-class aspects of his political beliefs which, in the early years of Fascist rule, were an important element of its ideology.

Rationalism emerged through the work and ideas of a group of young architects who graduated from the University of Milan. Sebastiano Larco, Guido Frette, Carlo Enrico Rava, Luigi Figini, Gino Pollini, Guiseppe Terragni and Adalberto Libera called themselves, collectively, Gruppo Sette (Group Seven). They launched the movement in December 1926 with a series of manifestos published in the magazine *Rassegna*. These echoed the avant-garde ideas of the European Modern architects but at the same time pointed to links with what the Group saw as the timelessness of Italy's traditional classical architecture. Thus, from the outset, Rationalism contained an element of "Italianness" that distinguished it from its European counterparts.

While housing was clearly on the agenda of the European programme, Rationalist architectural projects of the first few years were restricted to commercial buildings – the Bar Craja designed in 1930 by Luciano Baldessari with Figini and Pollini, and Persico's and Nizzoli's Parker shop of 1934–5 are among the best known examples – visionary projections of townscapes and housing projects of the future, and exhibition displays. Both the Biennale of 1927 and the Triennale of 1930 in Monza contained examples of work by members of the Group. In the Electric House of 1930, sponsored by the Edison company and designed by Figini, Pollini and Piero Bottoni, the modern Corbusian house merged with the rational principles outlined in the American theory of "scientific management", which examined the problems associated with the rationalization of industrial work. The all-electric kitchen, one of the house's most prominent features, was a modern Italian statement clearly derived from similar ones made earlier in Germany and the USA.

In the early years modern design, in its Rationalist guise, depended for support either upon the new industries or directly upon the Fascist government which, with its ideal of the corporate state clearly defined, in turn made every effort to subsidize the new industries and to imbue them with the power and authority to help run the country. One of the initiatives taken by Mussolini to help Italian industry was made in the early years of the Depression, in 1933. The IRI (Instituto per la Ricostruzione Industriale) was set up with the explicit aim of helping Italian industry expand in the hopes that the Italian nation would thereby become increasingly self-sufficient. The state took over much industrial investment from the banks and, by the end of the decade, the IRI controlled a number of large companies, among them shipping lines, electrical and machine-tools industries and the telephone system.

The State supported Rationalism both directly and indirectly at this time. Mussolini showed an interest in the work of the Rationalists when in 1931 he opened a group exhibition of their work in Rome, and in the same year Pier Bardi (a key Rationalist apologist) wrote a report for Mussolini, calling for State control of architecture. Terragni's Casa del Fascio was built in Como in 1934–36, a Rationalist building which was used by the Fascist party, while the appearance of a number of Rationalist designs for furniture constructed from tubular steel also had Fascist backing, although in a more indirect manner (steel received much State financial support in these years). By the middle of the decade, however, Rationalism, with its commitment to modernity and internationalism, had clearly lost out as the favoured style of the day to the twin ideals of nationalism and tradition. These were reflected in the neo-Classical movement in architecture and design, which was called "Novecento".

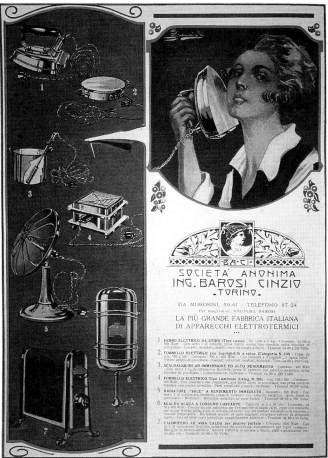

Rationalist designs for mass production were few and far between but a cluster of furniture and lighting designs reached the production stage and made a significant impact

Right and far right: Luciano Baldessari's "Luminator" light of 1929, made of chrome-plated steel. Designed as a "mechanized mannequin" for the Barcelona Exhibition of 1929, it offered a radical solution to the problem of lighting, and marked the first Italian venture into the area of "light sculptures" which were to have great importance after the Second World War.

Below: Plan for a radio-gramophone designed by Luigi Figini and Gino Pollini for a competition in 1933. They extended the idea of seeing new domestic technological products as furniture items but chose to use the new material, tubular steel. No ornamentation was allowed on the surface other than the accents created by the disposition of the essential controls and functional components.

on the Italian environment, both public and private. The "Luminator", a "light-sculpture" by Baldessari, a Rationalist designer a generation older than the members of Group Seven, was designed in 1926 but not manufactured until three years later when it was shown at the Barcelona International Exhibition of 1929. The first of what were to become a succession of expressive lighting forms, it was inspired by German experimental work, and conceived as an "illuminated mannequin" with a piece of curved tubular steel representing the arms.

The move from buildings to lighting and furniture was a logical one for Rationalist architects, since the unified environment was all-important and they were unable to obtain funds for many of their architectural projects. The use of metal in furniture inspired a number of designs: some, such as items for hospitals and offices, stressed the practical qualities of the material; others, such as chairs designed by the architects Gabriele Mucchi (his "S5" model), Terragni (his designs for the interior of the Casa del Fascio), Guiseppe Pagano, Bottoni and Gino Levi Montalcini, combined utility with the abstract sculptural possibilities of tubular steel. Even the design of the gramophone, an item still considered as a piece of furniture, succumbed to the attraction of the new, bright, chrome-covered tubular steel, as was demonstrated by Figini's and Pollini's entry for a competition organized by the National Gramophone Society in 1933. Devoid of the period detail and decorative trim that characterized many other such pieces in these years, theirs was a simple wooden box placed on four tubular steel legs.

While Rationalism succeeded, therefore, in influencing the design of a range of products, from chairs to radios and typewriters, its mass impact was minimal. Its essentially

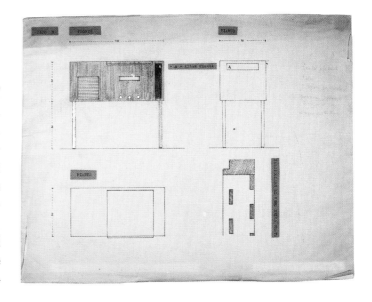

internationalist and revolutionary tendencies in the end caused it to fall from favour as the most appropriate style for the Fascist state. Although Mussolini had started out as a socialist – as the editor, in fact, of that movement's Italian newspaper – and his early regime was not centred upon middle-class ideals, by the mid-1930s it was clear that Italian Fascism had become the party of the bourgeoisie. This had strong implications for design since the twin values of nationalism and traditionalism became increasingly prominent in the course of the 1930s, and needed a style to represent them.

NOVECENTO

They found this in the Novecento movement, which evolved a new style based on a pared-down reworking of the classical idiom. Novecento was first and foremost an architectural school but, like Rationalism, rapidly extended its sphere of influence to the "lesser arts". Unlike Rationalism, however, the impact of Novecento was stronger in the area of the traditional applied arts than in the products of the new, technological industries, and it drew its inspiration from the decorative arts of France and Austria rather than from the "machine style" of Germany and the USA. The Novecento group, whose best-known members included Gio Ponti and Emilio Lancia, was officially formed in 1926. Later others – Giovanni Muzio and Tomasso Buzzi – also became associated

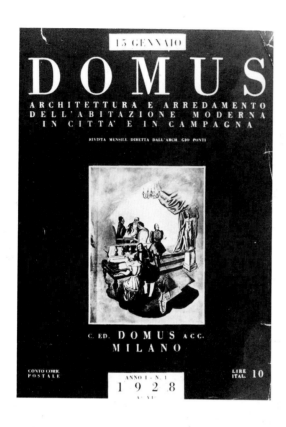

with the Group. One of the first Novecento architectural manifestations was Ponti's and Lancia's "Holiday House", which was financed by the newly formed Rinascente store. In 1927 Novecento was in evidence in the Biennale; in 1928 Ponti founded *Domus* magazine, which was to act as a mouthpiece for the movement; and during the following decade the style rapidly permeated the environment of the industrial bourgeoisie of northern Italy, particularly Milan, affecting the appearance of much of its architecture and its luxury goods. The influence of the work of the Austrian designers Josef Hoffmann, Dagobert Peche and other members of the Wiener Werkstatte (a Viennese workshop set up on the basis of the English Arts and Crafts example), as well as that of the French high-class cabinet-maker, Emile-Jacques Ruhlmann, dominated the formulation of the new style for the applied arts. However, in spite of these foreign influences the appeal of the Novecento style lay, ultimately, in its intrinsic "Italianness", contained in its appropriation of the indigenous classical idiom.

Until the mid-1930s, Rationalism and Novecento were the only contenders for the Fascist style and they vied openly with each other as possible guises for Modernism in Italy. They represented different tastes, and different social ideals. While both were essentially modern in spirit, they drew upon different references in their campaigns to transform the environment. By the middle of the decade it had become clear that the modern style favoured by Mussolini was the neo-Classical idiom, which combined Italy's glorious and imperialistic past with its authoritative present and future. It quickly became a modern imperial style, manifested not only in new towns such as Sabaudia and Littoria, which Mussolini constructed on the marshland south of Rome, but also in buildings on the numerous Greek islands which were annexed by Italian forces and which, in the 1930s, became

important components of the expanding Italian empire.

The growing popularity of the neo-Classical interior, much loved by the northern industrial bourgeoisie, encouraged the emergence of a range of interior artefacts to suit it, including furniture, ceramics and glass. The architect Gio Ponti, who spearheaded the Novecento movement in the applied arts, was responsible for bringing the decorative work of the Wiener Werkstatte to the notice of the Italians. Cultural links between northern Italy and Austria were still very strong as that region had been in Austrian hands for many years before the unification of Italy.

Although it contained a large element of historicism, the new decorative arts movement was essentially modern in spirit, reworking conventional forms and motifs in new ways. While Rationalism has frequently been seen by historians as the training-ground for post-war Italian design, inasmuch as it prepared the way for the architectural profession to dominate the formulation of a new style for consumer goods, the vogue for neo-Classicism was also influential in encouraging manufacturers – particularly those concerned with the production of the traditional applied arts – to use architects to propose new forms for their goods. Ponti, for example, collaborated for many years from 1923 onwards with the ceramics company, Richard Ginori, while at the end of the period Carlo Scarpa worked with the Venini glass company, a firm

Above left: The Palazzo Rinascente, Milan, built in the late 1920s. Among the first of its kind to cater for the new wealthy middle-class population in the north, in the highly authoritarian Novecento style, it dominated one side of the Piazza del Duomo and became a visible symbol of increasing affluence and consumption. From the outset it set high standards in design, a role that it developed after the Second World War.

Left: The main square of Littoria, built by Mussolini in the 1930s on reclaimed marshland south of Rome. Together with the neighbouring Sabaudia, it was constructed according to very formal plans, with all buildings in the Novecento style giving a strong visual coherence.

64

established in the 1920s that had from the outset embraced the concept of the "modern" in its glass designs.

A particularly fruitful cooperation between a designer and a manufacturer in these years was that of Pietro Chiesa with Fontana Arte, one of the more progressive producers of decorative arts. Many of Chiesa's highly innovative lighting designs harked back to the work of the Wiener Werkstatte. A hanging light from 1937, however, which employed a system of spherical weights to alter the height of the light source, owed much to contemporary abstract sculpture. Chiesa became the artistic director for Fontana Arte in 1933 but prior to that he had worked with architects, Tomasso Buzzi among them, on a range of glass designs for exhibitions. His first work in a more rational vein was created for Fontana Arte's exhibit at the Fifth Triennale of 1933, held in Milan in Giovanni Muzio's new "Palace of Art", built specifically to house the exhibition, which took place every three years. Chiesa's simple light designs set a precedent which many other designers followed. The most memorable was produced by Fontana Arte in 1936: his "Luminator" (not to be confused with Baldessari's light of 1929 which had the same name) was no more than a simple tube, fixed to a base, which opened up into a funnel form at the top where the light source was housed. The simplicity and visual potency of this standard light proved an inspiration to many. Chiesa's work spanned a spectrum from eclectic and expressive at one end to simple and classical at the other, and he remains one of the principal pioneers of the twentieth-century Italian lighting movement that flourished in the years after 1945.

Giò Ponti also played a vital role in formulating a new role for the designer in these years. He aimed to aid the transition, in the area of the traditional applied arts, from craft to industrial production and to help define the new role for the designer within this new context. At all times Ponti retained a strong sense of respect for the artisan and continued to see craft as the true basis for design. However, he also envisaged the possibility of designers working across a wide spectrum of projects and in this he showed the way. He not only worked for craft-based industries, such as Richard Ginori and Fontana Arte, but also designed an interior for a locomotive, manufactured by the Breda company, which was exhibited at the Triennale of 1933. His ceramic designs, which included highly decorative pieces and some simple designs for a range of sanitary equipment, demonstrated his abilities to work across a broad spectrum of products.

Ponti's role as spokesman for the new Italian design movement was backed up by the work he did in preparing and supporting the Triennale exhibitions of this period. As we have seen, they served as the principal means at this time of communicating the advances in design to manufacturers and the public by providing a shop-window in which manufacturers could display their most innovative wares.

Conceived by an art critic, Guido Marangani, who as of 1921 had worked very hard to establish it, the exhibition started out as a biennial, international event first held in Monza in 1923. While the original intention of the Biennale was to emphasize local, artisanal production it quickly became a much more sophisticated event, showing the latest

Above: A building for residences, offices and shops in the Corso Littorio, Milan, designed by E. Lancia in 1933–36 – a striking example of the way in which the Novecento style was made to look both authoritarian and modern at the same time. Lancia was a founder-member, with Gio Ponti, of the Novecento group.

Above: The Piazza della Vittoria, Brescia, between the wars. Under Mussolini's rule, architectural emphasis was firmly placed on public, rather than private, buildings, such as banks and post offices, which were seen as symbols of the grandeur of the State. Statues were widely used to enhance the mood of nationalism.

Right: A terrace setting designed by Luigi Figini and Gino Pollini in the exhibition of interiors at the Sixth Triennale, 1936. With its use of existing chair types and familiar materials such as wood and terrazzo, it combined an Italian indigenous tradition with the mood of modernity expressed by way of severe composition combined with simple forms.

Right: Pietro Chiesa's "Luminator" standard lamp, manufactured in 1936 by Fontana Arte, the company of which he became artistic director in 1933. This design, fabricated in varnished brass and producing a soft, indirect light, was among the most progressive – and simple – of his proposals.

designs. By the second half of the 1920s the exhibition also served as a show-place for both Novecento and Rationalist projects. In 1930 the "International Biennial of Decorative Art" was transformed into the "International Triennial of Decorative and Modern Industrial Art", thereby reflecting the transition that had taken place. By 1933, the year in which the event moved from Monza to Milan, the exhibition had become dominated by the products of the newly organized decorative art industries. In 1933 and 1936 the work of the Italian Rationalists had a strong profile there.

The change of emphasis at the Triennales from regional, artisanal craft work to the products of the new applied art industries mirrored a major development in the story of Italian design in the inter-war years. Increasingly a significant number of manufacturers who had begun by providing hand-made goods on a modest scale for local markets, started to increase the scale of their operations and to seek out national outlets for their products. This pattern was repeated for ceramics, glass, furniture and metalwork where, in each case, a few expanded companies came to dominate the field by the end of the decade. They used design as a means of penetrating the new markets they were seeking to conquer.

Like ceramics and glass manufacture, metalworking underwent a change in this period, not only in the heavy transport industries, but also in the area of smaller household goods. A number of workshops moved into larger-scale production while other companies were formed specifically to mass-manufacture goods in this sector. La Pavoni, for instance, had been set up in 1905 to produce machines making coffee by the espresso method. Its product for domestic use from around 1930 was a much simplified version of its earlier model manufactured for bars and restaurants.

One of the best-known and longest-lasting coffee-makers from this period was the little Art Deco, faceted "Moka Express" designed and fabricated according to new production techniques by Alfonso and Renato Bialetti. It was not until the post-war years, however, that Moka, led by Renato Bialetti, moved into large-scale industrial production and the little coffee-maker became a ubiquitous household object. Although in the 1930s its appearance had an avant-garde quality, it has today assumed the identity of a quasi-vernacular Italian object that seems to have been in existence indefinitely. Its success lies as much in its simple functionality as in its familiarity, and it has undoubtedly earned the title of a "classic" modern Italian artefact.

The *casalinghi* (metal household) goods manufactured at this time also reflected a hint of changing attitudes towards design and production which were to be consolidated in the

Below: "Moka Express" coffee-makers, designed by Alfonso and Renato Bialetti in 1930, in the popular, faceted, Art Deco style. The design was put into production in the early 1930s on an artisanal basis; after the Second World War it moved into mass production.

Right: "Octagonal line" tea and coffee service manufactured by Alessi in 1935, and influenced – like the "Moka Express" – by the faceted Art Deco style popular in the inter-war years.

Right: White porcelain vase designed by Gio Ponti for Richard Ginori in the late 1920s. In his work as artistic director for this illustrious ceramics company, Ponti introduced the neo-Classical style into a number of his designs, representing one aspect of the Novecento movement which was notable for combining neo-Classicism with modernity.

Left: Armchair model 231, manufactured by Cassina in 1938 and demonstrating the company's conservatism at that time: canework is combined with heavy upholstery and a flower-patterned fabric. Most of Cassina's furniture was made individually to customers' orders, and their taste was traditional.

post-war years. Whereas, up until this time, the metalware produced by leading manufacturers such as Krupp (an Italian subsidiary was established in Milan in the 1890s) had been manufactured almost exclusively for the aristocracy or the commercial sector, now the new wealthy middle-class clientele of northern Italy sought stylish metal goods to match their modern kitchens. Workshops that had previously manufactured objects only in eclectic and historicist idioms began to introduce goods in the "modern style" into their ranges and the catalogues of firms such as Cesare Marinai depicted simple, stylish ware which owed much to the innovative work of the Austrian and French designers, Hoffmann and Jean Puiforcat. Hand-making was still the norm, although in many workshops labour was reorganized along rational lines in order to meet the increased demands for goods and to satisfy a variety of aesthetic tastes. On a more mass-production basis, stainless steel was beginning to be introduced into the manufacture of cooking equipment: the Lagostina company produced a set of simple items in 1933 which have remained largely unchanged since that date.

The Alessi company, a large metal workshop established in 1921, began to expand beyond producing metal components for beds to simple, utilitarian items of household equipment. As with so many of the other metal workshops in Italy, tradition and utility alone determined the design of Alessi's early products. In 1929, however, the company began to concentrate exclusively on the production of specialized household ware for the table and the bar counter – cheese dishes, condiment sets, egg cups, sugar dishes, bread baskets and ice-buckets – and, in 1932, under the direction of Carlo Alessi who became responsible for design, the company began to develop a more individual approach towards the appearance of its goods. A coffee-set of 1935–7 with cylindrical components stands out as a striking example of Alessi design. From 1935 until 1948 a growing sense of the need to industrialize the workshop was in evidence but it was not until 1950, with a large order from America, that the move towards mass production was finally initiated.

Apart from the few Rationalist experiments in tubular steel furniture, and the strikingly avant-garde work (all destined for a wealthy clientele) of the group of designers known as the Turin Six – among them Gigi Chessa, Carlo Levi and Enrico

Below and right: The liner *Conte Grande* and its dining room in the early 1930s, showing the highly luxurious interiors of these first-class ships. They were designed to cross the Atlantic in only four days.

Paolucci – for the most part Italian furniture manufacture of the inter-war years continued to be dominated by regionalism, stylistic conservatism and small-scale production. Brianza was still the main furniture-making area in the north and numerous companies thrived there, growing significantly as mass consumption increased dramatically and large stores, like La Rinascente, began to deal in furniture.

While many of these firms had been established around the turn of the century, they were joined in the inter-war years by a number of new arrivals, eager to capitalize on the increased demand for domestic furniture from new, wealthy, middle-class customers. The Cassina Amadeo company, based in Meda, another suburb of Milan, was one of these. As Pier Carlo Santini explained, the first years of the company, which was formed in 1927, was the "time of the joiner-designer-draughtsman ... the decorator who had furniture made to his own design; the artisan workshop ... and the craftsman artist".[5] These categories represented the different ways in which furniture had always been made, traditionally, for different sectors of the market. The Cassina family had been joiners since the eighteenth century but in the early 1900s the firm moved from the manufacture of chairs and

barrels to the production of furniture items that required the skills of an upholsterer. In the early years of the firm's existence, production was organized on a modest scale and outside craftsmen were used extensively. At first only small tables in nineteenth-century styles were produced, appealing to the bourgeois taste of the time. The customers were "shopkeepers and retailers of furnishings in general, principally in Milan"[6] but many pieces were also sold to large-scale manufacturers who subsequently re-sold them. In the early 1930s the Rinascente store and the Mobilificio di Fogliano became major buyers and the company moved into the manufacture of armchairs and drawing-room suites.

As a result of the increasing demand for its wares, Cassina introduced rationalization into its workshops – in 1937–9 a new workshop was constructed and in 1940 French and German machinery was installed – and began to handle its own publicity and distribution. Stylistically the company began to move away from historical forms and to emulate the contemporary designs that were already in fashion, particularly in its upholstered items which owed much to the contemporary French decorative style. Many were commissioned by decorators for specific purposes and were then

copied for small production runs. This meant that, generally speaking, the tastes of the clientele dictated the appearance of the products so that in terms of design style the company tended to follow rather than lead, a tendency that characterized the approach of many manufacturers of domestic consumer goods in the 1930s. Only a very few were truly innovative in the styling of their products. Where manufacturing was concerned the stylistic variation of products necessitated great flexibility on the part of the workforce and a limitation on the degree of mechanization involved. By the post-war period, however, the expansion that had occurred before the war enabled the Cassina company to exploit the new political, social and cultural situation and to be ready to restructure both its production and distribution systems so that it could move confidently into the new era.

Up until 1940, however, the Cassina story exemplifies the way in which many Italian companies, in the area of the traditional applied arts, approached both production and design. The expansion of demand on the part of the newly affluent middle-class home market enabled companies to grow but, where design was concerned, required only that they catered for the most popular tastes of the day.

Although only a handful of manufacturers deliberately took up the challenge of the new "machine aesthetic", it was none the less evident in many of those products that stood outside the context of private consumption, but that were central, all the same, to the programme of Italian modernization in the inter-war years. Italian aeroplanes, boats and trains flourished as symbols of modernity, and they bore no traces of the decorative aesthetic that dominated applied art production. They were also the hallmark of the success of Mussolini's regime: the fact that during the Fascist era the Italian trains ran on time has been frequently reiterated. The Duce reorganized the railway system, primarily as a means of moving troops from one part of the country to another, and invested huge sums of money in the manufacture of items of transport that were intended to contribute to Italy's military might. The Fiat train of 1932, the Breda electric train of 1936 and numerous aeroplanes, trams and transatlantic liners from the 1930s were all among the most aggressively modern objects to emerge in Italy.

The picture of Italian design in the years between the two world wars is complex and extremely varied. The chasm between the traditional applied arts manufacturers and the new industries remained vast in spite of attempts to straddle it. Italy's self-sufficiency meant that there was little contact with foreign markets and there was, therefore, no stimulus from either foreign competition or the need to fulfil the aesthetic expectations of foreign customers. Yet in spite of this isolation there were a few signs of a desire to introduce modern design, in the European sense of the term, and modern production methods, in the American sense. Fiat's automobiles, Olivetti's office machinery and corporate image, as well as isolated instances of radio design and tubular steel furniture, stand out here and, in these instances, efforts were made to find a visual means of expressing the concept of modernity which was so vital to one face of Italian industry and culture.

Although this could as yet only be expressed within a context of nationalism, the close links that were established between industry, culture, economics, politics and design in the inter-war years proved crucial in allowing Italy to establish itself not merely as an expanding nation but as a world power. The encouragement of both large- and small-scale

production provided Italy with a strong base on which to move forward into the post-war years. In addition, the debate about the ideological content of style and design, initiated in the years of Fascist rule, provided an important theme: it was to prove a crucial element within the modern Italian design movement that emerged in the years following 1945.

Left: Locomotive made in 1937 by Breda, a company that adopted the American concept of streamlining but applied it in a much more restrained way. Chrome highlights and bulbous shapes were deliberately avoided.

Below left: 1930s poster for Fiat advertising rolling stock. Both the form of the locomotive and the way it is represented emphasize streamlining which, with its evocations of speed and modernity, was a concept Fiat developed in the inter-war years.

Left: Poster for a Ferragamo shoe from the 1930s, showing the widespread interest in Classicism that dominated the Italian decorative arts, including fashion and fashion accessories. When, in 1935, the League of Nations imposed sanctions on Italy and it had to rely on its own raw materials, Ferragamo turned to cork, Cellophane and raffia as replacements for the leather than he could no longer obtain.

Above right: Woman's shoe, from 1940, by Ferragamo. Made of black suede with a collar of red kid, and a cork wedge heel also covered in red kid, this fashion item used the colours of the uniforms worn by Fascist officers, reflecting the increasingly martial tendency of much Italian casual wear of the time.

CHAPTER 3

1940–1955

"THE FORM OF THE USEFUL": RECONSTRUCTION AND DESIGN

THE RICOSTRUZIONE

"This is the season of spring in contemporary Italian art with all the freshness and vitality and experimentation of a great revival," according to W. D. Teague in 1950.[1] Writing in the British magazine *Design* the previous year, the journalist Leopold Schreiber, just returned from a visit to the Milan Fair, remarked, "The Italians have undoubtedly a genius for reconstruction."[2] He had observed, at first hand, the huge effort which had been made, in the three years following the end of the war, to restore Italy, economically, socially and culturally, to its pre-war status.

Italy was completely devastated by the war, both physically and morally, and in 1945 the situation looked bleak. Over three million houses, and all their contents, had been destroyed by bombing and the three years which followed the end of hostilities were marked by a severe deprivation of all essential commodities.

By the end of the decade, however, there had been a remarkable recovery on a number of fronts. Rapid building programmes had been initiated to rehouse the homeless, and the wheels of Italian industry, undamaged for the most part by war, were turning once again, producing a wide range of goods essential to the country's material reconstruction.

Left: The "Isetta" car, produced by Iso in 1954. Strikingly compact, it was minimal yet stylish, and made an enormous impact. Its size and reasonable price placed it in the spirit of democracy that dominated the 1950s; it was later produced by BMW in Germany.

Left: The Galleria Vittorio Emmanuele (left) and a residential area
(right) after the bombing suffered
by the northern Italian towns during the Second World War.

Although characterized by hardship this was an enormously exciting period, dominated by faith in the new
democracy and hope for the future. Within this new age of
optimism the architect-designers played a vital role, providing a possible shape for that future and a form for the new,
democratic, Italian lifestyle. Hand-in-hand with manufacturing industry, the designers succeeded in turning a
dream of the future into a reality.

By 1949 pre-war levels of industrial production were re-
established (the 1945 figure had been only a quarter of that
for 1941) and a remarkable recovery from the devastation had
been achieved. In spite of the fact that changes in governmental policy, intended to combat growing inflation,
caused the transformation to slow down in the last couple of
years of the decade, by 1950 Italy was none the less established as a visible manufacturing force within Europe, and
Italian industry was producing goods geared towards the
market. The subsequent decade and a half witnessed an

export-led boom that transformed Italy into both a modern
industrial state and a mass consumer society on a par with
other European powers such as France and Germany. By
1966 industrial production was three times the level it had
been fifteen years earlier. Within this metamorphosis the role
of design proved vital. Particularly significant was the new
concept of industrial design that emerged as the new industries and, increasingly, some of the more traditional ones,
sought to organize their production along modern lines; to
make their goods look appropriate to the modern age; and to
use this as a means of persuading new customers to buy them.
Industrial design provided both a means of helping make
Italian goods competitive on the international market and, at
home, of giving the new Italian industrial culture a sophisticated and attractive image.

The story of the emergence of an Italian industrial design
movement in the decade following 1945 is inseparable from
the political events of those years. Alcide De Gaspari was

elected Prime Minister in December 1946, heading a coalition government formed of Christian Democrats, Communists, Socialists, Liberals and members of the Actionist party, all linked in their commitment to anti-Fascism and the new Italian republic.

Industrial reconstruction was effected largely through the implementation of State policy. The most significant decisions were those that opposed any form of direct State control over the affairs of private industry and those that encouraged a laissez-faire approach towards trading on the international market combined with a protectionist attitude towards the home market. Although these policies were generally followed, the state did take some direct steps to help industry get back on its feet by granting cheap credit, providing cheap energy and steel and, through the agency of the IRI, actually controlling a large sector of Italian industry itself, including the airlines, the telephone network and the manufacture of ships, cars (Alfa Romeo) and machine tools. Most import-

antly, perhaps, the government also helped manufacturing industry produce competitively priced goods, by implementing a low wages policy. Labour was plentiful (there was a constant supply from the south of Italy) and so trade unions remained weak.

American financial aid was also crucial to the rapid reconstruction of Italian industry after the war. Between 1943 and 1948 $2,200 million were supplied in the form of food and fuel, and between 1948 and 1952 $1,500 million were provided by the Marshall Aid scheme to help Italian reconstruction. In addition, the expansion of a middle-class home market eager to acquire as many consumer goods as possible after the deprivation of the lean war years helped industry get back on its feet. As the fully fledged export-led boom did not get off the ground until the end of the 1950s, the home market continued to play an important role in the decade immediately following the war. During that time manufacturers concentrated on modernizing their production systems,

manufacturing goods for the inhabitants of the new Italian republic and evolving a product style that encapsulated the hopes and aspirations of the new democratic Italian society, now rapidly emerging from the defeat of Fascism and the destruction of war.

However, in spite of the impact of industrial reconstruction the period was also inevitably one of great hardship and massive unemployment – factors that the new coalition government had to confront when it came into power. During the first few months of the regime the left-wing parties formed an important element within the combined government, but in 1947 the Communists and Socialists were excluded and the Christian Democrats – the party favoured by the industrialists – assumed a more prominent role.

DESIGN AND IDEOLOGY IN THE LATE 1940s

The change in the political picture of the second half of the 1940s was closely mirrored by changing attitudes towards design. With the dismissal of the left-wing parties from power the prevailing emphasis in design moved from an approach founded on a neo-Rationalist, democratic position to one based on an anti-Rationalist, bourgeois stance.

This was openly reflected in *Domus*, the leading architectural and design magazine of the day. In 1946

Ernesto N. Rogers took over editorship of the magazine, bringing with him a strong left-wing, anti-Fascist approach to the problem of design. Steeped in Rationalist principles, but fundamentally opposed to Mussolini's regime, he was careful to move beyond the ideological signification that the Rationalist style had acquired as the vehicle of Fascism. He was at pains to reinstate its original, more abstract, utilitarian, and democratic aims, articulated in the idea of the rational mass production of standardized units, both in architectural construction and the manufacture of domestic items. His ideas were developed within the context of the destruction of homes and the need to rebuild a society, in both a physical and a cultural sense. To this end interior furnishings were, for a short time, approached with a philosophy that stressed the Rationalists' belief in the necessity of mass production and design for industry.

Rogers was careful to talk in terms of process, rather than style, to emphasize links with tradition, and to stress the essential humanism of his programme. His aim centred on the need to give the architectural problem its proper context within the specific cultural, social and economic issues of the day, expressed in his assertion that "It is a question of forming a taste, a technique, a morality, all terms of the same function. It is a question of building a society."[3] This demonstrated clearly his commitment to the need for a renewed relationship between culture, society and design.

Two exhibitions of the early post-war years demonstrated this neo-Rationalist approach to the problem of design. The first, held in 1946, was the exhibition by RIMA (Riunione Italiana Mostre per l'Arredamento) of home furnishings, at which a group of young architects – among them Ignazio Gardella, Carlo De Carli, Franco Albini, Vico Magistretti and Vittoriano Vigano – displayed a range of simple furniture items. Made mostly of wood, these confronted the problems of serial production and the shortages of raw materials and small living spaces: chairs folded and stacked to meet the exigencies of the day. The Eighth Triennale, held in 1947, reiterated the same theme, taking "the home" as a focus and proposing a neo-Rationalist solution to the problem of post-war housing. As Pier Bottoni, a committed Communist, explained: "The programme of the Eighth Triennale . . . had to

Left: An intense desire for physical reconstruction was present after 1945, with Italy rebuilding itself from scratch. Housing was a priority, and many construction programmes were initiated with the help of American aid. The spirit of reconstruction was particularly apparent in the articles published in *Domus*.

Far left: Sella Valsugana De Gaspari on holiday in the late 1940s. De Gaspari headed the Italian government during the crucial years of post-Fascist reconstruction. In spite of hardships, the citizens of the new Italian republic were optimistic about the future, and De Gaspari succeeded in bringing Italy into line with other major international powers in a very short time.

Below: Chair designed by Gastone Rinaldi for RIMA in 1955, the tubular steel framework allowing it to be tipped on its back or used upright. Italian designers were inventive in grasping the opportunities of new technologies, but the use of a wicker seat suggests the continued presence of more traditional tastes.

take into account the social and economic climate created by the war . . . we must face and solve problems that interest the least well-off classes. The aim was a 'home for everybody'."[4] With the expulsion of the Communists and Socialists from the coalition government in 1947, however, Rogers' brand of neo-Rationalism gave way to a new anti-Rationalist design philosophy which took sculpture rather than architecture as its mother discipline and source of inspiration, and which defined itself as a movement with more pronouncedly bourgeois, rather than specifically working-class, tendencies.

Returning to the editorship of *Domus* in 1947 after a gap of seven years (during the war years he had put his energies into a magazine called *Stile*), Gio Ponti ignored the left-wing attempt to recuperate the Rationalist collective ideal, proposing instead a more overtly expressive, middle-class approach. This embraced both the individualism of the craft tradition and looked to the USA – an increasingly important source of cultural and design ideas in the late 1940s in Italy – for a model of design operating under a democratic system. Under the editorship of Ponti, *Domus* focused on the need for a renewed language for modern design that took its stimulus

from sources other than that of modern architecture. Ponti's statement that "Our ideal of the 'good life' and the level of taste and thought expressed by our homes and manner of living are all part of the same thing"[5] reflected the shift that occurred between 1946 and 1950 in Italian design ideology, providing a direct parallel with the changing political climate of those years and sowing the seeds for the events of the subsequent decade.

THE INFLUENCE OF THE USA

With the demise of the early post-war emphasis on neo-Rationalist themes, such as prefabrication and standardization, and the new concentration on "artistic" qualities, Italian design began to adopt a very particular visual identity, as witnessed by a group of industrial products that began to demonstrate to the rest of the world that Italy's reconstruction could earn a special place in world trade. These included Piaggio's "Vespa" motor-scooter, designed by Corradino D'Ascanio in 1946; Olivetti's "Lexicon 80" typewriter, designed by Marcello Nizzoli in 1948; Gio Ponti's espresso coffee-machine for La Pavoni of 1949 and Pininfarina's "Cisitalia" motor-car of 1951 – they were remarkable, above all, for their startling visual originality and their striking family likeness. Their sensuous curves expressed a voluptuousness and opulence which did not, however, discredit their essential utility. The body-shell aesthetic they advocated was not merely an attempt to turn industrial artefacts into sculpture objects: it also reflected another important factor which had wider significance within Italian culture and economy during this period – Italy's dependence on the USA.

This growing dependence had been behind the elimination of the left-wing parties from the coalition government. The USA provided not only the necessary funds but also the essential "know-how" and technology to enable Italian industry to get back on its feet. Thus the increase in the scale of production effected by the large Italian manufacturing companies – Fiat, Olivetti, Pirelli, Snia Viscosa (textiles) and Montecatini (chemicals) among them – were based entirely upon the implementation of American principles of Fordism

Below: Bookcase and folding armchair by Vico Magistretti, 1946. Both designs explored important themes in post-war Italy. The bookcase pushed forward the technological limits of furniture construction: it is formed of two steel tubes fixed between the floor and the ceiling, a system patented in Italy in 1946. The armchair is evidence of the increasing interest in flexibility and portability.

Left: The casino at San Remo in 1952 – both the building and the furnishings were designed by Gio Ponti. Into the fairly austere structure he introduced a playful note, with trompe l'œil playing cards on the surfaces of the upholstered easy chairs. Ponti became very interested in the application of such motifs to furniture, and worked with the illustrator and designer Piero Fornasetti on a number of projects recalling seventeenth-century examples of the technique.

Below: Section of the Montecatini exhibit at the Fiera di Milano of 1948, showing the use and development of plastics. Research into plastics technology absorbed a great deal of money; by the 1950s the results were seen in small household objects, such as those produced by Kartell.

in Italian manufacturing. Fiat's figures increased by 400 per cent, for example, between 1950 and 1961. Although this modernization process had been initiated in the pre-war years, it went through a much more intensive second phase of development in the 1940s and 1950s, enabling Italy to become a strong competitor on the international market, primarily in the areas of automobiles, textiles, office machinery and petrochemicals.

The influence of the USA went further than this. By the second half of the 1950s Italy had become a modern consumer society along American lines, capable of manufacturing those goods such as washing machines, dishwashers, colour televisions and food-mixers which the country required. The importance of the USA in the decade after the war was vital, as it provided both the industrial, cultural and economic model to which Italy aspired, and the means by which it could emulate it.

This was a two-way process. Just as Italy was impressed by all things American, the vogue for the "Italian style" grew rapidly in the USA, and indeed in a number of European countries, Britain among them, through the 1950s. This was linked to the large-scale emigration of Italians to other countries in these years.

Below: The Fiat 500B coming off the assembly line in 1948. Ten years earlier the Fiat company had opened its Mirafiore plant in Turin, modelled on Ford's factory at River Rouge. Larger and much more efficient than the one at Lingotto, it enabled Fiat to increase its production figures enormously in the post-war years.

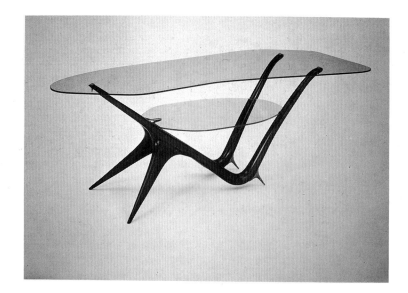

In the years immediately following the war a range of metal goods emerged that derived partly from the American idiom of streamlining yet were distinguished by a highly sculptural aesthetic – they came to be known as "the Italian line". Mass-produced objects with sleek, fluid contours, they were designed for the street, the workplace and the home. Widely disseminated, hugely popular and, above all, aggressively modern, they came to symbolize the new Italian democracy and to represent the essence of *ricostruzione*. The most prominent of this family of goods were Corradino D'Ascanio's "Vespa" motor-scooter, designed for Piaggio in 1946 (right); Gio Ponti's

THE FAMILY OF FORMS

coffee-machine for La Pavoni of 1947 (left); Battista Pininfarina's "Cisitalia" car of 1946 (right), and Marcello Nizzoli's sleekly sculpted "Lexicon 80" typewriter of 1948 (above). Furniture displayed similar organic forms – for example, the table from the late 1940s by the Turin designer Carlo Mollino (top).

Left: Still from the Hollywood film *Roman Holiday* (1953) starring Audrey Hepburn, Gregory Peck and a "Vespa" motor-scooter. Films such as this were instrumental in taking Italian design abroad to influence a whole new generation.

Hollywood took the Italian style on board wholesale, and films such as *Roman Holiday* (1953) and *Three Coins in a Fountain* (1955) helped to show to the rest of the world the strength of Italian contemporary culture. This manifested itself in the combined appeal of Italy's artistic heritage and its new modern image, represented by "Vespas" and coffee-bars.

The "espresso coffee" cult also grew throughout the 1950s, in both the USA and Europe. The proliferation of coffee-bars in urban centres everywhere by the end of the decade served as another means of introducing the new Italian products – furniture, coffee-machines and crockery among them – to a wide, and in particular to a young, international audience. The designer F. H. K. Henrion, just returned from a holiday in Italy, wrote in the British *Design* magazine as early as 1949 about the smart little coffee-cups that he had found in Italy.

By the end of the 1950s, Italian style had become increasingly important to the emerging youth culture in Britain, where the young not only rode "Vespas" and Lambrettas, and

drank espresso coffee, but now wore Italian suits and fashion accessories as well. Their image of Italy was, however, determined more by Hollywood's depiction of it than by the real thing. Italy's determination to export its contemporary material culture had, by the end of the 1950s, reaped enormous rewards.

On the other hand, the use of American production technology in the manufacture of Italian goods inevitably influenced their appearance. In 1950 the American industrial designer W. D. Teague made a trip to Italy to see the state of post-war reconstruction, thereby helping to seal the design connection between the two countries. A direct Italian borrowing from the USA was the concept of streamlining: this was visible in the die-cast or stamped, voluptuously curved casings (which had their origins in the aerodynamic, teardrop bodies of automobiles and other objects of transport) used to conceal the internal mechanisms of products such as typewriters, cars and radios. But whereas the Americans tended to decorate their body-shells with chromed details and other visual highlights, the Italian designers of the 1940s and 1950s favoured a simpler, less aggressive, more utilitarian and less elaborated "industrial aesthetic" for their products. Thus, for example, the cover concealing the rear wheel of the "Vespa" motor-scooter – the object which F. H. K. Henrion in 1949 described as "a new form and technique of locomotion"[6] – and the two-piece die-cast metal shell of the "Lexicon 80" typewriter were both simple, elegant solutions: they appealed to the eye in much the same way as the abstract, organic sculpture that was produced in the same period.

The USA was also behind the replacement of the term "industrial aesthetics", which had been widely used in design circles up until this time, by that of "industrial design", and was responsible for the export of the concept of the "consultant designer for industry". The Americans had pioneered the commercial application of art to mass production industry in the years of the Depression, using "design" as a means of enhancing product competition by increasing sales appeal. They found their "industrial designers" among the ranks of visually creative individuals attached to the advertising profession. By 1939, design had become a major factor in the manufacture of most of the high-technology consumer goods produced in the USA. While Italy was clearly indebted to that country for the invention of the concept of industrial design it appropriated it into a very different economic, social and cultural context, so that it became significantly transformed in the process. Italy's designers for industry were not affiliated to the world of advertising but were architects trained in the Rationalist tradition: they carried the heritage of the European Modern Movement into the post-war period. Their aims were inevitably much less overtly commercial than those of the Americans. In addition, the European market, with its class distinctions and cultural variation, was totally unlike its essentially homogeneous American counterpart. Goods manufactured with the collaboration of an industrial designer tended to be aimed at a sophisticated, wealthy, urban market, rather than at the mass of society, and thus aspired to the level of "high" rather than "mass" culture.

While the American model lay at the roots of the Italian post-war design movement, therefore, the latter moved quite quickly into a separate arena, developing in the process a unique identity for itself. This was already apparent in the group of mass-produced objects that emerged from Italy's assembly lines in the late 1940s and early 1950s.

THE STEEL INDUSTRY

These new "industrially designed" objects were all fabricated in metal, predominantly steel. The wide availability of cheap steel in post-war Italy enabled many industries to flourish – automobiles, electrical appliances, office machinery, and, to some extent, furniture. In 1945 a third of the Italian steel industry was owned by Finsider, a company itself owned by the IRI. After the war it established its manufacturing according to a new method based on the complete cycle, commencing with the raw material. As a result Italian steel became internationally competitive, and Italy saw an engineering boom. This facilitated the manufacture of new products in this sector, and a wide range of new consumer machines rolled off the production lines.

Italy's late arrival on the industrial scene, combined with the possibilities provided by American aid, put it in a position to be able to purchase up-to-date production machinery. The appearance of the "Vespa", the "Lexicon 80", the Pavoni coffee-machine and the "Cisitalia" motor-car (in addition to the sewing machines manufactured by Necchi and Borletti) owed much, therefore, to the new methods of working metal that were introduced in these years.

"THE ITALIAN LINE"

The uniqueness of what came to be called "The Italian line" cannot be reduced to the mere influence of technology. In the hands of highly trained and experienced designers such as Gio Ponti, Marco Nizzoli and Pininfarina, these massproduced metal consumer goods acquired a level of visual sophistication which had as much to do with prevailing aesthetic theory as with the constraints of the materials and production machinery used.

The catchphrase "utility plus beauty" came to characterize the Italian design aesthetic of the late 1940s and early 1950s. It implied that pre-war Rationalism, apart from being ideologically suspect, was no longer relevant in the post-war years, and that the domination of architecture should be replaced by the role of the fine arts. In practice, contemporary abstract sculpture – the work of artists such as Max Bill, Ben Nicholson, Antoine Pevsner, Alexander Calder, Hans

Arp and Henry Moore – which favoured the organic rather than the geometric as its source of abstraction, provided the main stimulus; suddenly, sculptural form was everywhere to be seen. The pages of *Domus* were filled with illustrations of organic sculpture. In an article published in 1950, Max Bill elaborated the aesthetic principles involved in the idea of "beauty as function" while the Ninth Milan Triennale of the following year included a section of industrial products entitled "The Form of the Useful".

The Ninth Triennale of 1951 consolidated the progress that had been made in the second half of the 1940s and showed to the rest of the world, for the first time, that the Italians were beginning to develop an industrial design movement all their own. The setting, designed by the architects L. B. Belgioioso and E. Peressutti, with a hanging sculpture by Max Huber, was as dramatic as the exhibits themselves: with balls suspended from thin wires transversing the space, it

engendered a strongly sculptural atmosphere for the utilitarian objects displayed within it. Exhibits included typewriters by Olivetti, among them the "Lexicon 80", the little portable "Lettera 22" (first produced in 1950, the first of its kind to be designed for standardized mass production in Italy), digital clocks by Gino Valle for Ritz Italora, the "Vespa" motor-scooter, Ponti's "Visetta" sewing machine, lights by the Castiglioni brothers, the "Cisitalia" car, and a wide range of domestic electrical appliances.

The strong sense of product form that characterized all the products at the Triennale was reiterated at the subsequent exhibition of that title, held in 1954, where the pendulum between the "artistic" and the "useful" had swung firmly in the direction of the former. This time the section devoted to industrial goods was called "The Production of Art" and the whole event was characterized by what has been described as a feeling of "abandoned playfulness".[7]

Left: At the Ninth Triennale of 1951, the display sign of "The Form of the Useful" (the section devoted to new industrial products) was as evocative as its contents. The wire structure, threaded with balls to intersect the space, was designed by the sculptor Max Huber, and clearly owed much to the Constructivists as well as to the mobiles of Alexander Calder.

Right: Marcello Nizzoli's "Lettera 22" typewriter, designed for Olivetti in 1950 and awarded the Compasso d'Oro in 1954. Italy's first portable typewriter was a simple little utility object, capable of fitting into any environment. Light in weight and compact in shape, it came in a carrying case with a handle, its uniform beige colour relieved by a single red tabulator key.

Left: "Visetta" electric sewing machine, designed by Gio Ponti for Officine Meccaniche Visa and produced in 1954. Finished in green, it incorporated the organic curves which characterized "the Italian line". Sewing machines were among the consumer durables greatly in demand by new markets.

Page 90: Stacking chair made of bent plywood designed by Vittoriano Vigano and produced from 1949. Capable of disassembly for transportation, this little chair was typical of the tendency towards simple, functional items to furnish new homes.

Pages 90–91: Interior designed by Carlo Mollino in 1944 for the home of Ada and Cesare Minola in Turin. It shows Mollino's developing idiosyncratic style, which has been described as "streamlined Surrealism". Heavily upholstered chairs, echoing the forms of the human body, achieved a sculptural presence in space.

THE FURNITURE INDUSTRY

By 1954 it was apparent that the Italian furniture industry had begun to align itself more closely with the concerns of the modernized sector of Italian industry, rather than with the craft sector from whence it had originally come. This represented an important breakthrough for the international image of Italian design.

The architect-designers who took on the responsibility of designing the products of post-war industry had, inevitably, a special relationship with the interior and the furnishings within it. As we have seen, the Italian furniture industry had traditionally been a highly localized, artisanal activity and furniture was largely made to order. While the companies based in Brianza had gone some way towards enlarging the scale of their production, working cooperatively with each other and introducing national distribution systems, they still remained modestly sized operations in the years immediately

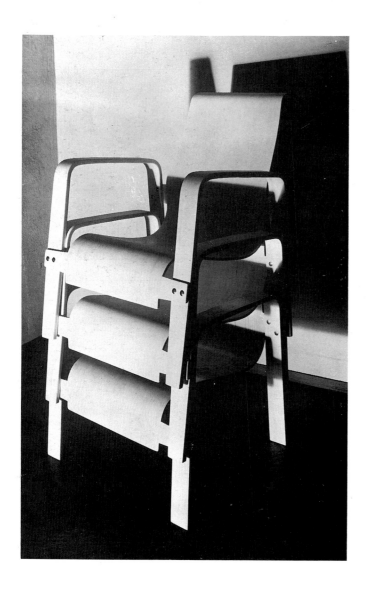

following the war. In fact, 90 per cent of the Italian firms still employed only five people or fewer in 1947. This dualism, created by the coexistence of a handful of very large, export-led companies with mechanized production systems and a huge number of small, family-owned firms that combined some mechanized production with skilled hand labour, characterized Italian industry in the decades after the war and became increasingly defined towards the mid-1950s.

While no furniture manufacturing company ever grew to the size of, say, Fiat or Olivetti, a number of firms did move into the modern age in the decade following the war. This was reflected in their approach towards both mechanized production and the appearance of their products. Inevitably design played an important role in this transformation. A number of existing companies modified their activities dramatically around this time; others were created from scratch, and defined themselves from the beginning as small-scale modern industrial operations. Like the large concerns, they were export-oriented and their products were designed from the outset with an eye on the international market.

The most significant change in the production of furniture was the adoption of new materials and modern production techniques. Thus, from the mid-1940s onwards, new types of Italian furniture emerged made of bent and moulded ply-wood, sheet metal, metal rod, rubber and, eventually, plastics. Here, once again, the USA provided a model and the early post-war editions of *Domus* featured the work of the American modern furniture designers – Charles Eames, George Nelson, Eero Saarinen and Harry Bartoia – to stimulate similar innovation on Italian soil. Italian versions were quick to appear, among them a moulded plywood chair by Vittoriano Vigano in 1946; a chair by Christiano and Frattino with rubber joints in the same year; and, in 1947, a folding metal chair by Marco Zanuso, and a metal-legged chair by Ettore Sottsass Jnr. In 1948 the Fede Cheti fabric company, one of the few progressive furniture companies, sponsored a modern furniture competition. It stimulated new designs from Zanuso, Vigano, Magistretti, De Carli, Gardella, Menghi and Albini. By the end of the decade it was quite clear that a new Italian mass production furniture movement had been born.

From the outset the Italians developed their own national version of what was clearly already an international idiom pioneered by the Americans. Like their consumer machines of these years, the Italian forms were more expressive and more sculptural than their foreign equivalents: quite quickly

Right: Small armchair with a re-clining back, designed by Carlo Mollino for the "House of the Sun" in Cervinia, 1947. Mollino combined bent laminated wood with upholstered cushions to create a chair that was modern and comfortable. His organic aesthetic contrasted strongly with the more rectilinear forms of Rationalist designs from this period.

Above right: The Apelli and Varesio joinery, Turin, in about 1950. This was where most of Carlo Mollino's important furniture was made; the components in the workshop show clearly how strongly his forms resembled organic shapes such as branches of trees and antlers' horns.

Far right: Sketch by Carlo Mollino for a cupboard with cheval glass, intended for the bedroom of the Minola house in Turin (see pages 90–91) – it demonstrates the joint qualities of inventiveness and fantasy that characterize so much of his work. All Mollino's furniture designs were for wealthy clients and produced on an artisanal basis.

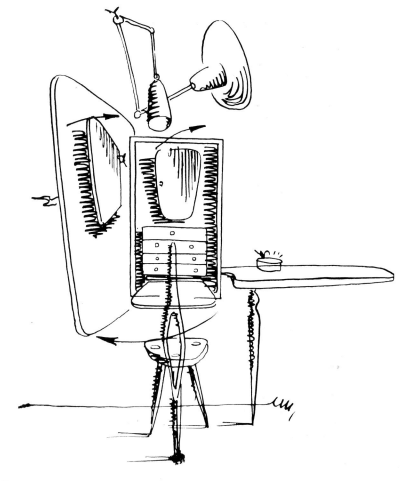

other countries began to look to Italy for aesthetic inspiration in the area of home furnishings. Unlike the Scandinavians and the British, who stressed the craft roots of their modern furniture movements, the Italian designers wholeheartedly embraced the aesthetic possibilities of the new materials, producing pieces that had no obvious links with the traditions of craft (other than the quality of their manufacture) and no visual inhibitions. Once again "beauty" was more important than mere "utility", and Italian furniture objects began to appear in the pages of sophisticated design magazines in metropolitan centres worldwide.

The most extreme examples of the expressive Italian furniture style of the late 1940s emanated from Turin where a small group of furniture designers, grouped around Carlo Mollino, created a highly extravagant set of "streamlined surreal" furniture pieces in carved wood and moulded plywood, in the spirit of the Turinese Baroque style. Designed to fit around the curves of the human body, the organic forms of the chairs, desks, tables and sofas recalled the twisted branches of trees and deers' antlers.

In Milan, where most modern furniture was produced, such extroversion was less apparent but the "organic" theme was equally popular, influencing the curved forms of foam-

Above: The "P40" settee, designed by Osvaldo Borsani and manufactured by Tecno in 1954. A highly innovatory design, it represented both increased flexibility (the back could be let down to turn it into a bed) and an interest in new materials – in this case, rubber and steel. (See page 100 for a reclining chair version of the same design.)

rubber sofas and chairs and the wooden, splayed legs of dining-tables, cupboards and coffee-tables. Apart from conforming to the aesthetic requirements of the day, these forms were the inevitable results of the use of the new materials – foam rubber and moulded plywood – which favoured the organic over the rectilinear.

After the war Cassina was one of the first pre-war companies to move into the production of furniture items in the modern style. In the early post-war years the company transformed itself into a manufacturer of modern furniture aimed at an international market. Two factors led to this dramatic volte-face.

One was a bulk order from the Italian navy, between 1947 and 1952, for the supply of furniture for its ships. In order to meet this requirement Cassina had to undertake a thorough rationalization of its production processes and instal new equipment to enable it to manufacture standardized furniture in sufficiently large numbers. This reorientation of the company and the assured revenue that it was guaranteed from such a massive order caused it to rethink completely its production philosophy. The growing prosperity of the early post-war period, with its emphasis upon exports, encouraged Cassina to think in terms of meeting the needs of a wealthy international clientele. It also began to sell its goods in the name of "modern design" – the hallmark, increasingly, of successful Italian goods abroad.

The second factor which persuaded Cassina that this was the right way forward was a series of meetings and collaborative exercises with members of the new generation of architect-designers. The first, short-lived liaison with Paolo Buffa was quickly followed by one with Franco Albini, which lasted from 1946 to 1947. The most fruitful relationship, however, was with Gio Ponti, with whom Cesare Cassina worked from 1950 onwards, on the design and production of a number of items including the "Distex" armchair and the well known "Supperleggera" chair. Based on a long-standing design that originated in the fishing village of Chiavari, Ponti's little wooden chair, with its finely tapered legs and caned seat, recalled Italian tradition but also ideally fitted the modernizing mood of the 1950s. It went into production in 1957 and quickly became a huge international success. It also sealed Cassina's arrival as a manufacturer of sophisticated modern furniture pieces for a wealthy, international, style-conscious clientele.

The Tecno company was established as such in 1954, although it had begun life several decades earlier as Borsani Arredamenti – a workshop-based, family-run company that worked on personalized interiors and their furnishings. Like Cassina it was quick to adopt the modern style in the post-war years and in the early 1950s it produced a range of designs by architect-designers; these included a circular armchair in plywood on steel legs by Roberto Mango and a mass-produced chair in foam rubber, designed by Osvaldo Borsani himself, which contained a mechanism permitting it to recline at different angles. This kind of innovatory thinking challenged the traditional concept of seating objects, as well as the materials from which they were made. It made Italian products highly visible on the international market and encouraged

Above: Bed-settee designed by Marco Zanuso and manufactured by Arflex in 1955. Zanuso used a metal structure to create an innovative mechanism for turning the settee into a bed and employed foam rubber for the upholstery, an ideal material for both purposes.

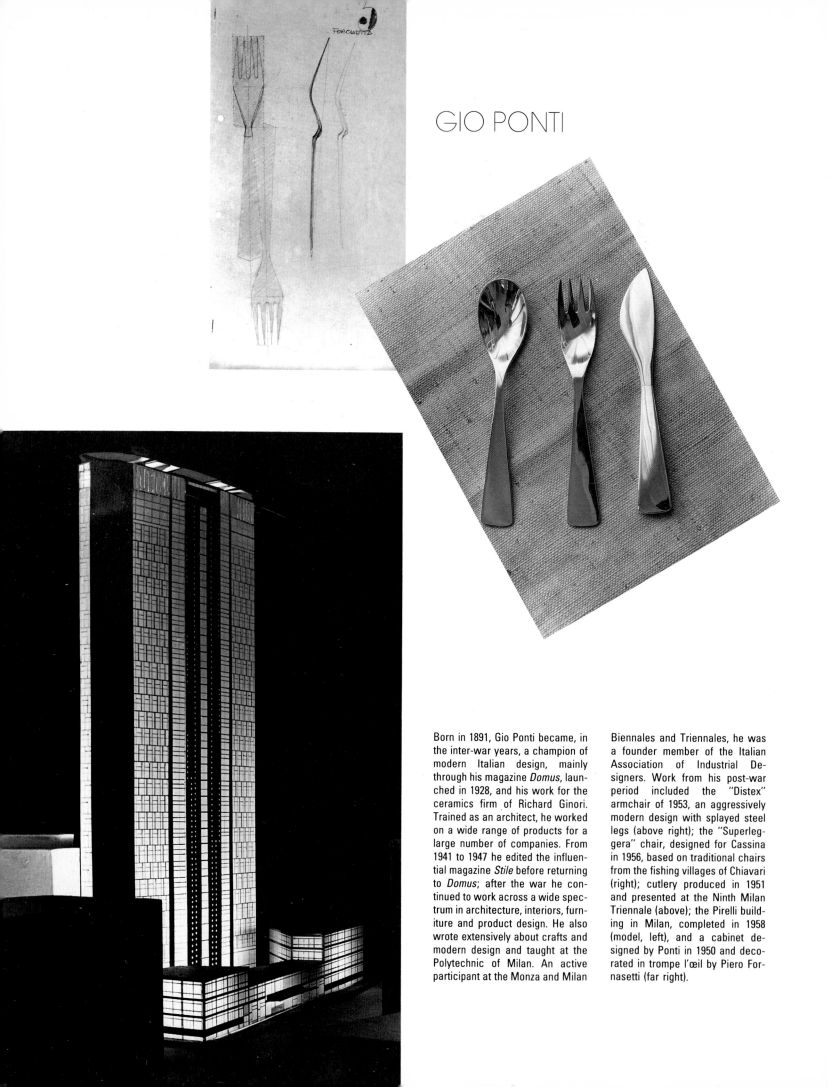

GIO PONTI

Born in 1891, Gio Ponti became, in the inter-war years, a champion of modern Italian design, mainly through his magazine *Domus*, launched in 1928, and his work for the ceramics firm of Richard Ginori. Trained as an architect, he worked on a wide range of products for a large number of companies. From 1941 to 1947 he edited the influential magazine *Stile* before returning to *Domus*; after the war he continued to work across a wide spectrum in architecture, interiors, furniture and product design. He also wrote extensively about crafts and modern design and taught at the Polytechnic of Milan. An active participant at the Monza and Milan Biennales and Triennales, he was a founder member of the Italian Association of Industrial Designers. Work from his post-war period included the "Distex" armchair of 1953, an aggressively modern design with splayed steel legs (above right); the "Superleggera" chair, designed for Cassina in 1956, based on traditional chairs from the fishing villages of Chiavari (right); cutlery produced in 1951 and presented at the Ninth Milan Triennale (above); the Pirelli building in Milan, completed in 1958 (model, left), and a cabinet designed by Ponti in 1950 and decorated in trompe l'œil by Piero Fornasetti (far right).

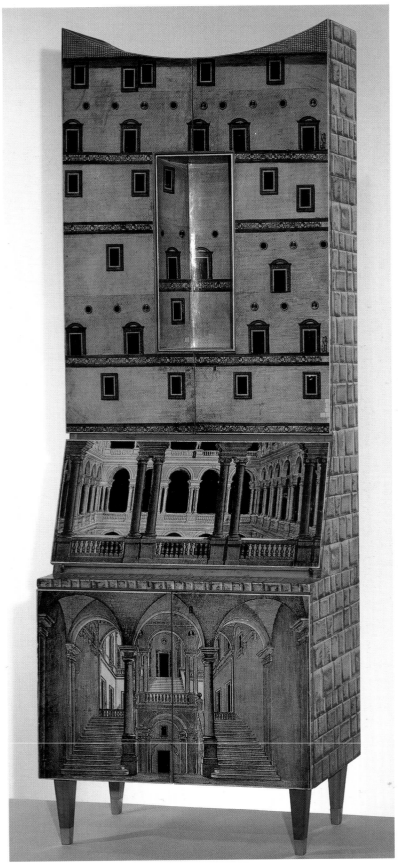

Below: Hanging light, model 2072, designed by Gino Sarfatti and manufactured by Arteluce in 1953. With its coloured Perspex discs, it was clearly influenced by the mobiles of Alexander Calder, who was the inspiration behind many of the more exotic "light sculptures" to emerge in these years.

other countries to look to Italy, and the Italian furniture manufacturers in particular, as a source of radical new ideas.

Experimentation with new materials, suited to serial production, provided the way forward for a number of new furniture manufacturers. It also provided a challenge to the first generation of architect-designers who, with the absence of architectural projects on which to test their freshly acquired skills, had moved from interior design into furniture design. Marco Zanuso, for example, was asked by Pirelli in 1948 to produce some designs that would make use of the foam rubber that the company had developed as a potential furnishing material. As a result of his work, the Arflex company was formed as an offshoot of Pirelli. Zanuso was given a key position in the new company and took his designs from conception right through the production process to the finished products.

The new model of design-led manufacturing had little in common with the artisanal tradition of furniture-making, which oriented its goods towards existing tastes and markets. The new approach had to create its own market and it concentrated on setting the pace stylistically. In 1949 Azucena was formed by three designers – Gardella, Caccia, and Magistretti. It too was committed to design innovation and provided an outlet for the designs of all three men. When in 1954 Zanotta was formed, it also concentrated on manufacturing furniture items proposed by leading designers of the day, among them the Castiglioni brothers.

Dino Gavina's first company was established in Bologna at the end of the 1940s, and it began by manufacturing experimental modern chairs and selling them directly to the public. Gradually retailers became interested in the work and a factory was built in San Lazzaro. Contacts with the State railroad, and with the army for the supply of hoods for jeeps, got the company moving into a larger scale of production.

The first designers with whom Gavina collaborated were little-known, local figures, but in the early 1950s he was introduced to Carlo Mollino, Carlo De Carli and Pier Giacomo Castiglioni, the last of whom he went on to work with very closely. Their first joint project was a chair called "Babela", designed for the meeting-room in the Chamber of Commerce in Milan. Gavina subsequently produced Castiglioni's trestle table, the "Cavaletto", one of his best-known pieces. Gavina SpA was finally born in 1960 and the company's main successes were achieved in the years after that.

Although they were geared to modern production methods in the way they worked the new materials, the furniture manufacturers remained relatively small in size. Most tended to concentrate on a single material or manufacturing process and to collaborate with other companies when other processes were needed. As a result the furniture industry based around Milan developed into a sort of halfway house between the large, mass production companies and the very small artisanal workshops. Using modern methods and modern machinery, firms produced stylistically advanced, exclusive furniture items aimed at a wealthy, sophisticated, international clientele, while remaining relatively small-scale in operations and retaining much of their traditional skilled labour. Thanks to the latter, the quality of their products remained very high.

The limitation of size and production numbers enabled furniture manufacturers to innovate easily, and frequently, without having to bear the huge costs of retooling to which mass production companies such as Fiat and Olivetti were committed. Above all it allowed for flexibility, stylistic variation, and quick decision-making, factors that were essential when design was the central element in both the image and the promotion of the furniture. Goods were exported through agencies, a principle of collaboration that was vital in this period and remained so throughout the highly competitive 1960s and 1970s.

By the mid-1950s Italian furniture had become one of the major, international symbols of an affluent, cosmopolitan lifestyle. It had even begun to challenge the dominance of Scandinavian furniture, with its ideology of democracy, tradition and craftsmanship.

Lighting too took on a special significance in Italy at this time, largely because of its sculptural potential. The highly expressive and aggressively modern "lighting sculptures" that emerged in these years – manufactured by yet another group of newly formed, small-scale companies, among them Arteluce, Arredoluce, O'Luce and Stilnovo – once again tapped the visualizing skills of the leading designers of the day, especially those of the Castiglioni brothers, Vigano, and Gino Sarfatti. Sarfatti's work for Arteluce has been described as "a typical combination of utilitarian ingenuity, exquisite workmanship and fantasy of conception".[8] These lighting designs quickly became international hallmarks of the Italian style. Not only did the fixtures prove eminently suited to the "utility plus beauty" formula, they also contributed to the expressive mood typical of numerous interiors at this time.

While countless small furniture firms confirmed their commitment to the fine art ideal in the 1950s, many of them justifying their prices through their products' association with Italy's fine artistic heritage, still only a handful were truly innovative. Many, as Andrea Branzi explains, simply emulated the work of the leading designers: "Even the smal-

Below: Table light designed by Gino Sarfatti and manufactured by Arteluce in 1954. The adjustable PVC shade balanced on the metal base allowed the light to spread in a number of different directions. One of Sarfatti's more minimal designs, it demonstrates the way in which appearance, however flamboyant, never diverged far from function in the so-called "heroic" years of Italian design.

lest joiner's shop soon learned how to make bar counters that looked like Gio Ponti's own designs; the smallest electric workshop soon learned to make lamps that looked like Vigano's and upholsterers played on armchair models that might be reminiscent of Zanuso's."[9]

By the mid-1950s Italian furniture had been transformed from an "aristocratic craft" to a "design product" and, through the agency of the Triennales and Italian magazines that focused on the concept of the interior, had acquired an admiring international audience. By this time, also, the links between interior furnishings and the modern lifestyle, which set such store by its material accessories, had been firmly established as the central source of the appeal behind the Italian objects that swamped the international market-place. Bearing the message of Ponti's "good life", these were entirely representative of the consumer boom that characterized the social and economic picture in many industrialized countries during the 1950s.

This extended beyond furniture to include smaller, domestic items and electrical appliances as well. In the high technology and new materials sector of industry, companies that focused on household appliances and plastic goods flourished. The Kartell company, for instance, was founded in 1949 with Gino Columbini as its own in-house designer. The small products – fruit-squeezers, washing-up bowls, buckets, dust-pans and brushes – that he developed for Kartell, all of them in bright colours which contrasted dramatically with the hitherto ubiquitous "peasant" brown of so many traditional household goods, showed that art could elevate the most menial tasks, such as cleaning, to a "lifestyle" status.

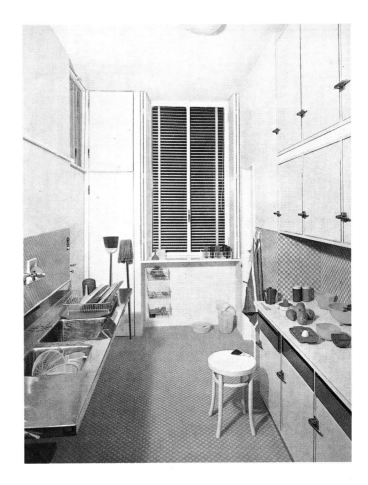

Far left: Borsani's "P40" reclining chair, made for Tecno in 1954. Among the most striking designs of the decade, it helped secure for Tecno an international reputation. (See page 94 for a bed-settee version of the same design.)

Above: Modern kitchen from *Domus*, 1954, showing how the new, brightly coloured, plastic items produced by Kartell had penetrated kitchen design and planning, which in turn were heavily based on American examples.

Left: Plastic lemon squeezer, designed by Gino Columbini and manufactured by Kartell in 1959. Columbini and Kartell produced the first of these brightly coloured, attractive household objects, initiating Italy's creative work in plastics which continued through into the 1960s. Items ranged from small, seemingly mundane household artefacts to furniture: no longer was plastic seen as a cheap, substitute material.

Franco Albini's and Franca Helg's "Margherita" armchair, manufactured by Bonacina in 1950. Modern in its form and yet very traditional in its use of cane as a material, it represents the twin pulls of the future and the past typical of many areas of Italian culture in the decade. Albini, in particular, moved into the post-war period with a confidence derived from his pre-war experiments.

Thermos containers designed by Gino Columbini and manufactured by Kartell in 1953. Kartell paid careful attention to the appearance of even the most mundane plastic items; with Columbini's help, the company created a reputation for plastics design that remained unchallenged for many years.

Even domestic appliances had been given a totally new look by the end of this period. In 1954 Rex Zanussi's company, which manufactured what the Italians call *elettro-domestici*, brought in the designer Gino Valle to restyle its ranges of "white goods", refrigerators in particular. Zanussi's scale of production was expanding enormously, but the appearance of the refrigerator had remained unchanged for several years and needed a complete face-lift. Valle was already established by this time, mostly on the basis of his clock designs for Ritz-Italora and Solari. His work for Zanussi, of simplifying and rationalizing the appearance of its products, helped make that company a market leader in subsequent decades.

THE APPLIED ARTS

The traditional Italian applied art industries also entered the modern age in the decade following the war, but they were not influenced so dramatically by the new technology and were not to hold on to their international reputation for very much longer. In fact, after 1960 they tended to become somewhat peripheral to the Italian modern design movement, with only a few notable exceptions. In the 1950s, however, some remarkable modern work was produced in the applied arts, and the Triennales of the 1945–55 period continued to be dominated by the Italian "decorative arts".

The workshop still dominated this area of production in Italy, and many could still be found supplying local needs. The importance of craft work to the image of Italian goods abroad in the early 1950s cannot be over-estimated. The production of leather goods – shoes, belts, handbags – was particularly strong and was organized entirely on a small-scale, regional basis, mostly supplying local needs but also, in a growing number of cases, penetrating further afield into foreign markets as well.

The primitive and "surreal" work of Picasso and Miró had an enormous influence on Italian ceramics. At the 1951 Triennale Italian ceramics had a room to themselves, demonstrating their commitment to an artistic avant-garde and their strong allegiance to contemporary sculpture. The work of two artists, Lucio Fontana and Agenore Fabbri, stood out from the rest of the display, demonstrating the growing alliance between ceramics and sculpture.

Apart from exceptions like the Milan-based Fontana Arte, Italian glass production in the early 1950s was still based in workshops in Venice and Murano and dominated by companies such as Venini, Vetri d'Arte, and Barovier and Toso. The same highly sculptural aesthetic dominated the artistic end of the glass spectrum, with vivid colour playing a vital role in completing the highly expressive style of much of the Italian glass that emerged in the decade after the war.

On an even more artisanal level the craft-based areas of

Above: Majolica vase produced in Faenza by A. Bucci in the 1940s. With its simple textured surface, it shows the strong emphasis on craft characteristic of one branch of Italian culture in the immediate post-war years. Paralleling the search for a new design language for mass-produced goods, this renewed interest in the craft tradition, much encouraged by Gio Ponti, served to guarantee quality of workmanship.

Above right: Blown glass bottles with hand-made bands, designed by Fulvio Bianconi in 1956. Their bright colours make a link between expressive, aggressively modern images and traditional skills.

Right: Poster for Olivetti by Pintori, 1949. The highly creative team of in-house graphic designers brought in by Adriano Olivetti before the Second World War continued to produce work that reinforced the company's high design profile.

enamelling and metalwork also made an aesthetic impact in the early 1950s. Metal vases by Paoli De Poli and anodized aluminium vessels manufactured by Azucena functioned as expressive household objects, completing the stylish modern interior of the day. Wickerwork and canework – other examples of Italy's strong, artisanal tradition – were also represented in 1951, and Albini's famous "Margherita" chair succeeded in extending this tradition into the modern context. "Italian flair" was evident, therefore, in a wide spectrum of goods from the simplest craft wares to the most sophisticated high technology products. A unity of aesthetic purpose and a sense of vitality characterized the entire range of Italian goods.

The architect-designer Gio Ponti was the strongest supporter of Italian craft, and of the importance of the link between the output of the artisanal workshop and mass production industry. He was committed to the retention of traditional skills and aesthetic values alongside the formulation of new ones. His own work, from elaborate furniture pieces decorated with Fornasetti prints in imitation of sixteenth-century examples, to streamlined forms of his industrial products, demonstrated the breadth of his interests and his belief in the need to work on both fronts simultaneously.

Right: The Fiat "Nuova" 500 at Monza in 1957, designed by Dante Giacosa to replace the much-loved "Topolino". Still a very basic, extremely small, two-door car, the new model, now with four seats, provided a cheaper alternative to Giacosa's 600 of 1955.

Below: The Lancia "Aurelia" B20 Coupé, designed by Pininfarina in 1953. His "Aurelia" range demonstrated the way in which coachbuilders continued to work with small manufacturers to produce large, luxury cars aimed at an affluent market. Their fluid, elegant and sophisticated lines contrasted dramatically with the much more elaborate forms of American cars of the time.

Far right: The Montecatini building in Milan, designed in 1937 by Gio Ponti with the engineers Eugenio Soncini and Antonio Fornaroli, which by this time had become a symbol of Italy's progressive approach towards new materials and new technologies.

Italy at Work was the title of an exhibition of Italian work goods that toured the USA in the early 1950s, representing a wide spectrum of artefacts from craft to mass production. The event helped to carry the message of Italian design abroad at this early stage of its evolution.

THE MASS PRODUCTION INDUSTRIES

While the "culture of the home" provided one main area of focus for the design-led Italian manufacturing industries of the post-war decade, it did not detract from the importance of design to the mass producers of such engineering-based goods as automobiles and typewriters, destined to transform the street and office both at home and abroad. As in the pre-war years Fiat and Olivetti led the way in these areas. Outside the home, where it was more relevant to talk in terms of undifferentiated mass markets, and where individualism was less important, product standardization was more viable. Thus in the 1950s both Fiat and Olivetti developed products designed for the large-scale production systems that both companies had evolved in these years. At this time, too, Olivetti consolidated its relationship with Marcello Nizzoli who, although still a consultant, had become very closely

integrated into Olivetti's process of design and manufacturing. His portable "Lettera 22" typewriter of 1950 broke down the distinction between equipment for the home and for the office, and introduced an element of flexibility into the concept of office organization.

The other well-known car manufacturers of the day, Lancia and Alfa Romeo, continued to produce exclusive models with the help of the coach-builders, or body-stylists, notably Pininfarina. In addition to his highly praised "Cisitalia", he was also responsible for the design of the Alfa Romeo 55, the Lancia "Aprilia" and the Fiat 1100. In 1949 F.H.K. Henrion commented that in his view the Italian car designers "have found a way to combine the general American trends with elegance and with certain classic standards of aesthetics".[10] He went on to describe how Pininfarina had succeeded, in the Alfa Romeo 55, in coping with the width of the car by including two lamps juxtaposed on each side of its front elevation. This kind of attention to visual detail became the hallmark of Italian car-styling. Like Italian furniture, it earned a reputation for exclusivity by virtue of its sophisticated, essentially simple, yet highly expressive forms, combined with an ability to provide exactly the right symbolism for the wealthy clientele at which it was aimed.

Right: The working environment inside the Montecatini building. Gio Ponti designed all the furnishings for the building; the desks were made of sheet steel and the chairs of tubular steel.

Right: Marcello Nizzoli's "Divisumma 24" adding machine, designed for Olivetti in 1956, and innovatory in that it visibly consisted of two parts, the top one being obviously removable. The use of dark purple for the top part of the shell was a brave and surprising choice, and the keys are composed with great clarity and balance. The "Divisumma 24" demonstrates the close relationship between artist and technician that was a hallmark of the Olivetti company.

THE DESIGNERS

Manufacturers across a wide spectrum of mass-produced goods, therefore, played a vital role in creating the concept of "Italian design". Their willingness to use design as one of the key factors in their export programmes was vitally important to its high profile in the decade after the war. This would not have been possible without the cooperation of a group of individuals whose training and dispositions made them best qualified to confer this image on the products of a range of Italian industries.

The Italian designers for industry who emerged in the decade following the end of the war were a handful of young men trained in the Rationalist architectural language of the 1930s. The architectural possibilities offered to them, after 1945, were few and far between. Apart from the State-run and Marshall Aid-funded INA-Casa scheme which, in the late 1940s and early 1950s, set out to provide homes in those areas of Italy that had been particularly badly deprived of housing during the war, there was little money available for reconstruction requiring the cooperation of architects. The housing that was constructed on the outskirts of the industrial centres was "spec"-built and achieved on a tight budget with little architectural input. Thus the graduates of the polytechnics of Milan and Turin saw few architectural challenges before them in post-war Italy, which is why many of them turned to the alternative, but related, profession of interior design.

The growing prosperity of the northern cities and the expanding "bourgeois" market associated with industrialization offered numerous opportunities to create stylish interiors for a new status-conscious clientele. For this reason many architects set themselves up as freelance designers, often operating from their own homes. Many combined interior work with the design of prototypes for mass production indus-try and, in a few cases, with work of a more personal, experimental nature as well. Exhibitions also provided a chance for them to develop a new aesthetic. Furniture, though, afforded the first new mass production opportunity, with technical goods following quickly on its heels.

A few designers, notably Ponti, Bottoni, Nizzoli and Albini, had already made a mark for themselves in the pre-war years but they moved now into the post-war period with renewed vigour. Breadth of activity was part of their special contribution. Following in the footsteps of the American industrial designers of the 1930s who designed everything, in Raymond Loewy's words, "from a lipstick to a steamship", the Italian designers spanned a similar spectrum, expressed in Ernesto Rogers' phrase, "from a spoon to a city". The Italians adopted a more high-minded, less overtly commercial approach than the Americans, and were sustained at all times by a strong critical and theoretical framework. A number of critics and academics, among them Carlo Argan, Gillo Dorfles and Umberto Eco, devoted considerable effort to evolving a language-based theory of design that would justify, inform and enrich Italian design practice. The magazine *Civiltà delle Macchine*, founded in 1953, served as one of the ways in which theorists provided designers with a means of allying their work to the broader cultural debates of the period. Post-war anti-Rationalist architecture had its apologist in Bruno Zevi, whose book *Towards an Organic Architecture* was published in English in 1950 and went on to influence architectural practice worldwide throughout the decade.

Ponti produced some strikingly modern forms in a number of projects, including cutlery for Krupps and wash-basins for Ideal Standard. He also designed textiles for Fede Cheti and, in 1954, executed a study for a car for Alfa Romeo. In 1947, in his book *Towards the Exact House*, he argued the case for standardization; in 1949 he designed the settings and cos-

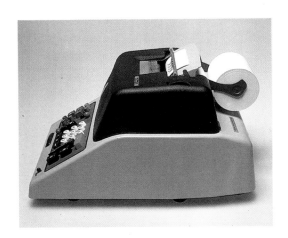

Right: "Lady" armchair designed by Marco Zanuso and manufactured by Arflex in 1951. This elegant armchair was among the first to exploit the aesthetic implications of using foam rubber to replace conventional upholstery. The new material's potential for soft curves and lightness made it the ideal means of translating the streamlined aesthetic of objects made of metal into comfortable furniture items.

Franco Albini's "Luisa" armchair of 1955. Its dramatic profile demonstrates his continued interest in the application of "architectonic" forms. Elegantly proportioned, it is both visually satisfying and ergonomically highly researched.

Left: Small living-room tables by Vico Magistretti, 1949. Made of birch, plywood and mahogany, their neat, stackable shapes made them highly flexible in confined spaces. Easy to manufacture, they had the simple forms which preoccupied many of the young postwar designers.

tumes for the Scala's production of Gluck's *Orfeo ed Eurydice*. He was one of the few to be involved in a number of architectural projects at this time: examples include the Columbus Clinic in Milan of 1940–48 and the second Montecatini building, also in Milan, of 1951. Perhaps his best-known work, the Pirelli skyscraper, was under construction by the mid-1950s. Ponti's commitment to the principles of standardization and mass production remained constant, informing even the most individual of his projects. Thus while he directed much of his effort to interiors he also evolved what he called "typical solutions", which could be duplicated indefinitely.

Franco Albini earned a reputation for himself before the war with his highly innovative designs, among them his transparent radio and a range of elegantly formed chairs that were shown at the Triennales of the late 1930s: a cleverly structured, suspended shelving-system stood out as one of his most original designs. Trained as an architect at the Polytechnic of Milan (he graduated as early as 1929), Albini turned to furniture design as a natural extension of architecture, and his pre-war pieces showed both a commitment to new materials and the beginning of an interest in the curved, organic forms that were to succeed Rationalism and dominate the immediate post-war years.

After the war Albini extended his experiments, working on interiors – among them the Zanini fur shop in Milan in 1945 – and a number of furniture items, demonstrating his great versatility in this area. The strong visual contrast between, for instance, his cane "Margherita" chair of 1951 and his

highly refined "Luisa" armchair of four years later bears witness to his abhorrence of a single stylistic solution to the problem of design. In 1964, with Franca Helg (with whom he collaborated on a number of projects) and Bob Noorda, Albini worked on a scheme for the Milan underground railway. Like Ponti he could embrace craft traditions and the modern spirit in a single breath.

While Ponti and Albini evolved their ideas about industry in the context of the pre-war period, a generation of younger designers – the Castiglioni brothers, Marco Zanuso, Vico Magistretti, Ettore Sottsass Jnr and, on the fine art periphery, Bruno Munari – developed their own particular approaches within the framework of the years of industrial reconstruction. All of them had graduated in architecture around the beginning of the war and a number of them had spent the war years in the armed services. Sottsass, for example, served with the Alpine troops in Yugoslavia; his confrontation with peasant architecture there had a profound influence on him.

Marco Zanuso graduated from Milan Polytechnic in 1939 and set up his own office in Milan in the mid-1940s. His first post-war experiments were designs for chairs made of metal tubing; he moved on to investigate the possibilities of rubber as a material for mass-produced furniture. He exhibited the results at the Triennale in 1951: among the furniture pieces was his "Lady" armchair, made from foam rubber and "nastricord" in imitation of car seats, which developed a new typology for a piece of domestic seating. Zanuso's earlier metal and rubber chairs, designed for a competition at the Museum of Modern Art in New York in 1949, had already

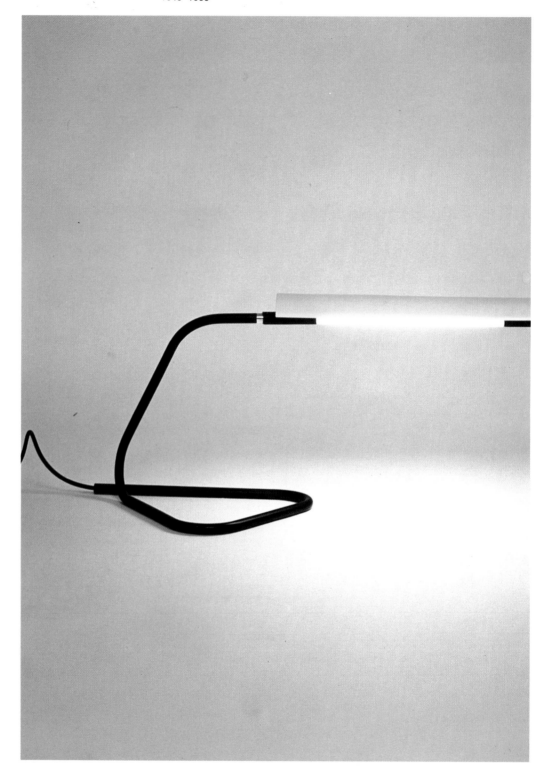

Right: The "Tubino" desk light of 1950 by Achille and Pier Giacomo Castiglioni, manufactured by Flos and shown at the Milan Triennale of the following year. With its basic structure and simple mechanism for altering the direction of the light, it was an early example of "techno-functionalism". This design principle required that the appearance of an object be dictated solely by its technological and utilitarian constraints, with nothing included that did not have a vital functional purpose.

shown the way forward in their use of softly curved lines defining their contours. While they were essentially exposed frame structures, the "Lady" was enclosed in fabric and stood on four short metal legs. It combined an image of comfort with a visual sophistication which had much in common with contemporary abstract organic sculpture. Other projects by Zanuso from this period included the interior of Filiale (a shop specializing in rubber flooring), which was strikingly minimal in its effects, and yet more seating experiments in foam rubber, including a folding lounge chair that made use of rubber webbing as well. Zanuso's involvement with this new material was an important breakthrough in the decade folllowing the war, opening a door through which many others were to pass.

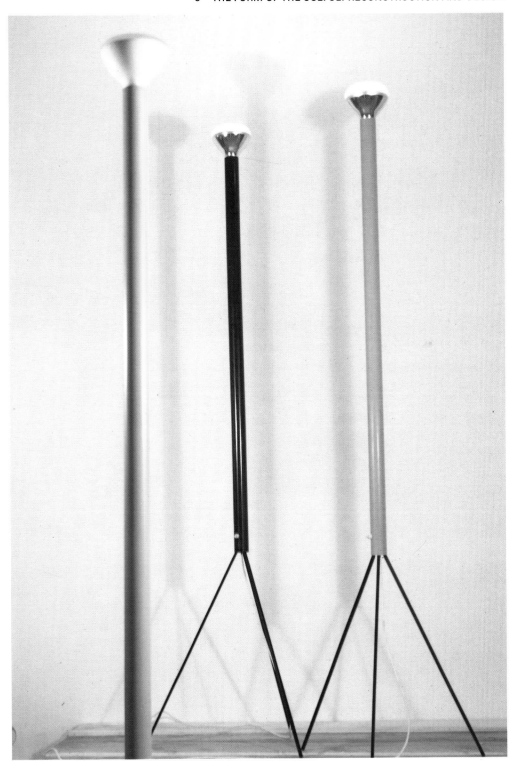

Left: The "Luminator" by the Castiglioni brothers, manufactured by Gilardi e Barzaghi in 1955. Another example of the brothers' commitment to "techno-functionalism", its design required simply a stand, a column and a light bulb.

Achille Castiglioni was the youngest of three brothers, Livio, Pier Giacomo and Achille. After the war, until Livio's death in 1952, they all turned to industrial design. Like his peers, Achille Castiglioni worked across a range of design disciplines including product design, interior design and exhibition display. Early projects included a radio receiver of 1950 and a couple of lights for Arredoluce that helped to establish the brothers' reputation as innovative industrial designers. Unlike the lighting designer Sarfatti, who tended towards fantasy in his sculptural creations, the Castiglionis stressed the technical and functional aspects of lighting while engendering radical new forms. While their philosophy was essentially neo-Modernist their forms were sculptural: the term "rational expressionism" has been used to describe

Above: Ceramic vases and a table lamp by Ettore Sottsass, dating from the late 1950s. Although trained as an architect, Sottsass began his professional career as an interior designer, and was com- missioned in 1956 by Raymors of New York to design ceramics. His forms were inspired by primitive designs, and he used brightly col- oured glazes to give a raw feeling to the simple shapes.

Right: Wire flower-holder by Ettore Sottsass, mid-1950s. As a sculptor, Sottsass evolved some highly abstract Constructivist pieces from wire and Perspex: this flower-holder provides the minimum functional element in what is otherwise an exercise in spatial manipulation.

their work. "Tubino", a little desk light, was exhibited at the 1951 Triennale while a standard lamp, named "Luminator", was created in 1955. Both were radical designs inasmuch as they meshed together the form and function of the objects in new ways.

While a number of other designers emerged in the exhibition listings and magazines from these years – among them Gardella, De Carli, Vigano, Ico and Luisa Parisi, Alberto Rosselli, Roberto Menghi and Roberto Mango – only two were destined to become major figures throughout the post-war decades, their professional careers coinciding exactly with the post-Fascist era. Vico Magistretti and Ettore Sottsass, while not producing anything outstanding in these early years, represented two instances of young men starting out on new careers within the context of economic and cultural

reconstruction. Both of them concentrated on architecture, interior design and furniture, finding wealthy clients in Milan to act as patrons for their early experiments in new materials.

While Magistretti went on to produce a number of important mainstream modern designs in the years after 1960, Sottsass, perhaps more than any other of his generation, had a personal reason for moving beyond the design ideal of the pre-war period. His father had been a member of the Rationalist architectural movement and represented something that Sottsass Jnr felt he had to abandon. He himself was trained in the Rationalist tradition, in Turin, but very early on was drawn to the spontaneous, anti-rational approach towards creativity manifested by painting and sculpture. Early experiences in the Fiat carriage-works before the war and in Guiseppe Pagano's architectural practice after the war led him to Milan, where he set himself up as an independent freelance designer at the end of 1945. For the next decade he combined interior projects with personal research, the latter manifesting itself in a number of pieces of abstract sculpture, occasionally transformed into simple utility objects such as bowls, vases and lampshades. Colour, texture and the emotive impact of form became increasingly vital for Sottsass as he developed his skills and ideas in this early formative period.

In the 1950s, Sottsass also made an incursion into the area of ceramics, in collaboration with the firm of Bepe Fiore. Traditional materials appealed to him because of their pre-rational associations and he set out to attempt to instil the same quality in new materials. By 1955 he had investigated a number of strategies for moving beyond Rationalism, across a wide range of design media, including work for the INA-Casa scheme (1948–53) to interior design and industrial design.

By 1955, therefore, many of those designers who were to make the strongest impact on post-war Italian design had established professional practices, and had begun to develop their own, individual approaches towards design and to make contacts with clients and companies that were to support them. Their names were used as a means of guaranteeing "artistic" input and individualism for mass-produced objects, and this became the basis on which many goods were promoted. As a result the Italian designer was seen as a kind of magician, capable of transforming a chair into a fashionable "lifestyle" accessory.

While this was clearly a hard-headed commercial strategy aimed at creating an image for Italian products that increased their desirability and saleability, and justified their prices, it also served to enhance the status of the designers and to provide them with a system of patronage and a level of appreciation unrivalled elsewhere. In the eyes of the media at least, they became reincarnations of Renaissance artists – all-powerful, creative individuals who could transform the physical environment.

EXHIBITIONS, COMPETITIONS AND PUBLICATIONS

The support system for design also improved in the decade after the war and played an important role in promoting the concept of Italian design at home and abroad. As in the pre-war years the Triennales provided a focus, but these exhibitions were no longer the only means of creating a public space for design. The retail trade also expanded to meet the needs of the growing market in Italy and played a vital role in sponsoring design and designers. La Rinascente, the largest department store in Milan, assumed a very active role in this respect; in 1953, for example, it mounted an exhibition called "The Aesthetic of the Product". In the following year it introduced a system of annual awards for the best designs of the year: called the Compasso d'Oro (The Golden Compass), this quickly became a highly prestigious prize, and the successful designs of 1955 included examples by most of the best-known designers of the day – De Carli, Nizzoli, Sarfatti, Albini and the Castiglioni brothers.

Specialist magazines also played a crucial role in disseminating the concept of design. While *Domus* had the highest profile, both at home and abroad, the stylish *Stile Industria* was launched by Alberto Rosselli in 1954 and for just under a decade it remained a vital force. It helped to establish Italian design as a concept with its own distinctive theoretical base and high aesthetic standards.

Right: Hanging light designed by Ettore Sottsass for Arredoluce in 1958. Made of metal and plastic, it represented Sottsass's interest in creating utility objects by manipulating pieces of material into simple forms by minimal means: the two elements are joined by connecting threads. His researches grew out of an interest in Constructivist sculpture.

Left: Bucket in polythene designed by Roberto Menghi and made by the Smalterie Meridionali in the mid-1950s. The attention given to the appearance of this simple object was intensified by the way in which it was presented in the pages of *Stile Industria*. It succeeded in rising above the status of a mere utility object to that of an "art" object, helping Italy acquire a reputation for attention to visual detail in all its products, whether luxury or otherwise.

Right: A page from the magazine *Stile Industria* in 1954, the year of its launch. Even such a mundane object as a door handle – designed here by Sergio Asti – was treated as if it were a piece of sculpture. Together the designers and the magazine presented an image of Italian design that concentrated on its aesthetic rather than its technological inventiveness.

While the main impact of Italian design, both at home and abroad, lay in its aspirations to join the ranks of high culture (in this respect it can be compared to the neo-Realist cinema which earned Italy a strong international reputation in these years), it succeeded none the less, in this early period, in penetrating a more popular level of culture as well. The motor-scooters, typewriters, coffee-machines and items of modern furniture in coffee-bars and other public areas succeeded in influencing the mass environment and in helping to re-create a culture from its very roots.

A democratic base characterized modern Italian design. When Branzi described it later as a "harmonious relationship between production and culture"[11] it is to all levels of culture that he is referring. Design in the years 1945–55 did, it seems, genuinely reflect the character of Italian aspirations. While export figures were increasing (by 10 per cent between 1948 and 1952) most of the goods manufactured at this time continued to find their principal outlets in the home market. As Gillo Dorfles wrote in 1986: "I think we can say that Italian design, formulated just after the war, by a very few examples, like Olivetti's typewriters and the Vespa and Lambretta scooters, was within everyone's reach and became part of every home."[12]

In the following decade, however, this sense of democratic idealism faded into the background. As export figures grew dramatically, the best of Italian design turned increasingly towards foreign markets and became associated more and more with exclusive cultural messages. The period during which design had functioned as an intrinsic element within the general cultural and economic reconstruction of Italy had come to an end. Although design remained a vital part of the economy, from now on it tended to play a much more peripheral role, and had less influence on Italian society and mass culture as a whole.

modelli per maniglie
disegno Sergio Asti, arch., dello studio Asti Favre

Due considerazioni hanno guidato lo studio e la realizzazione di queste maniglie. Si è tenuto conto, in alcuni pezzi, della funzione puramente meccanica di una comoda presa della mano, in altri, della esigenza di dotare la forma di un valore plastico particolare. Infatti dei tre modelli che presentiamo, i primi due rappresentano soluzioni per porte di abitazione; la terza invece è stata studiata per porte di negozio. Con tutto questo, il risultato non è stato, nel primo caso di una maniglia semplicemente anatomica, o, nel secondo, di una astratta scultura, bensì di pezzi che hanno tenuto conto della diversa funzionalità, o meglio della diversa destinazione, con le conseguenti necessità formali.

These handles have been studied and created considering two different factors. In some pieces attention has been paid only to the purely mechanical function of a comfortable hand-grip; in others, to the necessity of enriching the shape with a particular plastic value. In fact, of the three models shown here, the first two are meant for use on doors in the home, while the third has been studied for shop doors. In the first case we do not have as a result a simply anatomical handle, nor, in the second case, an abstract sculpture; on the contrary, these pieces have been created in consideration of their different functions, one would even say different destinations, with consequent different formal requirements.

30

La realizzazione in lega leggera è ottenuta mediante fusione in conchiglia e susseguente anodizzazione in differenti colori.

The moulded model in light alloy is anodised in various colours.

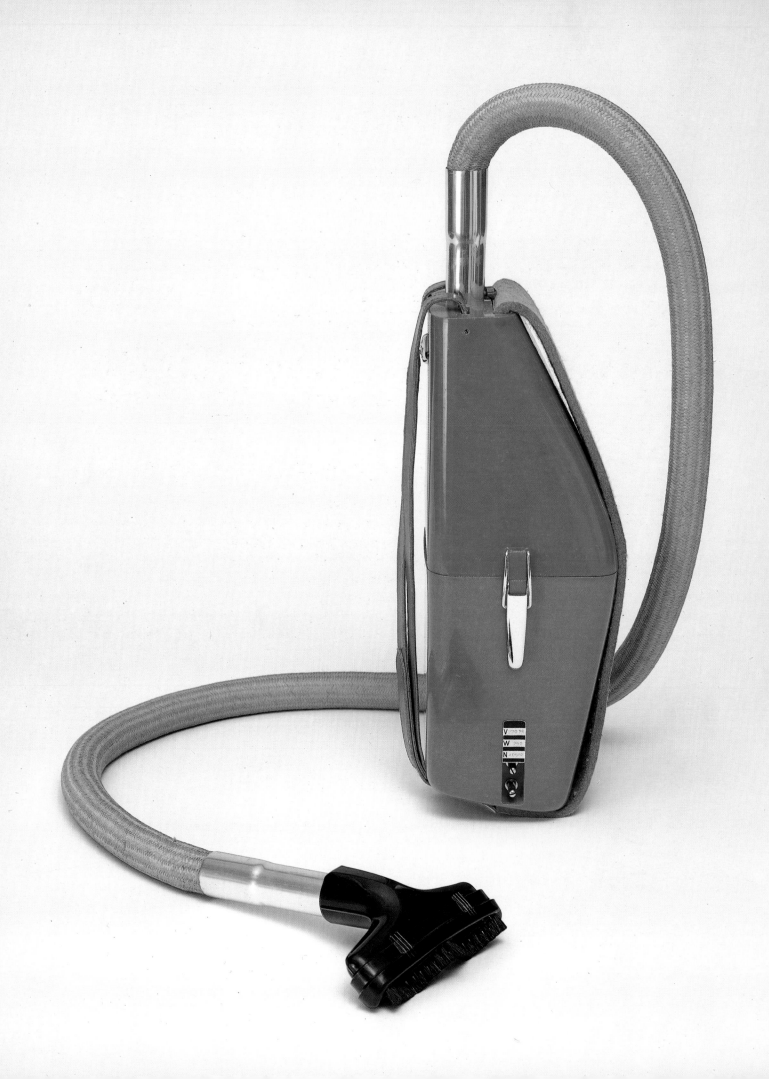

1956–1965
"THE GOOD LIFE": DESIGNING THE ITALIAN MIRACLE

THE CONSUMER SOCIETY

The full flowering of Italian design, as the rest of the world came to know it, occurred during the period that historians of modern Italy have called that of the "Economic Miracle". The years 1958–63 represented a period of sustained economic growth, the climax of the movement of reconstruction and expansion that had begun immediately after the war and developed steadily through the 1950s, accelerating rapidly as it reached the end of that decade and the beginning of the next.

The boom was characterized by huge leaps in productivity (between 1959 and 1963, for example, car production increased five-fold, fridge production four-fold, washing machines three and a half-fold, and plastic products fifteen-fold) and by a higher standard of living for the Italian population, at least the middle classes. This triggered the emergence of mass consumption – an entirely novel phenomenon in Italy which was modelled, inevitably, upon the American model of private consumption. All the material accoutrements of modern urban living – the consumer machines (fridges, washing machines, television sets) – filled the new block apartments in the suburbs of large, industrial towns, built to house the expanding working-class population. Stylish furnishings became, increasingly, the norm in countless middle-class Italian homes. Urbanization itself was one of the features of these years, with growing numbers of people crowding into the northern industrial cities. Films such as

Left: "Spalter" vacuum cleaner designed by Achille and Pier Giacomo Castiglioni and manufactured by Rem in 1956. It was radical in its use of ABS plastic for the casing and aluminium for the internal mechanism, as well as in its form. This was evolved so that the machine would be comfortable when slung across the user's back from a strap, and easy to pull across a carpeted floor.

Right: Traffic on the "Motorway of the Lakes", linking Milan with the mountains to the north, in 1962. Increasing affluence meant not only that more people than ever before owned cars, but also that they could afford to take more frequent holidays and weekend breaks.

Federico Fellini's enormously successful *La Dolce Vita* (1960) communicated to an international audience the suddenness of the incursion of the new values into Italy.

The increase in demand for "consumer durables" inevitably necessitated their production in greater numbers. This led manufacturers in the high technology consumer goods sector, producing cars, typewriters and electrical household equipment, to intensify their production along Fordist lines, seeking ever more rational means of doing so, and demanding more and more from the workforce. Even in the furniture sector the emphasis was upon increases in production figures and the implementation of product standardization as a way of achieving it. Style, however, in these status-oriented goods, remained all-important: the question of standardization was balanced carefully against the need for aesthetic variation and individualism – a delicate task that necessitated a sensitive integration of design into the production process.

Although the emergence of an Italian mass market in these years was a vital element in the growth of production figures, the most crucial factor was the increase in exports. In the years after the war the initial decision about which manufac-tured goods to concentrate on had been directly related to the need to develop an export trade, and the government had chosen to subsidize only those manufacturing concerns that were producing goods competitive in the European and American market-places. Thus cars, for example, were favoured over agricultural machinery, and fridges over more basic goods needed by the Italian population.

Italy developed, from scratch, industries producing goods required by rich countries – cars, light household goods and petrochemical products. By the late 1950s the success of this strategy had become evident, with Italian goods of this kind competing favourably in their selected markets. Entry into the European Economic Community in 1957, and the conse-quent abolition of tariffs, also helped to consolidate Italy's role in the European market. Design became the most impor-tant means of market penetration: although Italy adopted second-hand technological know-how, it was able to make its goods look more appealing, with a level of design sophistica-tion unequalled elsewhere.

While the manifestations of sustained economic growth included increased production figures, growth in urbaniza-tion and rises in the living standards of many Italians, its root

Left: Artisan's workshop in Brian-za, late 1950s. Much of the furni-ture industry based in Brianza, just north of Milan, consisted of small workshops such as this which had not changed since the turn of the century. But by this time the indus-try was beginning to expand and become modernized, with many in-stances of advanced machinery being used alongside hand-work. The furniture industry, however, never grew to the size of that of cars and office machinery.

Above: Cooker designed by Gino Valle and manufactured by Zanussi in 1958. In Valle's work for Zanussi in the 1950s he grouped objects together and provided neat, minimal solutions to the problems of designing the details of body-shells and operating controls. His approach was a rejection of the much more ostentatious contemporary American aesthetic.

causes were embedded within government policy decisions dating from the previous decade. By far the most significant of these was the fact that Italy remained a low-wage economy. The absence of any governmental decision since the war to increase wages, combined with the presence of weak unions and strong management, made Italian goods highly competitive abroad on price. The availability of huge reserves of labour in southern Italy exacerbated this situation, decreasing the power of the workforce. The implementation of this policy meant that while living standards were increasing in certain social sectors during the 1950s, the phenomenon did not on the whole affect the Italian working-class population. This disparity was an important factor in creating the unrest that exploded towards the end of the period.

The working class was not entirely excluded, however, from the possibility of purchasing the new consumer goods. The increasingly low prices of such products made them widely affordable. Often, indeed, they were more accessible in terms of price than the produce which was, at this time, geared to the home rather than to the export market. Meat, for example, was relatively expensive while fridges and television sets were not. This dualism within the Italian economy was accentuated rather than reduced during the years of the "miracle".

The State also had a direct part to play in the economic miracle through the agency of two State-run bodies – the IRI and the ENI (Ente Nazionale Idrocarbonari). Together they continued to create an infrastructure for industrial growth by providing cheap steel, cheap petrochemicals, and a motorway system which was to prove invaluable. Through the companies it owned, the IRI became an important force (by 1962 it was the second largest industrial group in Europe) and the ENI, the state hydrocarbon company, moved into petrochemicals, plastics and synthetic rubber – all materials that played an important role in the production of export goods, and that previously had been dominated by the huge Montecatini company. Thus, in these years, publicly owned industry aided industrial expansion in the private sector by ensuring a supply of energy and materials, and providing a road system that facilitated extension of the market down into southern Italy.

The large-scale companies – Fiat, Olivetti, Pirelli, Snia Viscosa, Montecatini and Edison – grew ever more powerful in this period of mass consumption, and many of the small, and medium-sized, firms became increasingly dependent upon them. The profits of the car industry, for example, increased by 45 per cent in the years 1953–60, while those of the chemical industry grew by 54 per cent. It was to be a short-lived experience, however. By the mid-1960s a number of factors had emerged – among them the revitalization of the trade unions, full employment, and an increase in factory wages – that brought inflation and a crisis of profitability on the part of large-scale industry. As Italy had achieved its position of strength through low wages rather than through investment in technological research, it was unable now to combat the problems. Only a relatively low level of technology had been required to produce the household electrical goods that had played such an important part in Italy's economic success in foreign markets, and it now felt sharp competition, both from countries with a commitment to technological progress, namely, Germany and Japan, and from Third World countries where labour was still plentiful and cheap. From 1963 onwards, as credit became less widely available and demand for goods increased, the Italian economy went into a depression. By the middle of the decade, the economic miracle had come to a close.

DESIGN FOR CONSPICUOUS CONSUMPTION

Design played a central role in the transformation of the Italian economy from the mid-1950s to the mid-1960s. Not only did it constitute an important form of market penetration, it also succeeded in creating, both at home and abroad, an appropriate visual symbolism for the conspicuous consumption that was so essential to Italy's economic achievements. The individualism and elitism of Italian goods made them highly desirable and competitive in the European market, and this was true of even the most technologically advanced products. "The Italian line", which emerged in the decade after the war, to be disseminated throughout the industrialized world, became increasingly minimal, formal

Above: "Candy" washing machine, designed by Piero Geranzani, manufactured by Eden Fumagalli in 1959 and awarded the Compasso d'Oro in 1960. Unlike furniture, domestic appliances were manufactured in vast numbers in Italy in the 1950s and 1960s; their minimal, neat appearance represented the need for standardization – a prerequisite when production was on a huge scale.

and sophisticated. There was no longer the feeling, which had pervaded the earlier period, that the new organic forms stood for a particular political and cultural Italian reality – the defeat of Fascism and the birth of democracy. In sharp contrast, this visual formalism represented an idea of "international chic" which became increasingly synonymous with the materialistic lifestyle desired by affluent, style-conscious consumers in metropolitan centres all over the world, not just in Italy.

Between 1955 and 1965, Italy created a highly persuasive neo-Modern aesthetic of consumption, which replaced the earlier international success of the Scandinavian style. Like that earlier style it too focused on the "culture of the home", but differed from it in espousing what Vittorio Gregotti has described as "neo-modern materials and types"[1] rather than recalling traditional values. The idea of modernity communicated by the Italian style proved to be highly acceptable, as it provided a new image for the home that confirmed the optimistic values inherent in economic growth.

In these years the concept of "art" remained fundamental to the Italian definition of design, which continued to take contemporary abstract sculpture as its aesthetic model. In its sensuous curves an appropriate form was found for Italy's industrial artefacts, which were in turn, by implication,

Above left: Intersection on the newly constructed *Autostrada del Sole* in 1963. This masterpiece of engineering enabled northerners to travel "to the sun" for leisure, but also, very importantly, opened up new markets in the south for manufactured goods.

Above: The production line of "Divisumma 24" adding machines at the Olivetti factory in Ivrea, 1956, after the factory's reorganization along rational lines inspired by American examples.

themselves transformed into "art" objects. This was nowhere more apparent than in the highly formalized photographs of products that filled the pages of magazines such as *Domus* and *Stile Industria*. Divorced from any form of meaningful context, and photographed with only empty space as a backcloth, industrial objects such as typewriters, chairs, and even plastic buckets, were presented as if they were items of sculpture on show in an art gallery, their voluptuous curved surfaces providing the only point of contact between them and their audience of potential consumers. The intention was to raise the status of even the most mundane household object to that of an exclusive "art" form and to transform it, in the process, from a utility artefact into a covetable object. The message of conspicuous consumption was subtly integrated into the aesthetic of Italian products which became, as a result, the material symbols of international "good taste".

The important question of function was not abandoned, however. Instead, it was integrated so closely with form that it became inseparable from it. In an article in *Stile Industria* in

1954 entitled "Forma, Funzione, Bellezza" (Form, Function, Beauty), the sculptor Max Bill outlined an aesthetic theory which became highly influential on much Italian design. Form was defined in a neo-Platonic sense, as an abstract ideal which could be seen as synonymous with absolute beauty and pure functionality; for Bill, art was "the harmonic unity of the sum of all the functions"[2] and could therefore be present in the design of everyday useful objects. The theory was entirely formalistic in nature and made no reference to the socio-cultural context of objects.

This formalist approach was much criticized by a number of writers who could see that designers were becoming the slaves of industry and commerce. Writing in *Stile Industria* in 1959, for example, Alberto Rosselli claimed that "not only economic and production but also social factors have to be considered inasmuch as these factors evolve as a function of the much more complex environment of contemporary life".[3]

A new emphasis on science, rather than art, as the principal pivot for design represented another critical reaction to

Far left: Gino Columbini's plastic dustbins, manufactured by Kartell in 1955. Highly utilitarian objects, they were designed in plastic with vertical ribs for strength and handles in the sides for ease of use. Their appearance, therefore, exactly reflects their function, a characteristic of many of the plastic objects being made at the time. They became ubiquitous in all kinds of working environments – such as greengrocers (left) and workshops (below left).

formalism. This was manifested once again in the pages of *Stile Industria*, in the form of a tribute to the design school at Ulm in Germany. The achievements at Ulm were the contextualizing and systematizing of the design process in such a way that it had moved away from its limited associations with "art" and "form" to become a much more abstract, rational discipline. The work of the Argentinian design theorist, Tomas Maldonado (who succeeded Max Bill as director of the Ulm school), in the area of what he called, somewhat mysteriously, "scientific operationalism" – a complex term describing the rationalization of the design process – was seen as one way of integrating the designer with the production system without making him totally subservient to it. The most important thing, according to Rosselli, was "to go beyond a teaching which excludes the critical function of the designer within industry".[4]

Thus while the political debates of the years immediately following the war had faded from view, there was still a possibility of the industrial designer defining his role in some degree as an essentially critical one, this time in the context not of political ideology but of capitalistic big business. Despite the presence of this critical element, the design of most products at this time continued to align itself directly with the aims of the manufacturer who produced them. The element of visual fantasy, which had characterized many of the enthusiastic projects of the first post-war decade, was tempered by a much less naive, more urbane aesthetic which emphasized the plasticity of the object and re-stated the aims of Modernism, albeit with new forms, new materials, and within a new economic and political climate. This new aesthetic quickly developed into a highly sophisticated, extremely sensuous and, above all, elitist idiom that became, by the mid-1960s, the visual status symbol of international stylish living.

PLASTIC FURNITURE

New materials, particularly plastics, were widely exploited and came to play an important role in the modern Italian design movement of these years. With cheap energy and the success of the Italian petrochemical industry, synthetic materials were made increasingly available, and provided an obvious challenge to designers keen to express the essence of modern industrial Italy to the rest of the world.

Kartell was the first company to manufacture plastic consumer goods for the home; the work of its in-house designer, Gino Columbini, quickly established a standard for Italian plastic products that stressed both quality and modernity. While, in the early 1950s, the moulding technology available had made it possible only to manufacture small plastic products, by the turn of the decade plastic furniture had joined other smaller items to become one of the most striking of the new Italian exports.

One of the first plastic chairs to emerge was still relatively small in size. Marco Zanuso's little polyethylene child's stacking chair for Kartell, developed in the early 1960s, and available in orange, green and white, was fabricated in a number of easily assembled moulded elements. The seat and back, striated to make the chair lighter and to give it some flexibility, were in one piece while the legs slotted on individually.

The other important plastic chair to be developed was Magistretti's full-size domestic dining chair, "Selene", designed for Artemide in 1961. Made of glass-reinforced polyester, its subtle curves both reflected the moulding technique used in its manufacture, and provided a comfortable and pleasing form. It was not until 1967, however, that the chair was finally put into production by Artemide, by which time the reinforced polyester had been replaced by ABS, a much stronger plastic which proved more appropriate to this particular design.

The use of plastics for furniture had the effect of expanding the base of many furniture manufacturing companies. Plastics production was a capital-intensive, industrialized operation that required expensive tooling, rather than one based on traditional craft skills and organization. Thus plastics, along with the use of metal, effectively transformed one sector of the Italian furniture industry.

THE FURNITURE MANUFACTURER

As well as plastics, a number of explicitly "luxury" materials, most of them traditional but new to this context, were creeping into furniture production. Daniele Baroni explained:

> By the beginning of the '60s some of the better qualified firms were already at an industrial level and well advanced in technology and in the planning of production. The Italian furniture trade began to do well on the market and to attract favourable international attention. New materials began to be used in design, such as chrome fittings, luxurious leather upholstery, smoked glass, marble, mirrors, multi-coloured Perspex and futuristic shapes. Italian design and fashion were hailed all over the world and the "Italian look" became so popular that many talked of Italy as the "home of design".[5]

Many of the existing manufacturing companies expanded, intensifying their relationships with key designers in their efforts to capture new markets abroad. On the basis of its successes with designers in the 1950s Cassina, for example, initiated relationships with Vico Magistretti in 1960, and with Tobia Scarpa in 1963. In 1965 Cassina reproduced a set of "classic" furniture designs by Le Corbusier. Registering its commitment to modern design and its sympathy with the ideals of the European Modern Movement from the first half of the century, this represented at the same time an attempt by Cassina to raise its own production to the level of "classics" in their own lifetime.

Left: Sergio Asti's soda syphon, manufactured by Saccab in 1956. This elegant object, with its flowing contours, won a silver medal at the Eleventh Triennale of 1957. Exhibited in the "Production of Art and Industrial Design" section, it was a good representation of the highly sculptural aesthetic that dominated the event.

Left: Child's stacking chair, designed by Marco Zanuso and Richard Sapper and manufactured by Kartell in 1961. Although not produced in quantity until 1967, this little chair was one of the first Italian plastic objects of any significant size. With its striations for increased strength and its flexibility, it was a good example of a plastic object whose form reflected both its intended use and the manufacturing process involved. Available in orange, black or white, it typified the Italians' vision of plastic as a new, colourful, exciting material.

Above: Chair model 917, designed by Tobia and Afra Scarpa and manufactured by Cassina in the early 1960s. The Scarpas, husband and wife and one of the key Cassina design teams, were responsible for a number of simple yet sumptuous designs that epitomized the image of modern luxury so closely associated with Italian furnishings at this time. Model 917 was available in walnut or ash, with either fabric or leather upholstery.

Right: Chaise longue of 1929, re-produced by Cassina in 1965 to the original design by Le Corbusier, Pierre Jeanneret and Charlotte Perriand. Cassina's decision to put these classic items from the 1920s into production reinforced its commitment to Modernism and, by implication, equated its contemporary products with the work of the masters of the earlier movement. Italian furniture was beginning consciously to look back to its roots in European Modernism.

Below: Achille and Pier Giacomo Castiglioni's "Mezzadro" chair, designed in 1957 but not manufactured by Zanotta until 1971. The tractor-seat chair was a perfect instance of the Castiglioni brothers' philosophy of taking "ready-made" objects and turning them into designed artefacts. Strikingly original, it remained a distinctly avantgarde object until the 1970s, when it became very popular for use in high-tech interiors.

The company formed by Aurelio Zanotta in 1954 was committed to using architects and designers from the outset. Although "design" became a byword for the firm it avoided the pursuit of a single style: Zanotta's products were distinguished by their technological and typological inventiveness and originality. The Castiglioni brothers' little "Mezzadro" tractor seat stool, first produced in 1957, was one such example. The company rapidly earned a reputation for original, experimental design and found enthusiastic, albeit highly specialized, audiences abroad. It earned its bread-and-butter income by producing more mainstream sofas filled with expanded polyurethane foam which it manufactured at its small plant in Nova Milanese.

The Gavina company went from strength to strength, forming relationships with Carlo Scarpa and subsequently with his son, Tobia, as well as with Mario Bellini and Vico Magistretti; Carlo Scarpa was chosen to be president of the new Gavina company when it was formed in 1960. The firm played an important role in the development of Italian de-

Below: Chair model 892, designed by Vico Magistretti and manufactured by Cassina in 1963. Magistretti began his collaboration with Cassina in 1960; his first projects were for a number of simple designs in wood. In spite of its modern appearance, the 892, available in beech or walnut with a stained or lacquered finish, had great traditional appeal.

sign, particularly through its decision to manufacture Marcel Breuer's side chair, designed at the Bauhaus forty years earlier. This alone brought the company into the international arena.

LIGHTING DESIGN

Dino Gavina, by the early 1960s a central figure in the modern Italian furniture movement, initiated the formation of a new company, Flos, to focus on lighting alone. He had seen a gap in the market, and gave Pier Giacomo Castiglioni and Tobia Scarpa the responsibility of designing the first models for the new company. Partially financed at the outset by IRI, Flos quickly became one of the most prestigious manufacturers of lamps in the world.

Myriads of other smaller companies emerged on the contemporary wave of enthusiasm for all things Italian, eager to manufacture pieces of sophisticated modern furniture for a growing international market that had developed a taste for it.

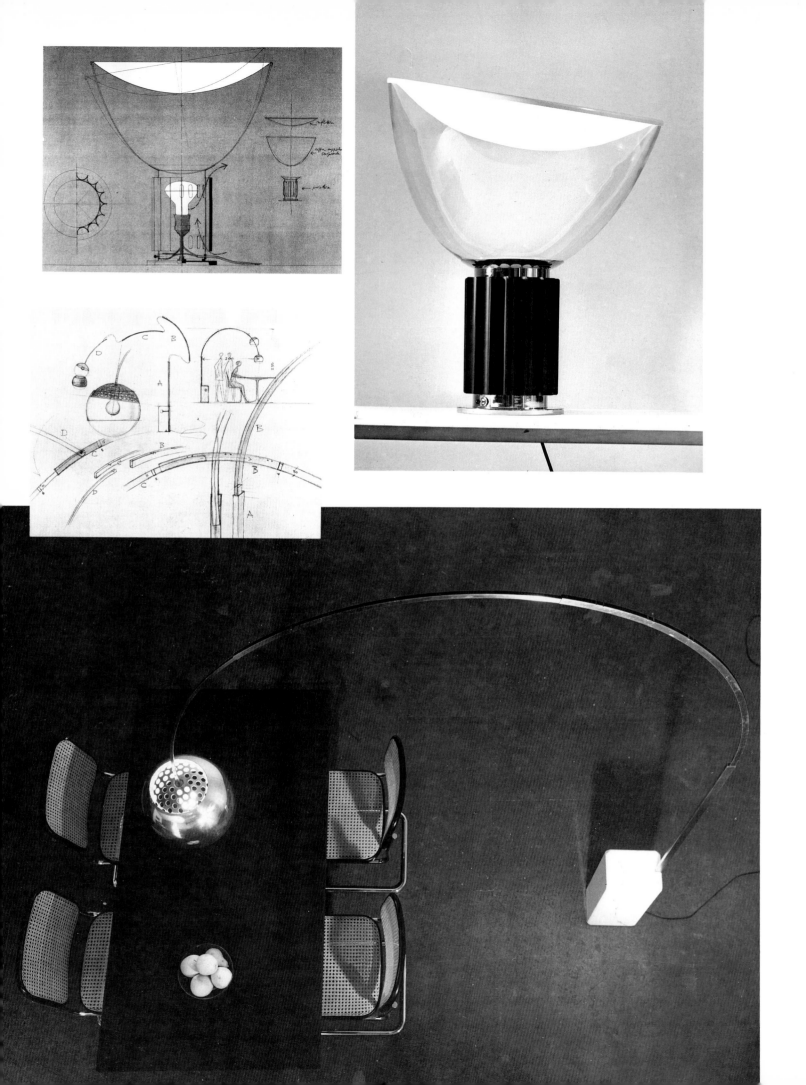

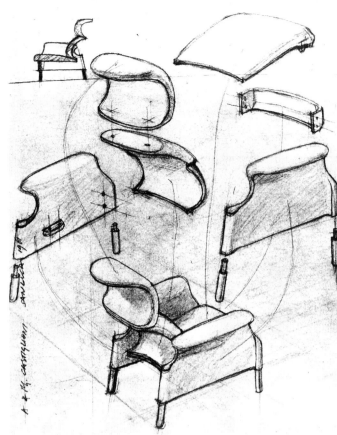

THE CASTIGLIONI BROTHERS

Livio (1911–1979), Pier Giacomo (1913–1968) and Achille Castiglioni (born 1918) all trained as architects and worked together on a number of projects, mainly in exhibition and interior design. Pier Giacomo and Achille collaborated most closely, after 1945, on a range of products that earned them an international reputation – lighting for Flos and Stilnovo; radios, televisions and record players for Brionvega; furniture for Kartell, Bernini, Zanotta and Gavina. Their highly personal philosophy was based on the idea (borrowed from the artist Marcel Duchamp) of the "ready-made", anonymously engineered object, while their rigorous approach towards the design of technological products has gained the name "techno-functionalism". Some of their most lasting designs are shown here: the neo-Liberty "San Luca" armchair, manufactured by Gavina in 1961 (this page); the "Arco" lamp, perhaps the best-known of all their designs (left), and the "Taccia" table lamp (above left), both manufactured by Flos in 1962.

Light fittings went from strength to strength, with ever more inventive forms evolving to express their role as "interior sculpture". The Castiglionis' famous "Arco" light, for example, designed for Flos and first manufactured in 1962, epitomized the way that Italian lights served both as a source of illumination and as a means of transforming an interior into a formalized, luxurious and dramatically modern setting. The combination of traditional marble and glass with ultra-modern steel, chrome and aluminium served to reinforce this message.

The late 1950s and early 1960s represented the high point of the Castiglionis' involvement with lighting design. Numerous hanging models, such as those designed in 1958 for the interior of the Splügen Brau restaurant in Milan, and the simple "Teli" model, made of fabric, accompanied a wide range of table lights, among them "Taccia", designed in 1962. The Castiglionis experimented widely with the possibilities of using the bare technological prerequisites of lighting to create new formal solutions. A standard light of 1958, which consisted of a number of small bulbs wired into a transparent sphere, owed much to imagery derived from space research, while the giant bulb produced by Leuci in 1957 and the "Toio" light of 1962, consisting of a car headlight, a metal tube and an exposed transformer, were both examples of "ready-mades", a concept borrowed from the artist Marcel Duchamp in the early part of the century.

The young architect-designer Joe Colombo also produced some highly original lighting designs, among them his "Spider" light of 1965 designed for O'Luce. Lighting provided a perfect vehicle for Italians to demonstrate their mature approach to the problem of the modern technological object, while remaining firmly within the preferred and familiar sphere of the "domestic landscape".

OLIVETTI: PATRON OF MODERN DESIGN

Although Italy did not participate in the advanced technological research undertaken by other countries at this time, it did succeed in evolving sophisticated aesthetic solutions for a wide range of consumer machines the technology for which had been perfected elsewhere. By the late 1950s a number of such products – among them radios, sewing machines, television sets and vacuum cleaners for the home and typewriters and adding machines for the office – had appeared in both the domestic and international market-places, reinforcing the idea that Italian design was by no means confined to the area of the traditional applied arts.

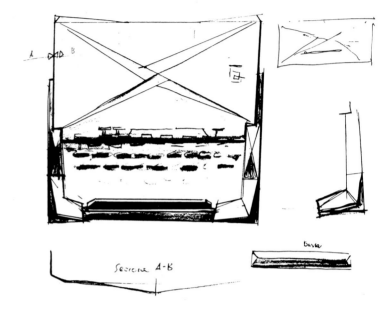

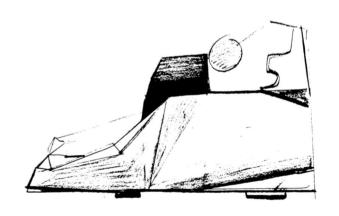

Above: Marcello Nizzoli's sketch for the "Diaspron 82" typewriter of 1959, his first foray into faceted, rather than curved, forms. This new approach was the final phase of his collaboration with Olivetti which had begun before the Second World War.

Above: Ettore Sottsass's "Elea 9003" computer of 1959, his first project as Olivetti's consultant designer. He met the new challenge by colour-coding the control panel, lowering the height of the cabinets and providing overhead links between them. He suggested a number of different configurations for the layout of this system.

The Olivetti company continued to develop, expounding its unique ideas about the role of industry within modern culture and society as a whole. It was alone at this time in concentrating on machines for the office, rather than for the home, a market emphasis that reinforced Olivetti's commitment to mass, rather than batch, production. In 1959 it bought up a third of the American company, Underwood, and fused its US affiliate, Olivetti Corporation of America, with the older firm. At the same time it moved into the rapidly expanding area of computer technology. Roberto Olivetti, son of Adriano, began to exercise his influence within the company and to define the way he felt that the industrial designer should operate. In issue 37 of *Stile Industria* he wrote that "no industry would dream of entering a market (let alone a European one) with a line that had not previously been handled, in one way or another, by an industrial designer".[6] He added, however, that he felt that design was more than just a means of selling something: for him it was a responsibility of central management, the primary means of both forming, and improving, public taste, and of creating contemporary culture.

Nizzoli continued, through the 1950s, to produce designs for office machines for Olivetti. A close friend of Persico, one of the most articulate and forceful of the theoreticians of Italian Rationalism in the 1930s, he had had no technical experience before he began working with Olivetti but this had not prevented him from designing some of Italy's most striking post-war office machines. One of Nizzoli's last designs for Olivetti was the "Diaspron" typewriter of 1959, the replacement for the "Lexicon 80". Technically superior, it transformed the curves of the earlier model into sharp angular forms, an idiom which was also used in the "Summa Prima 20", a hand-operated adding-machine from the early 1960s. These designs seemed to lack some of the fluidity and confidence of his earlier products and received much adverse criticism at the time.

A very important stage in Olivetti's evolution was the introduction of Ettore Sottsass Jnr as a consultant designer for the newly formed electronics division. It was a courageous and, in some ways, unexpected choice. Approached by Adriano Olivetti in 1958, Sottsass had had little or no technological experience, and had spent the previous decade evolving a highly "artistic" approach to design. However, his appointment was in keeping with Olivetti's broad-minded approach to the cultural role of design. Olivetti's first request was for Sottsass to design the company's new electronic computer, the "Elea 9003". The most difficult problem presented by the project was that of combining the necessary standardization of the components with the flexibility required for individual installations. Sottsass responded by providing standard aluminium racks to hold the electronic and mechanical components and repeated motifs to provide visual unity. Other innovative features included the lowering of the major elements to just below eye-level so that operators could see each other while they worked. A rigorous commitment to rectilinear form characterized the overall design, reinforcing the essential rationalism of the system.

The relationship between Olivetti and Sottsass was a special one. The latter remained an independent consultant, with all the freedom he required to avoid becoming ensnared in what he himself called the "hierarchic-bureaucratic structures of industry".[7] He headed a team of designers, engineers and draughtsmen who were employed directly by Olivetti. The team was divided into two groups, one based inside the company and the other in Sottsass's office in Milan. Sottsass was also assured immediate contact with the small number of people who enjoyed powerful positions at Olivetti, through a Department of Cultural Relations, Industrial Design and Publicity; in this way, the design process was integrated into the very structure of the company.

Olivetti's commitment extended beyond attention to the visual detail of the products to the use of modern architects for its factory buildings and showrooms. Marco Zanuso, for example, was commissioned to design the company's plant in São Paulo; the New York showroom (1954) was the creation of the Milanese architectural group, Belgioioso, Peressutti and

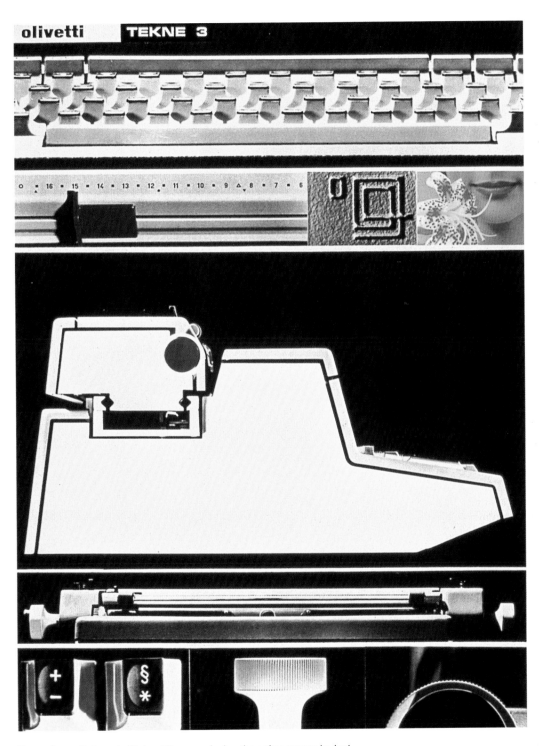

Above: Ettore Sottsass's "Tekne 3" typewriter, manufactured by Olivetti in 1964. It demonstrated his interest in creating a strong profile from straight lines and sharp radii, replacing the softer curves he had used in the previous decade. This new approach was made possible by developments in the machinery for manufacturing metal.

Above: The Olivetti showroom in Düsseldorf in 1960, designed by Ignazio Gardella. The company's concern with the visual aspect of its corporate identity extended to commissioning well-known architects to design its showrooms all over the world. Gardella provided a simple area, with spatial and constructional details to show the products in their best light.

Rogers, and the Düsseldorf showroom (1961) that of Ignazio Gardella. When Adriano Olivetti died in 1960 at the age of fifty-nine a number of individuals, including his son Roberto, took over the management of the company. It provided a model for numerous other Italian manufacturing firms which at this time were seeking ways of integrating design into the manufacture and sales of their consumer goods.

ELECTRICAL APPLIANCES

Companies manufacturing consumer machines collaborated increasingly with designers in the years between 1955 and 1965, demonstrating one of the ways in which Italy was now able to ensure for its products a key position within the European market-place. The sophisticated goods created by these joint efforts all espoused the same expressive and formalist aesthetic that had characterized Nizzoli's early typewriters for Olivetti. One of the most memorable objects of these years, the "Mirella" sewing machine, was designed by Nizzoli for the Necchi company in 1956. It exhibited the by now familiar subtly curved forms, partially determined by the position of the mechanical components beneath the metal skin, and partially by Nizzoli's skills as a sculptor. It combined a sense of rationalism with an expressive use of form, and careful attention was given to the positioning of the knobs and levers. The body was sectioned off in various differently coloured components with the joints left visible – a hallmark of Nizzoli's personal style.

The confidence of the exclusive "Italian line" was shown in a number of products, among them the Borletti sewing machine of 1957, designed by Marco Zanuso, and the little "Spalter" vacuum cleaner designed for Rem by the Castiglionis. The latter had a curved profile designed to be pleasing to the eye, was capable of being pulled across a carpeted floor easily, and was comfortable when carried by a strap on the user's shoulder.

Radio design had been a particularly progressive area for designers in the 1930s and the television set played a similar

Above: Television set designed by Sergio Berizzi, Cesare Butte and Dario Montagni, manufactured by Phonola in 1956. This strange, hybrid object combined current ideas about the design both of furniture and of technological products, by separating the functions into two distinct elements. It is a striking example of the experimentation of Italian designers during the 1950s.

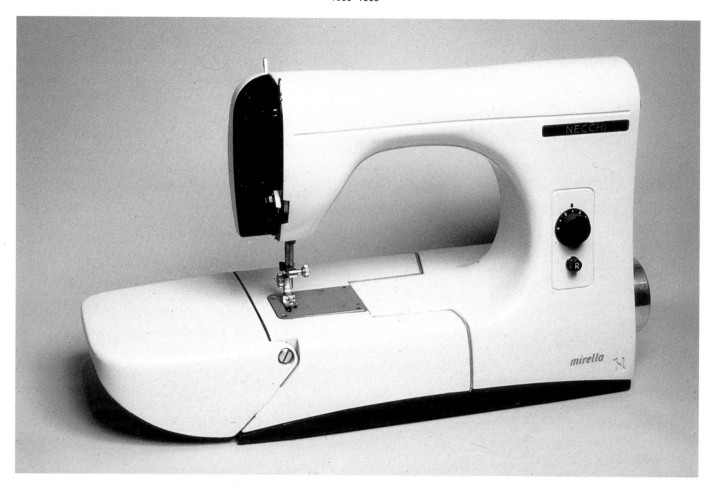

Above: "Mirella" sewing machine designed by Marco Zanuso and manufactured by Necchi in 1956. The elegant form of its casing allied it with other "streamlined" Italian objects from this epoch. Gentle curves were combined with attention to detail over the placing of controls and surface components; the machine's internal mechanism was also innovatory in its use of aluminium.

Left: The "TS 502" radio, designed by Marco Zanuso and Richard Sapper in 1964, and available in orange and white. A compact little radio with two hinged sections, it closed to form a simple box that concealed the controls and the loudspeaker; even the handle fitted neatly into the outer case.

Left: Marco Zanuso's and Richard Sapper's "Doney 14" television, manufactured by Brionvega in 1962. The first fully transistorized television set to be produced in Italy, its reduced size made it portable, and Zanuso and Sapper designed it in such a way as to make it extremely compact.

role in the post-war period, providing a new challenge for designers. By the 1960s television had become a universal phenomenon in Italy. One of the more extraordinary design solutions from these years was provided by Montagni, Berizzi and Butte for Phonola in 1956. This television set displayed the same sculptural curves as Nizzoli's sewing machine and the Rem vacuum cleaner, thereby claiming a place within the same "family of forms". Its particular contribution lay in the way the receiver was separated from the rest of the machine and it managed to combine the functions of both "furniture item" and "piece of domestic equipment" in a single object.

A few years later, in 1962, the Brionvega company produced the first of a number of television sets designed jointly by Marco Zanuso and the Bavarian Richard Sapper, who had settled in Italy in the late 1950s. Brionvega had started production in 1945, at first concentrating on producing complete radio sets. With the advent of Italy's first television

network the company moved into the production of the first all-Italian television sets in 1952. But it was not for another decade that it began to work with designers – Zanuso, Sapper, Castiglioni and Bellini – all of whom became closely involved with the technical aspects of Brionvega's production. Since that time Brionvega has continued to demonstrate a strong commitment to design and has promoted its goods on that basis.

Named "Doney 14", the new television set by Zanuso and Sapper completed the evolution from furniture item to piece of equipment: it was the first totally transistorized set in Italy and won a Compasso d'Oro in the year of its appearance. While retaining soft curves at its corners, it was a much less extravagant, more rational solution than its predecessors. In 1964, once again with Sapper, Zanuso designed another television for Brionvega – the "Algol 11" – which, apart from its angled screen, moved one step further towards the neo-

Modernist box forms that were to characterize Brionvega's production ten years later. The little radio receiver – the "TS 502" of 1964 – again by Zanuso and Sapper, was another highly original design: its two hinged compartments closed to make a single unit that concealed the controls. This gave the object the appearance of an anonymous box which had no explicit function, yet which communicated the sense of mystery associated with advanced technology.

This gradual move from exuberant sculptural forms to more rational geometric shapes was a result of improved production facilities in the areas of plastics and metal manufacture, as well as of a growing awareness of the presence of the neo-Modernist German electrical goods in the European market-place. While retaining their own subtle cultural identity, the Italian products did none the less move one step nearer to their German competitors in the ever-intensifying battle for market supremacy. In these years the Italian electrical goods industry succeeded in establishing itself as a force to be reckoned with, on the level of typological, rather than technological, innovation, as chic Italian *elettrodomestici* made their dramatic appearance in style-conscious homes everywhere.

THE AUTOMOBILE MANUFACTURERS

Italian cars continued to flourish. Fiat continued to expand in both home and foreign markets, producing a wide range of models, from the compact "Nuova" 500 of 1957 and the 600 of a year earlier, both designed by Dante Giacosa, and the larger 1100, 1200, 1500, 1800 and 2300 automobiles. Between 1950 and 1961 Fiat increased its production by 400 per cent and by 1961 the company accounted for 90 per cent of all car sales in Italy.

The Italian motorway system, developed at the end of the 1950s, made the south of Italy easily accessible for the first time, and brought an increased demand for cars there. The concentration on small cars proved a highly successful way of withstanding foreign competition: the little Fiats became ubiquitous in Italian cityscapes and landscapes, providing substitutes for motor-scooters and a means of transport for large numbers of people who had hitherto been considerably less mobile. Abroad, the little Italian cars began to compete with French and German models (the Renault "Dauphine" and the Volkswagen "Beetle" in particular). They succeeded in conveying an image of contemporary Italian culture to an increasingly wide audience.

Production of more exclusive, highly styled cars also continued. The Alfa Romeo and Lancia companies, still dominating the picture, made extensive use of the well-known Italian body-stylists to give the cars their sophisticated look. The Lancia "Flavia" saloon of 1962, for instance, exemplified the way in which, in contrast with contemporary American practices, Italian car designers concentrated on smooth contours, keeping excrescences to a minimum. Both Zagato's GT sports "Appia" coupé and the Flaminia Gran Turismo coupé, designed by Touring of Milan, were examples of streamlined design. The same graceful curves were evident in Alfa Romeo's models, notably the Giulietta "Sprint" and the "Spider".

Italy had now become the home of not only the most elegant saloon and sports cars available on the international market, but also of the world's fastest and most visually impressive racing cars. Bugatti is probably the best-known name from the pre-war years, but all the other well-known manufacturers had involved themselves in this area as well. The company headed by Enzo Ferrari, who had himself moved from car racing to car production in the early years of the Second World War, concentrated almost exclusively on racing cars. Following the bombing of his first two plants the

Right: Poster advertising the Fiat 600D of 1956, a variation on Dante Giacosa's simple little 600, which had been launched in 1955.

Maranelo factory was constructed in 1947 and, from the early 1950s onwards, some of the most advanced racing cars of their day were produced there. In 1951 a Ferrari won the British Grand Prix and, from the basis of this success in motor-racing, the company went on to develop a number of sports models – many of them, such as the 250 GT and later the famous "Testarossa", styled by Pininfarina. With their low, sleek, flowing forms and integrated features, they quickly became associated with an international lifestyle of affluence and sophistication.

DESIGN PROMOTION

The strong emphasis upon visual elegance and aggressive Modernism was sustained and encouraged by a dense system of exhibitions and publications that played a vital role in disseminating the message of Italian design. As in the earlier years, the Milan Triennales acted as the main focus for Italy's foray into design culture, and the Eleventh, Twelfth and Thirteenth Triennales, held in 1957, 1961 and 1964 and devoted to the themes of "Europe", "Compulsory Schooling"

Left: Four important Italian industrialists – Alberto Pirelli, Vittorio
Valletta, Giuseppe Bianchi and
Gianni Agnelli – celebrate the
launch of Autobianchi's new
"Bianchina" car, at the Science
Museum, Milan, on 16 September
1957. The late 1950s saw the height
of the Italian "economic miracle".

Below: Alfa Romeo's little "Spider"
sports car from the mid 1950s
epitomized the idea of the elegant
Italian two-seater, closely associated with the image of "the good
life".

and "Leisure" respectively, reflected a number of key issues in Italian design activity and thought. The European emphasis, for example, at the Eleventh Triennale, coincided with Italy's entry into the EEC and stressed the need for Italian manufacturers to concentrate on providing the right goods for an expanding European market. The section devoted to mass-produced consumer products, "The Production of Art and Industrial Design", contained a range of goods, among them Sergio Asti's soda-syphon for Saccab and the streamlined petrol tank of a motor-cycle, all of which displayed the same sculptural curves and sleek profiles. The section organized by Gillo Dorfles, Leonardo Ricci, Alberto Rosselli and Marco Zanuso, however, set out to be more than a set of formalized objects. It was also intended to provide information about ways of analysing objects, and about the technical and economic context of design. In 1957, a strong intellectualizing note was present, an essential part of the general attempt to ally design not simply with industry and commerce but also with the fundamental culture of modern Italy. The emphasis upon "art" and the creative contribution of indi-

vidual designers such as Ponti and Nizzoli also served to provide a cultural justification for industrial design.

The Twelfth Triennale brought to a head the burning question of design education and the need for a Milan-based school of industrial design. The models of the Hochschule für Gestaltung at Ulm, the Institute of Design and Syracuse University in the USA, and the Royal College of Art in London, were discussed at length in periodicals of the day, and the lack of an Italian equivalent was much bemoaned. However, Italian industrial designers continued to emerge from architectural backgrounds for many years to come.

By 1964, the year of the Thirteenth Triennale, the concept of consumption had become firmly embedded in Italian design culture, the pendulum having swung away from the earlier accent on production as the heart of the concept. The idea of design as a formal solution to technical problems had given way to design as lifestyle and, as a result, Italian design was increasingly perceived as being associated with conspicuous consumption. The sensuous forms of the furniture items, consumer machines and, to a more limited extent, small luxury products such as ceramics, glass and metalwork, had become synonymous with cosmopolitan affluence and stylish living.

The central theme of the 1964 Triennale was "Leisure", a sign of this new emphasis upon social, rather than technological or aesthetic, concerns, with exhibits examining ways in which the number of leisure hours could be increased and their quality improved through their re-design. A strongly didactic tone pervaded the Thirteenth Triennale. It made an all-out attempt to relocate design within culture and society, away from the aestheticism that had dominated the Triennales of the 1950s. It stressed the totality of the environment, rather than isolated objects within it, and many of the countries involved exhibited their products in settings that encouraged audience participation. The Italian products on display were all selected to relate to the central theme. They included a wide range of objects in current production, among them Zanuso's child's chair for Kartell; a motor-cycle manufactured by Gilera; a television set by Albini and Helg for Brionvega; Roberto Sambonet's "Centre-line" set of metal bowls, and furniture by Colombo, Zanuso and Albini.

Their position on round plinths served, however, to

Left: Wooden child's puzzle, designed by Enzo Mari in 1957. Mari applied the "problem-solving" design approach to the most basic and educational of objects. This wooden jigsaw, with its animal shapes, fits neatly together into a square.

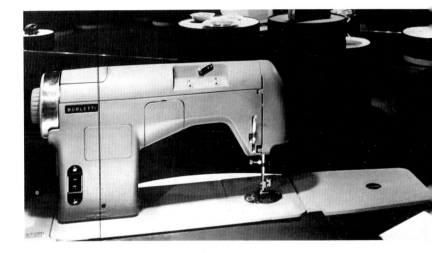

Above: Sewing machine designed by Marco Zanuso for Borletti, set on a round plinth at the Eleventh Milan Triennale of 1957. It was one of a number of highly innovative objects in the industrial design section (called "The Production of Art and Industrial Design"), which were dramatically displayed, isolated and spotlit, as if they were items of sculpture in an art gallery.

emphasize their formal qualities and to distinguish them from the more conceptual nature of the bulk of the exhibit. The idea of the isolated, formal object, photographed without anything behind it and discussed outside any socio-economic or cultural context, had characterized many design manifestations and its influence continued. A growing number of specialist design magazines projected an image of Italian objects likened to exhibits in art galleries. Careful lighting, expert photography and the use of quality paper combined to turn the most banal product into a fetishized object, an essential component of the mood of conspicuous consumption. In the pages of *Stile Industria* everything became an art object, imbued with the Platonic concept of beauty and, through the magical act of consumption, capable of raising its owner to a higher aesthetic plane (and, by implication, into a more elevated position in the social hierarchy).

Stile Industria, more than any other magazine of this period, served to reinforce this special role for the mass-produced design object. It promoted design as one of the most important cultural forces in modern Italy. Launched in 1954 under the editorship of Alberto Rosselli, it quickly became an important force in the Italian neo-Modernist design movement, providing a platform for discussions about the aesthetic and meaning of modern design in an international context. Its demise in 1963 was an early sign of the beginning of a revised attitude towards design in Italy.

The proliferation of Italian magazines dedicated to design was of vital importance to both the domestic and international dissemination of ideas and images. *Domus* and *Casabella* continued to link design issues with those of architecture, while *Casa Vogue*, *Abitare*, *Interni* and others showed just how sumptuous and progressive modern Italian interior de-

sign could be. On a more critical level two periodicals, *Edilizia Moderna* and *Civiltà delle Macchine*, became mouthpieces for the design intelligentsia of the day. *Edilizia Moderna* was a general critical magazine, which had been the house organ of Pirelli Linoleum since 1929; *Civiltà delle Macchine* was established in 1953 as a bi-monthly house magazine for the IRI-owned Finmeccania company and, under the editorship of Leonardo Sinisgalli, combined mathematics, poetry and industrial design. Both periodicals helped to elevate the subject of design in Italy to the status of "high culture". In its eighty-fifth issue, published in 1964, *Edilizia Moderna* dedicated its entire contents to the subject of design: it asked eight designers – Mario Bellini, the Castiglionis, Roberto Mangiarotti, Roberto Mango, Ettore Sottsass Jnr, Gino Valle and Marco Zanuso – to discuss their discipline and their methods of working. These discussions were given a critical context by Gillo Dorfles, Filiberto Menna and Enzo Fratelli.

THE CONSULTANT DESIGN PROFESSION

By the late 1950s the design profession not only had the backing of specialist periodicals but was also supported by a professional body, the ADI (Associazione per il Disegno Industriale), founded in 1956. There were also a number of competitions, prominent among them Rinascente's Compasso d'Oro, which continued to play a vital role by bestowing special status on certain objects that it deemed to be exceptional in their design. In the late 1950s and early 1960s the judges tended to isolate the objects they were looking at from the contexts in which they were produced and used, thereby reinforcing the aestheticization of the product. Everything conspired to emphasize this tendency and, by the beginning of the 1960s, certain Italian products had achieved worldwide status as "cult objects" – for example, Castiglioni's "Arco" lamp and Ponti's "Superleggera" chair.

Page 152: Roberto Sambonet's "Centre Line" set of cooking utensils, 1965. Made of stainless steel, these circular stacking utensils, including variously sized saucepans and a steamer, demonstrated a high level of design sophistication, both functional and aesthetic, in an area of production that was usually very conservative.

Page 153: Gino Valle's "Cifra 3" digital clock, manufactured by Solari in 1966. Trained as an architect, Valle made his reputation while working for Zanussi, the electrical appliances manufacturer, in the 1950s and 1960s. The innovative digital clocks he designed for Solari were destined for public spaces.

Above: Design for a ceramic plate by Ettore Sottsass from the late 1950s. Sottsass's interest in ideographic signs was inspired by the work of contemporary American abstract painters who were trying to evolve a pre-verbal sign language. The designer saw this as a means of returning to spontaneity in design and of rejecting the self-consciousness of so much of the work he saw around him.

Above: Painting by Ettore Sottsass, 1964. Although primarily an architect–designer, Sottsass also painted in order to develop visual themes which he then applied to surfaces of objects such as rugs, trays, ceramics and glass. His 1964 series expressed his interest in the imagery of Indian mystic culture and in the work of the second generation of American Abstract Expressionists.

This was a time of great fertility and creativity on the part of those architect-designers who had had to struggle in the early post-war years to find industrial patronage, and who were now winning international applause. Increasing numbers of manufacturers sought out designers who could transform their products into covetable objects and lend their names to promotional activities. Designers from the early period continued to dominate: Marcello Nizzoli, for instance, worked for the Necchi company from 1953 to 1961, and Ponti went from strength to strength. Vico Magistretti designed furniture for both Cassina and Artemide, and the Castiglioni brothers produced some of the most stunning designs of these years for a number of manufacturers, including Kartell, Gavina, Phonola, Brionvega, Zanotta and Flos.

Ettore Sottsass Jnr and Marco Zanuso played very different but equally active roles, making important contributions, through their divergent thinking, to the period. With the assistance of Richard Sapper in many cases, Zanuso integrated himself totally into the spirit of "techno-functionalism"[8] which dominated the Italian mainstream. He worked for Kartell as well as for Brionvega, the most adventurous of the firms producing audio and visual equipment for the domestic environment. As well as acting as design consultant for Olivetti, Sottsass continued to work on his own experimental furniture and ceramics and to develop a critical attitude towards the relationship between design and indus-

Above: "Ceramics of Darkness" by Ettore Sottsass, 1963, a search for a new primitivism that would return design to its original cultural function and remove it from its growing link with the world of conspicuous consumption. The dark colours of this particular series reflected the designer's severe illness at the time.

try and the whole question of conspicuous consumption. A trip to India in 1961 confirmed his anxieties about the fetishistic approach towards objects and the total absorption of the designer into industries that functioned as part of the system of advanced capitalism. He noticed that in the east, in contrast, "love and attention take the place of manipulation and use".[9] He began to associate the formalism of Italian design with an unthinking acceptance of the economic and cultural system that made objects function only in terms of status and money, and he set out to circumvent this in his own work. Form, for Sottsass, was seen not as an end in itself, but rather a starting point for an interaction with the user. In contrast to the stark neo-Modernist aesthetic of so many Italian objects from this period, Sottsass began to show an interest in colour, pattern and texture, and he developed abstract sign-systems (inspired by contemporary American abstract painting) which he applied to the surfaces of enamelled dishes, ceramics, trays and other small objects.

A trip to the USA in 1962 brought Sottsass into contact with the work of the second generation of Abstract Expressionist painters and the early Pop Artists with whom he felt a strong affinity and whose discoveries he soon set out to integrate into his design work. In 1963 he combined the lessons he had learned from both India and the USA in a series of ceramics entitled "Ceramics of Darkness". These coincided with a severe illness, but were followed the next year by the much more optimistic "Ceramics to Shiva" (the goddess of life). Ambitious experiments in post-Functionalist design, they represented, in the light of what Sottsass was to do later, an important stage in the evolution of his œuvre. In 1965 he designed a set of furniture pieces for the Poltronova company, which were produced as prototypes and exhibited in a gallery in Milan. They were again indebted to American Pop Art, as they used the images of banal objects in the everyday mass environment (traffic lights, bank-safes, etc.). They made no claim to be part of the world of "high culture" and began to suggest an alternative role for design. By the mid-1960s Sottsass had reached a level of maturity and had evolved a design philosophy that was "rooted in human values"[10] and that was to prove seminal in the post-Functionalist atmosphere of the subsequent decade.

Left: "Ceramics to Shiva" by Ettore Sottsass, 1964. In the wake of the dark ceramics of the previous year, these new designs were dedicated to the goddess of life and reflected both Sottsass's return to health and his continued interest in a meaning for design other than as a prop for industry.

The numerous young designers who emerged between 1955 and 1965 included Mario Bellini, Rodolfo Bonetto, Gae Aulenti, Cini Boeri, Sergio Asti, Gino Valle, Gino Stoppino and Joe Colombo. Colombo provided some of the most memorable icons from the period, among them his "Rol" chair of 1964, and all of these designers contributed prolifically to the mass of chic Italian products that were flooding the European market.

Their unmitigated and unchallenged success was, however, relatively short-lived. By the mid-1960s the socio-economic system that had fuelled the "miracle" and underpinned the Italian modern design movement had become a little shaky. A rise in inflation between 1960 and 1963 brought renewed efforts by Italian trade unions to challenge the low-wage policy that had been so significant in creating the boom of the late 1950s and early 1960s. In 1962,

Below: Alfa Romeo metal engineers on strike in 1962, one of the first signs that the government's low-wage policy was beginning to backfire. Workers were also developing strong grievances about working conditions and the poor provision of social services and housing.

Right: Interior by Joe Colombo with "Spider" lamps, manufactured by O'Luce in 1965, and his plywood chair, model 4801, of 1963. Colombo found minimal, technological solutions to the problem of illumination. The "Spider" could be attached to the wall or placed on a flat surface. Taken together, his furniture designs, set in highly selfconscious interiors, created a strong, neo-Modernist aesthetic of affluence that came to characterize mainstream Italian design of the 1960s.

with full employment, the trade unions were able to negotiate a wage rise of 10.7 per cent following a series of strikes. Although this did not immediately stem growth figures, the State introduced a programme of deflation and made it increasingly hard for manufacturers to obtain credit. As a result there was a decrease in demand, but this hit firms geared to the home market rather than those that directed their goods abroad. A significant part of the economic miracle had been achieved not by the handful of large-scale Italian companies but by small firms, which in many cases had been set up by former employees of those companies who had been sacked during the left-wing purges of the mid-1950s. With the credit squeeze of the early 1960s, many of those small firms found themselves in financial difficulties and, as a result, a number of mergers took place in the middle of the decade.

Although the crisis of the mid-1960s did not damage the image of Italian products abroad, it did transform the Italian industrial picture quite dramatically and put a halt to the easy mass production of competitively priced status goods. For the next ten years these problems intensified, creating a new and difficult situation for Italian manufacturers. This was exacerbated by an additional crisis, which emanated from the design profession's reaction to the changing socio-economic picture. A number of designers themselves became part of the "revolution" of the late 1960s which was sparked off by union activity and student rebellion. An "anti-design" movement emerged, which challenged the alliance of design with advanced capitalism and conspicuous consumption and which sought instead a renewed definition of the social, political and economic function of design. The Italian design movement, far from being destroyed, acquired a renewed energy and purpose that revitalized what might otherwise have become just a set of rather tired and meaningless gestures.

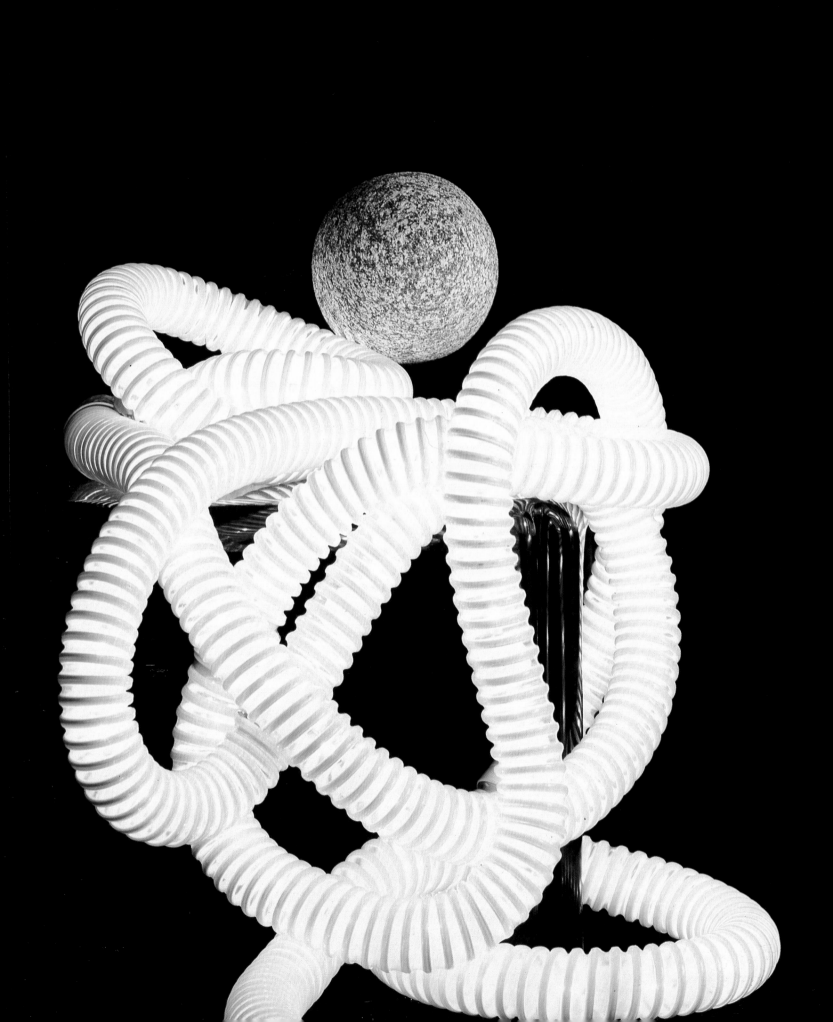

CHAPTER 5

1966–1975
CONSUMERISM AND COUNTER-CULTURE

STYLE AND SOCIAL CRISIS

In September 1969, James A. Michener wrote: "A style hurricane has hit Italy.... 'La linea Italiana' (the Italian line) is all the rage and if you haven't met up with it yet, you soon will."[1] His comment was made during the last week of an Italian electoral campaign. Immediately after a television debate between the leading candidates, switchboards had been jammed with people enquiring, not about the policies, but about where they could buy a particular table lamp that was seen on the programme. "Bright new lamps, colourful chairs, dashing automobiles and heavenly clothes are seen everywhere," Michener went on, "and knowing stores in other countries are laying in stocks for their customers." Style, or rather "stylishness", had become a *sine qua non* within the everyday life of an increasingly large proportion of the Italian population, particularly those in the north. Its significance as a mass cultural force was unprecedented, and it clearly vied with politics as a topic of everyday conversation.

While the proliferation of interest in the "Italian line" was closely linked with growing materialism and changing patterns of mass consumption both in Italy and the rest of the industrialized world, it was also directly related to changing economic, industrial and political patterns and events within Italy itself. The earlier period – the heroic years – of Italian design had been rooted in economic and industrial expansion at home and competitiveness abroad, but the late 1960s and

Left: "Boalum" lamp, designed by Gian Franco Frattini and Livio Castiglioni and manufactured by Artemide in 1969. This six-foot (two-metre) long, flexible structure, made of a plastic skin with the lighting elements inside, twisted snake-like through the fashionable, high-style Italian interiors of the late 1960s and early 1970s.

Left: Demonstration in the Piazza del Duomo, Milan, in February 1969. Students joined forces with industrial workers to express grievances concerning pensions, salaries and working conditions in factories.

Below right: Fiat 500, painted in 1968 by Nino Aimone. This evocative depiction of the popular little car, shown here as a leisure object, demonstrates the way it combined a highly utilitarian design with a distinctive visual character.

early 1970s witnessed a very different situation. By the mid-1960s Italy was experiencing a severe economic recession caused by a number of factors, among them wage rises and inflation. Rather than acting as the icing on the cake, as it had in the years of plenty, design became instead an essential means of survival, as it had been in the early post-war years of reconstruction. As exports became increasingly vital, and Italian technological achievements failed to keep up with those of Germany and Japan, the emphasis on design became more and more crucial. The reputation for tastefulness, for sophistication of colour and line, and the commitment to modernity that had by the mid-1960s earned Italy a world-wide reputation, now became the means by which the country fought to retain its position within world trade. On one level design continued to flourish, helping Italy sustain its earlier reputation, while on another it went through a severe crisis of confidence and of conscience.

Concurrently with these renewed efforts to integrate design into industrial production, an energetic, critical response to the strong alliance between design and manufacturing industry was articulated in the second half of the 1960s. Rooted in the debate that had begun in the previous decade, a "crisis of conscience" informed many of the design discussions which took place after 1965, resulting in the creation of an alternative Italian design culture that was less significant for the objects it inspired than for the ideas it stimulated. The "crisis of the object" that lay at the roots of much of the debate

brought an explosion of activity, which earned Italian design a parallel but quite different reputation from the one that had derived from its earlier commitment to good taste, new materials and artistic form.

This crisis of design values was not an isolated phenomenon. It was linked inextricably to social, political and economic events of the later 1960s, in particular the students' and workers' demonstrations of 1968 and 1969 that rocked Italian society and became a major source of critical debate in Italian political and cultural life.

Factory strikes were precipitated by a growing dissatisfaction with the de-skilling that had come about with an increased use of automation in the large firms. In addition the pressure of the rationalization process was making working conditions more and more disagreeable for the majority of the workforce. As the unions were still fairly ineffective in the mid-1960s, the first signs of protest came from a new generation of workers who had no union links but who gradually joined together with the trade unions, thereby strengthening them considerably by the early 1970s. The protests reached a head in 1969 with the activity of the "hot autumn" of that year.

Militancy in the factories in 1968 and 1969 was joined, and in many cases supported by, riots in the universities. Entry into universities had become open to an increasing number of students by the late 1960s, resulting in overcrowding and inadequate teaching staff and facilities. With full employment, graduates were less and less able to find work after completing their studies, and a growing dissatisfaction erupted into a series of protests, riots, marches and demonstrations which began in 1968, stimulated by the events in Paris in May of that year, and which carried on into the 1970s.

This crisis was a legacy of Italy's exceptionally rapid industrial growth and the accompanying social and cultural changes it had experienced in the years since 1945. With the demise of the low-wages policy, Italian industry could no longer compete so effectively abroad; and moves on the part of large-scale manufacturers to instil rational principles into their factories meant a dramatic and very rapid de-skilling of the Italian workforce. Many skilled workers left the large companies and sought alternative means of earning a living.

Another factor that greatly aggravated Italy's economic instability was the oil crisis of 1973. Severely disrupting the international economy as a whole, it hit Italy particularly badly – with few natural resources, the country had no alternative fuel. Without coal or nuclear power, Italy had

only natural gas which, though adequate back in the 1950s, was no longer so; the country had to continue to import oil at enormous cost. The hitherto thriving plastics industry was badly affected: all those manufacturers who had depended upon plastics for their modern products – furniture, appliances and household goods – had to think again about the viability of continuing to produce them.

In 1973 the lira was "floated" and in 1975 Italy's gross national product fell by 3.7 per cent, the first time that it had fallen for thirty years. The state could do little to alleviate the situation. Many state-owned companies, Alfa Romeo among them, sustained huge losses. Backwardness in research and technology meant that other countries were rapidly overtaking Italy. To many it must have seemed as if all the efforts of the early post-war years had been in vain.

Where design and its ability to carry the Italian flag abroad were concerned, however, the picture was not quite so bleak. Many members of the new generation of architects and designers dedicated their efforts to utilizing design to

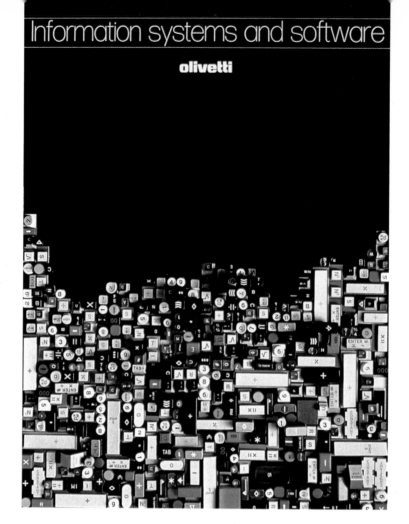

Right: Poster for Olivetti by F. Bassi, 1974. Bassi's poster was one element in the total corporate design exercise that Olivetti launched to promote itself abroad in the 1960s and 1970s. This attention to visual detail, not only in its products but also in its promotional material and its architecture, marked Olivetti out from competing companies of the time.

Right: Folding furniture manufactured in the 1970s, designed by Lomazzi, D'Urbino and De Pas. This range of furniture items – tables, chairs and cupboards – in natural or lacquered beechwood and canvas, was based on the notion of flexibility.

communicate dissatisfaction with the status quo. They sought to extract design from the tight hold of manufacturing industry; and certain areas of Italian design, in particular furniture, fashion, fashion accessories and domestic electrical products, continued to sustain the sophisticated image they had built up.

This was largely due to the special nature of Italian industry, which was characterized by what is called "industrial dualism". A gap was emerging between the large, capital-intensive, unionized, technocratic firms, and the growing number of much smaller companies, often family concerns, which were usually non-unionized and export-oriented. While some produced finished goods, primarily fashion garments and leather goods (shoes, belts, handbags, etc.), others were highly specialized manufacturers, subcontracted to provide components for large firms which, with so much unrest in their ranks, sought increasingly to decentralize their production.

In Italy in 1971, for instance, 81.8 per cent of manufacturing firms had fewer than five workers.[2] Their working patterns were characterized by what came to be called "flexible specialization" – the production of a small range of goods with a high use of manual labour combined with flexible machinery. They succeeded in maintaining a high level of craftsmanship, alongside the use of high technology machinery where appropriate. The fruits of this system did not, however, in this period at least, benefit the "official" Italian economy to any great extent. Instead, it formed part of the "submerged economy", outside the Italian tax system.

Because these small firms aimed their goods at international markets, and because their flexibility made it easy to bring innovation into their production processes, design flourished in this context, although it was often introduced anonymously. For the most part, goods were often copies of stylish originals rather then innovations, and were sold without the name of a designer attached to them. As the historian Martin Clark explains, "these were competitive workshops where the clothes were made that were later sold in the fashionable boutiques of New York or Paris."[3] But it was primarily this system, rather than that of the established Italian industry, that made possible the "style hurricane". Many of the more innovative products also depended upon the small firms and upon subcontraction for their very existence, as well as for their high design profile.

THE FURNITURE INDUSTRY

The furniture industry had expanded dramatically in the years following 1945, but because of the essentially individualistic nature of the product, the decision to appeal to the expensive end of the market, and the relatively small scale of production, the industry had never expanded to the scale of the firms that produced automobiles and office equipment. Furniture production had therefore remained a relatively flexible activity and cooperation between firms was fairly widespread. Tecno, for example, one of the largest companies at this time, which had moved at an early date into the production of office furniture, remained essentially a woodworking concern. Although it introduced some metalworking into its factory, it also subcontracted out much of the work needed to manufacture its products. Among its subcontractors was a foundry outside Brescia run by the Cervati family which supplied it with all its aluminium castings. In addition Tecno's work in interiors necessitated collaboration

with a number of other firms for the supply of materials such as marble and glass.

At the Triennale of 1968, Tecno introduced its "Graphis" office furniture, a dazzling white desking system that in the 1970s became a very successful project for the company. Tecno was most effective in combining aspects of large-scale production with craft traditions and subcontraction. It sustained the formula for a number of years and was able because of it to retain a high design profile.

Because of the huge investment costs involved in buying new machinery, many furniture firms tended to concentrate on one particular technology and to subcontract out work involving other materials. Zanotta, for instance, concentrated on plastics, a material that determined the emergence of three of their most successful designs: the "Sacco" seat of 1969 by Paolini, Gatti and Teodoro, which was filled with small pellets of polyurethane (the story goes that it began as offcuts thrown into a sack); the "Throwaway" sofa by Willie

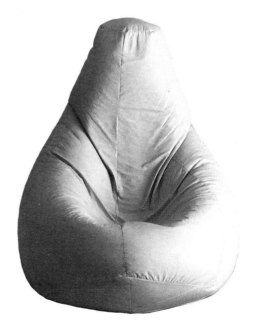

Above: "Plia" chair, designed by Giancarlo Piretti and manufactured by Castelli in 1970. A folding and stacking chair, with an aluminium frame and a plastic seat and back, it was available in red, green and transparent versions. It became a ubiquitous object during the 1970s in a number of public and private environments, its lightness and simple functionality making it an extremely useful addition to any interior setting.

Left: "Graphis" office system, manufactured by Tecno in 1968. Launched at the Milan Triennale of that year, it presented a brand new, all-white image for the modern office. Its modern appearance was combined with a new approach towards the planning of offices, which stressed increased flexibility and the use of advanced technology.

Above right: "Stadio 80" table, designed by Vico Magistretti and manufactured by Artemide in 1968. This smart plastic table, designed in reinforced polyester to accompany the earlier "Selene" chair, exhibited the same curved surfaces and high finish. The radii of the corners helped to give it strength and to avoid any appearance of a dished surface.

Right: "Sacco" seat, designed by Gatti, Paolini and Teodoro for Zanotta in 1970. Filled with thousands of small polyurethane pellets, it became one of the icons of the Italian anti-design movement. Its complete flexibility and formlessness made it the perfect antidote to the static formalism of mainstream Italian furniture of the period; it was one of the few anti-design experiments to be put into mass production.

Landels, made entirely of polyurethane foam, and the "Blow" armchair by Lomazzi, D'Urbino and De Pas, which was fabricated in transparent PVC.

In 1963 Giulio Castelli, managing director of the plastics company Kartell, wrote that "the furniture industry is a result of craftsmanship, which one can hardly consider in terms of industrial production."[4] This fact alone prevented the furniture industry from confronting the problems that were fast hitting the larger companies.

From a consumption point of view, it was also vital that furniture for private use remained subject to rapid turnovers in style. Furniture could not, therefore, be manufactured on the same scale as cars and typewriters. Some companies, such as Tecno, used moulded plastics only in such large-scale projects as auditorium seating, while others, including Artemide and Zanotta, used them in the domestic sphere. Inevitably, given the conflict between the laws of production and consumption, their pieces remained expensive and ex-

clusive – qualities that were not previously associated with plastics, that most democratic of materials. To justify their high prices, plastic furniture items had to become "de luxe" objects rather than cheap accessories. To this end skilled designers such as Magistretti, Colombo and Rosselli set about evolving slick modern forms. The shiny surfaces and voluptuous curves they created symbolically transformed plastic from a cheap into a luxury material, and earned Italy a reputation as the first country to find a truly modern idiom for plastic. No longer was it merely an imitator of other more expensive materials, but one with its own seductive aesthetic – determined, for the most part, by its own production processes.

Careful thought was given to the design and manufacture of all these pieces. The hole in the back of Colombo's chair, for instance, was no arbitrary detail but an essential means of extracting the chair from the mould in which its main body was fabricated. The complexity of the manufacturing process of plastic items forced designers to become increasingly integrated into it, with the result that their forms inevitably reflected the means of production. This commitment to the laws of technology, and the forms created by them, characterized many Italian products in these years.

But plastic products still exhibited an essentially introverted aesthetic that ignored the socio-economic context and aspired to the role of art. Umberto Eco provided an instance when he cited the example of a sophisticated Italian fork design from this period: it looked very modern and elegant (inspired in fact by Danish models), but its prongs were too small to cope with the staple diet of the Italian nation – spaghetti. By implication, therefore, it could only be used in very wealthy homes where meat was eaten. Its symbolism was linked more with its potential as a chic status object than as an item of utility, and this was true of many other Italian products from this era.

Plastics continued to influence other areas of production besides furniture. The housings of mechanical and electrical household objects, such as kitchen scales and food-mixers, were increasingly made from plastic rather than metal. The "Valentine" typewriter designed by Sottsass for Olivetti in

Left: Joe Colombo's stacking chair, model 4860, manufactured by Kartell in 1968. Made of ABS plastic, it reflects the manufacturing process involved in its making: the hole in the back was there to extricate it from the mould. Its confident shape made it a popular object in the 1970s.

Above: "Poker" card table designed by Joe Colombo for Zanotta in 1968. Made of laminated wood and stainless steel, with detachable legs and a green baize top, it was a new design based on an old theme, and provided a totally new image for a conventional item of furniture.

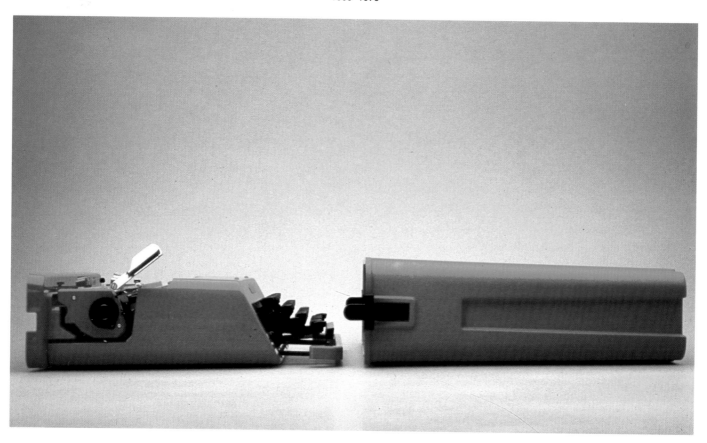

Above: "Valentine" typewriter designed by Ettore Sottsass and
manufactured by Olivetti in 1969.
This little red plastic typewriter
was not only radical in its appearance, but also in the way it proposed a new role for the typewriter
as a light, portable appendage of
the modern "pop" environment. Its
carrying-case was designed so
that it could be easily retrieved
from among books and records on
a shelf.

Right: Air conditioner designed
by Joe Colombo for Candy in 1970.
A free-standing redesign of an
earlier model which fitted into a
window, its neatness of line was
combined with a clear display of
controls. Its manufacture and
assembly were simple – it combined
a sheet metal body with a plastic
front – and its use of symbols made
it potentially an international product. When it was awarded the
Compasso d'Oro in 1970, it was described as being both "sufficiently
neutral and at the same time
expressive".

Above: Kitchen scales designed by Marco Zanuso for the French company Terraillon in 1970. A radical yet simple solution to the problem of weighing cooking ingredients, it registered the weight in the bowl on a digital dial. Both mechanically and visually it is a highly integrated artefact.

Right: "Dada" tableware, designed by Sergio Asti and produced by Ceramica Revelli in 1972. A simple, sculptural design with a small, Hoffmannesque motif, it was available in matt white and black. Progressive ceramic designs of this period tended to conform to the aesthetic developed by products and other interior items, rather than perpetuating the "craft" ethos which was so important in the 1950s.

1969 had a bright red ABS housing and carrying case, to stress its affiliations with the world of pop culture, as did Mario Bellini's little automatic record player of the same year.

Enzo Mari's vases and desk accessories for Danese, also made from ABS, were among the most inventive examples of work in this material. His purple reversible vase of 1969, for instance, developed for plastic a refined aesthetic which has remained unsurpassed. Other examples of his work in PVC exploited to the full the formal flexibility and fluidity of plastic as an expressive medium.

In many ways, Mari's experiments in plastics reached greater heights than parallel achievements in ceramics and glass. Only Sergio Asti, working for a range of ceramics and glass manufacturers, among them Cedit and Salviati, succeeded in evolving modern forms for those materials that were in keeping with the other Italian design successes of the time. In the area of metalwork Robert Sambonet and Roberto Mango – the former with a range of containers, the latter in the area of flatware – reached similar heights. These isolated examples of modern design in the decorative arts confirmed the desire of a number of firms to provide goods to fit with modern interiors, which were strongly influenced by the appearance of the new furniture and lighting.

"Glasses for Alice", designed by Sergio Asti for Salviati in 1978–79. Simple and elegant, with small black expressive details, they confirmed Asti's position as one of Italy's leading glass designers. Italy's achievements in product design were tending to eclipse developments in the more traditional decorative arts; Asti was keen to ensure that the latter were not forgotten.

Vase model 3087, designed by Enzo Mari and manufactured by Danese in 1969. Made of shiny, high-quality ABS plastic, it helped create a new elegant aesthetic for what had hitherto been considered a cheap, substitute material. The unusual colour, and the fact that the vase was reversible, top to bottom, reinforced this new image.

THE AUTOMOTIVE INDUSTRY: FROM STYLE TO DESIGN

During this period the leading styling studios, among them Pininfarina, Bertone and Zagato, continued producing special models for the more exclusive end of the market. Lamborghini, established in 1963 on the basis of an existing concern that had dealt only with industrial oil burners and agricultural equipment, produced a number of highly luxurious sports cars, challenging the established leadership of Ferrari. Two outstanding models, the "Miura" of the late 1960s and the "Countach" of the early 1970s, both styled by the Bertone studio, turned the concept of the dream car into a reality and set new standards for the alliance of stylishness and fantasy in Italian car production. In 1967, at the Biennale of San Marco, the designer Pio Manzù organized an exhibition entitled "The Line of the Italian Automobile", showing how important this phenomenon had become to the culture of Italian design in general. But all did not go uniformly well for the luxury car manufacturers. Alfa Romeo got into severe trouble; in 1979 Lamborghini went bankrupt.

The concept of the body-stylist was also beginning to be challenged by the rise of the Italian car designers who worked with mass production and took a more integrated approach towards the creation of automobiles. Giorgetto Giugiaro had been the chief designer for Bertone between 1960 and 1965, after which he worked for Ghia for a short period and then moved on to head his own company, Italdesign, in 1969. The products of his studio crossed the style spectrum from, at one end, exotic dream cars such as the Alfasud "Caimono" of 1971 and the Maserati "Boomerang" of 1972, to, at the other, more practical projects, among them a prototype taxi for Alfa Romeo, sponsored by the Museum of Modern Art in New York, and the Volkswagen "Golf" – perhaps his greatest achievement – which was launched in 1974.

Pio Manzù, a graduate of the Hochschule für Gestaltung in Ulm, became a consultant designer to the Fiat Styling Centre in 1966 and worked there on the problems associated with designing very small cars. His "City" taxi of 1968 was a radical new proposal both for its compactness and for its simplified production process. A year later, Manzù was killed, ironically, in a road accident.

Left: Prototype for a city taxi, designed by Pio Manzù, head of the Fiat Styling Centre, in 1968. Manzù, who worked according to the neo-Rationalist principle of problem-solving, was interested in public transport replacing private car ownership to combat the crisis of urban traffic.

Far left: Alfa Romeo "Carabo", designed by the Bertone studio in 1968. Nuccio Bertone gave his chief stylist, Marcello Gandini, a completely free hand in the design of this ultimate fantasy car. Its highly evocative, sculptural form was achieved through careful attention to every visual feature – the curve of the body-shell, the wedge-shaped front and the dramatic positioning of the air vents.

Above: Fiat "X1/9", designed by Marcello Gandini of the Bertone studio in 1972. A small, convertible sports car, its sharp, facetted shape was a novel replacement for the sculptural curves of the previous decade. The roof could be lifted off and placed in the boot.

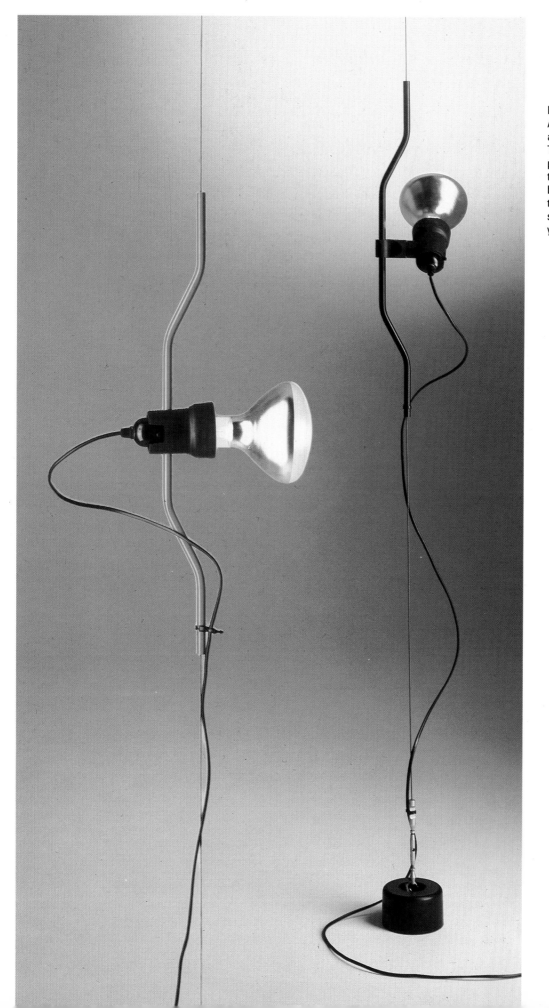

Left: "Parentesi" light designed by Achille Castiglioni and Pio Manzù and manufactured by Flos in 1970. This innovative little light, suspended on wires and adjustable so that light could be shed in a number of directions, epitomized the techno-functionalist aesthetic of so many Italian objects of these years.

DESIGNING THE MAINSTREAM

A number of young designers came to the fore during these years, joining the existing ranks of established mainstream designers. Stalwarts such as Marco Zanuso and Achille Castiglioni continued to work with those companies that were still prepared to invest in design innovation and to act as patrons for individuals whose design philosophies had reached a new maturity.

Zanuso, for instance, was responsible for a number of highly sophisticated goods, among them the "Grillo" telephone and television sets for Brionvega (designed with Sapper), while Castiglioni stretched his own brand of techno-functionalism to new limits in his designs for Brionvega and Flos. The reputations of these men were sustained and enhanced and they reaped all the benefits of long, successful careers and deep relationships with a handful of companies which appreciated their efforts and treated them well.

In appearance, many of their designs reached new heights of sculptural minimalism, as demonstrated by Zanuso's and Sapper's "Black 13" television set for Brionvega – the first Italian "black box" – and Sapper's "Tizio" light of 1973, which was to become one of the most publicized cult objects of the 1980s. This super-rational idiom owed much to the prevailing dominance of German technical goods, but the Italian designs were still distinguished by the elegance of their lines and the subtlety of their compositions.

One of the younger designers to inherit this classical approach and to make it work through this turbulent period was Mario Bellini. From 1963 onwards, following a couple of years in the design office of Rinascente, Bellini threw in his lot with the Olivetti company. He started as the designer responsible for its systems, machine supports, terminals and teleprinters, but later moved into typewriters. Bellini's special contribution to the world of Italian design lay in his evolution of the "stretched membrane", a "skin" that covered his pieces of highly complex electronic machinery, as well as the chairs and sofas he designed for Cassina. Bellini treated his objects as if they were skeletons, covering them with a protective layer which also served as an expressive surface. Following in the footsteps of his predecessor, Marcello Nizzoli, Bellini evolved a sensual, sculptural aesthetic for products that, through the liberating force of miniaturization, offered the possibility of becoming beautiful additions to the landscapes of the office and the home.

The highly anthropomorphic references of Bellini's work for both Olivetti and Brionvega became his hallmark through the 1960s, while his designs from the 1970s – serious,

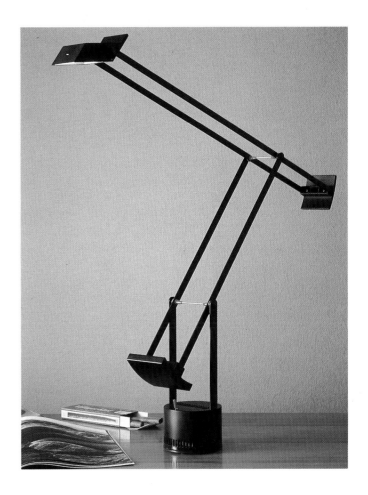

Above: "Tizio" light, designed by Richard Sapper and manufactured by Artemide in 1972. A sophisticated solution for a flexible desk light, it was weighted in such a way that it could rest in any position. Demonstrating a balance of functional and aesthetic concerns, it became a classic object internationally in the 1980s.

Left and below: "Snoopy" table lamp, designed by Achille Castiglioni and manufactured by Flos in 1967. As can be seen from its complete and its disassembled form, Castiglioni's lamp was a solution to the technical problem of creating a concentrated light of controllable intensity. The weight of the marble base combined with the thick glass disc gave it a stability belied by its appearance.

professional-looking typewriters such as the "Lettera 82", and tactile pieces of office equipment, including the "Divisumma 18" calculator of 1972 and his cassette deck for Yamaha of 1974 – became more architectonic and wedge-shaped. This transformation had much to do with the fact that Bellini abandoned clay as a material for his models and began to use polystyrene, which he cut with a heated wire. His "Totem" stereo system of 1970 and the "Triangular" television set of 1968, both designed for Brionvega, were striking, highly minimal designs. Their serious tone and visual purity confirmed the sophisticated role played by

Italian products in world markets, which helped, at this time of crisis, to sustain the idea that, in Italy, unlike in other countries, good design was synonymous with industry and culture.

Other mainstream designers who consolidated their careers and established firm links with Italian industry included Rodolfo Bonetto, and two women, Gae Aulenti and Cini Boeri. All of them worked with manufacturers and contributed to the stylish reputation of Italian design. Their work remained serious and elegant but did not in any way challenge the cultural status quo.

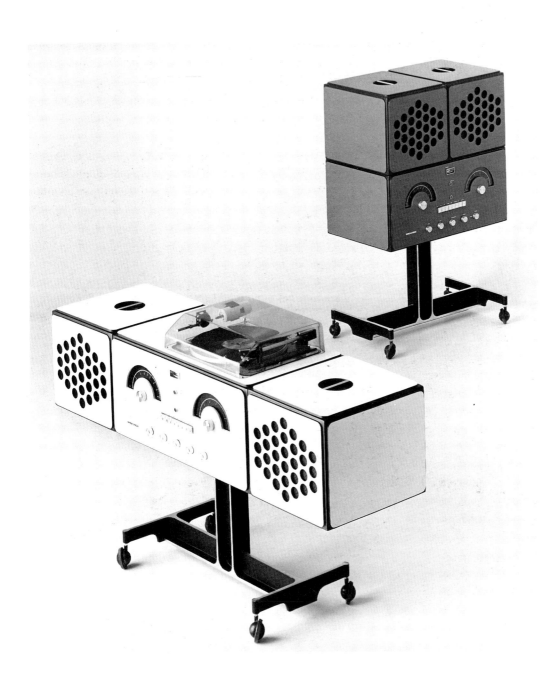

Left: Stereo radio-gramophone, model RR 126, designed by Achille Castiglioni for Brionvega in 1965. This free-standing system, based on a steel frame, allowed the speakers to be positioned beside the deck element when in use, and packed away on top of it to create a complete box. The dials and controls resembled a face.

MARIO BELLINI

Born in 1935, Bellini graduated in architecture in Milan in 1959. He taught at the Higher Institute of Industrial Design in Venice from 1962 to 1965 and emerged as one of Italy's leading architect–designers in the mid 1960s. In his work for Olivetti and Cassina (from 1963) and for Brionvega (from 1965) he proved himself to be one of the most able manipulators of forms

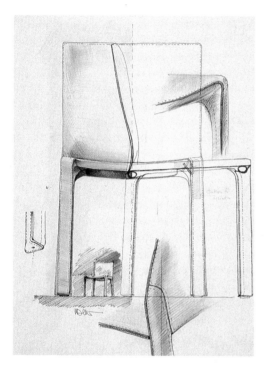

for mass-produced goods. His early work exhibited a typically organic form, which he justified by reference to the natural world, but later his objects became more faceted and rectilinear. Some of his most successful products were his chairs, including the "Amanti" for C & B Italia of 1967 (above); the "Cab" chair for Cassina of 1967, which zipped up at the leg like a boot (above left), and the model 932 leather armchair, based on the traditional club chair but aggressively modern, also for Cassina of the same year (left). Bellini has also worked extensively in the electronics field, designing the "GA 45 Pop" automatic record player with Dario Bellini for Minerva in 1969 (above right); and the "TCV 500" video display terminal (above far right) and the wedge-shaped "TC 800" cassette deck of 1975, both for Yamaha.

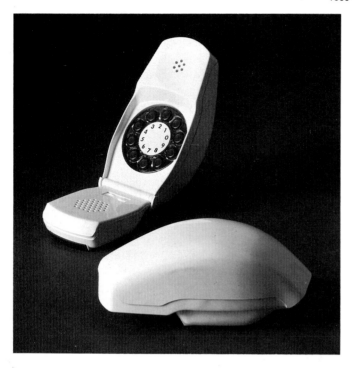

ANTI-DESIGN: THE CRISIS OF THE OBJECT

However strong the continued commercial impact of Italian goods on the international market through these years of social and economic turbulence, within Italy itself, on an ideological level, design experienced a severe crisis. While Italian furniture, cars, household appliances and fashion goods continued to impress the rest of the world with their "high style", innovative forms, sophistication and unerring respect for functional and technical requirements, the democratic idealism that had underpinned the early post-war efforts was less and less evident in the formula. The "educational and reforming" role of modern Italian design as it evolved through the 1950s and early 1960s[5] had, by the end of the 1960s, burned itself out and been replaced by an empty formalism which came to symbolize nothing other than the commercial and consumeristic values associated with advanced capitalism.

New debate now centred on the concept of product formalism which, for the protagonists of what came to be called the "counter-design" movement, characterized all that was corrupt and misguided in the Italian design achievement. Just as, several decades earlier, when it was transferred to the USA and used by the large corporations to communicate their values, the European Modern Movement had lost its original ideological strength, so, in the second half of the 1960s in Italy, a number of architects, designers and related professionals sensed that increased consumerism both at home and abroad had appropriated the products of Italian manufacturing industry to its own ends. Designed objects had been emptied of any vestiges of the democratic idealism that had initially inspired both their fabrication and their forms. In its attempt to ally itself with the most sophisticated end of international urban culture, and to escape from its pre-war provincialism, Italy had "sold out" to the twin forces of advanced capitalism and consumerism. In so doing it had lost

Above: "Black 201" television set, designed by Marco Zanuso and Richard Sapper for Brionvega in 1969. This ultimate "black box" became an important icon in Italy in the early 1970s. By positioning the controls on the top of the set and making the screen invisible when it was switched off, the designers emphasized the technological mystique of the object.

Top: "Grillo" telephone, designed by Marco Zanuso and Richard Sapper and produced by Siemens in 1965. Its radically new form, in which the earpiece and dial were combined on the same unit, was inspired both ergonomically and sculpturally. Its sophisticated profile made it one of the most successful Italian products of the 1960s.

Right: "Serpentone" seating designed by Cini Boeri and manufactured by Arflex in 1970–71. In keeping with the vogue for flexibility and the feeling for "anti-design", Boeri's foam-rubber seating could be used both indoors and outside. It was available in a number of lengths and could be fitted into a number of different kinds of environmental space.

Right: "Mickey Mouse" table, designed by Ettore Sottsass and produced by Bonacina in 1972. Based on designs produced as prototypes only a few years earlier, Sottsass's table – named "Mickey Mouse" because of the shape of its "foot" – incorporated ideas inspired by pop culture in a mass-produced, designed artefact.

sight of its earlier attempt to develop a design movement that would have a more educational and cultural function. Back in the 1950s "designing meant being engaged in politics and helping to solve social problems", in the words of Umberto Eco,[6] but by the mid-1960s this sense of engagement and idealism had lost its way.

The problem with the formalist aesthetic lay in the successful way in which it had divorced objects from their socio-economic context, thereby facilitating their appropriation by another ideological framework. As a result, the architect-designers who set out in the late 1960s to redefine Italian design and renew its earlier cultural and political role had first to employ a number of strategies to undermine the unmitigating "good taste" of so many Italian products. Most importantly, on a number of different levels, they wanted to negate the idea that an object's aesthetic function is more significant than its more abstract socio-cultural role.

As we have seen, the crisis of design in the second half of the 1960s was part of a wider economic, social and cultural crisis that dominated Italian everyday life. The university protests, for example, influenced architectural and design events since students in the architectural faculties in Florence, Rome, Turin and Milan played a vital role in the activities. One reason for their particular grievances lay in the expansion of the numbers of trained architects, making it harder for them to get work when they graduated. This was allied to a strong disillusionment with the older generation of architects and designers, who were moving into the vacuous area of "international chic" and losing their early pioneering spirit.

Even before 1968 there were some signs of an emerging "alternative" Italian design movement – one that drew on pop-inspired ideas from abroad, in particular the USA, Great Britain and Austria where the pop revolution had had an important impact upon art, architecture and design. Ettore Sottsass's two ranges of furniture for the Poltronova company, which were exhibited in prototype form only, drew heavily on

Above: "Yantra" ceramics by Ettore Sottsass, 1970, one of a series of ceramic vases in which Sottsass combined his interest in reviving popular styles from the past with his commitment to Eastern mystical thought. The forms of 1930s radios, for example, were linked with motifs inspired by Indian religious culture.

the ideas of the American Pop Artists Andy Warhol and Roy Lichtenstein, and, in the case of the second series, of the American Minimalist sculptors Sol Le Witt and Don Judd. Sottsass was attempting to translate a number of complicated ideas – about the renewal of form, the appeal of the objects of mass culture, the irrelevance of "taste" and the ideological neutrality of the object – into a range of simple furniture items. This was an example of "design about design" and it remained, as a result, far removed from the context of the mass production industry which Sottsass felt had gone too far in dictating the ideological content of Italian design.

Sottsass's designs were highly significant in that they took the ideological debate about design out of the magazines and integrated it into the designed artefact. In this he was providing a parallel to what was going on in avant-garde fine art at this time, where Conceptualism was fast taking over from traditional painting and sculpture. His alliance with fine art was not, however, simply a way of finding seductive sculptural forms, as it had been back in the 1950s, but rather a means of introducing a dialectic element into the design process. This became a key strategy in the activities of the Italian "anti-design" movement right up until the 1980s. It represented a blurring of the boundaries between design practice and design criticism, and resulted in a kind of "meta-design" that has remained an important parallel activ-ity to design for industry in Italy.

A new generation of architectural students re-asserted their medium as a valid activity – less in the context of built forms, however, than in the form of sketches, manifestos, exhibitions and projections of future utopias, used as a means of introducing cultural criticism into the practice of archi-tecture and design. Their initial inspiration came largely from the comic-book visions of future environments of the English architectural group, Archigram, and from the fantasy projects of the Austrian architect Hans Hollein. Rather than isolated objects or buildings, whole environments became the focus, as a means of avoiding the old dangers of "decon-textualization".

In 1966 two radical architectural groups, Superstudio and Archizoom, were formed in Florence. In the same year, the work of both groups was represented at an exhibition of so-called "Superarchitecture" which was held in Pistoia. In 1967 a second exhibit on the same theme was on show in Modena. The ideas of the radical architectural movement rapidly began to crystallize in the work of these two groups.

Superstudio, made up of Cristiano Toraldo di Francia, Alessandro and Roberto Magris, Piero Frassinelli and Adolfo Natalini, worked through the second half of the 1960s and into the 1970s on a series of real and utopian architectural, design and film projects. Drawings and photomontages com-

Right: Superstudio's "Quaderni" table, manufactured by Zanotta in 1971. Simple tables were covered with plastic laminate on to which Superstudio imposed the grid pattern developed in its visionary architectural projects; placed behind one another, the tables seemed to stretch into infinity.

Below left: "Audio-Visual Jukebox" designed by Ettore Sottsass and Hans von Klier for Olivetti in 1969. A multi-viewing film exhibition system, it was designed as part of a major Olivetti exhibit that toured France, Spain and Britain – a public relations exercise to show Olivetti's commitment to modern design.

Below: Superstudio's "New-New York" collage from the series entitled "The Continuous Monument" of 1969. In the late 1960s the Superstudio architectural group proposed, in two-dimensional form, the utopian concept of a "neutral grid" that could be imposed on the existing environment. This idealized vision was conceived as a means of freeing the environment from its ideological content, and allowing the construction of a new one, founded on a new set of values.

Left: Giant ceramics by Ettore Sottsass, 1967. Exhibited in a gallery in Milan, Sottsass's stunning ceramic forms proposed a new Pop-inspired environmental aesthetic that moved beyond the limitations of craft, emphasizing the dominance of image over form. These objects could as easily have been made of plastic as of clay, although the latter was employed for its cultural associations.

Right: "The Planet as a Festival" by Ettore Sottsass, 1972. This depiction of the "Irriwaddy river" was one in a series of lithographs depicting a utopian future environment. Motifs were borrowed both from American Pop culture and from Eastern mystical religion at a time when Sottsass had temporarily stopped making objects and was rethinking his ideas about the role of design in contemporary culture.

Below: "Grey" furniture, designed by Ettore Sottsass and made by Poltronova in 1970. Only ever produced as prototypes, this group of radical furniture items was inspired by American minimal sculpture, but it also proposed the possibility, through the use of an "anti-commercial" colour, of sidestepping the conventional pattern of furniture manufacture and consumption.

municated the essence of "Continuous Monuments" and "Ideal Cities" into which they injected their theories about the "neutral surface". Pessimistic about the possibility of politics being able to solve the social, cultural and ecological crises around them, Superstudio envisaged an environment in which everyone has a basic, neutral space to inhabit, without the necessity of production or consumption or the use of objects as crutches to support them.

The minimal grid system in their visions of future environments represented a paring down of space to a basic neutrality which, by implication, opened up the possibility of the creation of a new set of values. As one critic explained in 1973, "Superstudio is interested in what its members term 'evasion design' – as opposed to product design – which implies the eventual elimination of formalized design and architecture and a transition at some future time into its projected life without objects."[7] Throughout the period 1966 to 1973 Superstudio gathered together its proposals into a number of catalogues that represented a gradual disillusionment with the hope that architecture could ever change the world. "Architecture", they explained, "never touches the great themes, the fundamental themes of our lives."[8]

Increasing pessimism, in fact, characterized many of the "counter-design" manifestations during this period. It was paralleled by an accelerating retreat from the object and the built structure, and a growing internalization of the critical process. In the early 1970s Sottsass moved further and further away from the furniture and ceramics of his earlier years (recent projects included his "Grey Furniture" of 1970, his giant ceramics of 1967 and 1969 and his "Tantra" and "Yantra" series of 1970), towards two-dimensional work. His series of lithographs of 1973 entitled "The Planet as a Festival" brought together in graphic form many of his obsessions, favoured themes and motifs, among them the worlds of urban pop culture, and eastern spiritualism. As in the world of fine art, the concept was beginning to become more important than the object.

Archizoom's objects from the late 1960s functioned as ironic, post-Functionalist commentaries on the Modern Movement and the close alliance of Italian neo-Modernist design and consumerism. Its "Dream Beds", designed in 1967, contained visual references to popular culture, "bad taste" and stylistic revivalism, employed as strategies for undermining the ideology of Italian formalism. The "Mies" armchair of 1969, with its elastic seat, served as a succinct comment on the inadequacies of the Modernist aesthetic. In 1968, at the ill-fated Fourteenth Triennale which closed prematurely due to disruption caused by workers' strikes, Archizoom presented its "Centre for Eclectic Conspiracy", another ironic stab in the back of the Italian modern design movement. Like Superstudio's "Continuous Monument" project, Archizoom's "No-Stop City" also extended the idea of the city into infinity.

The alliance of the anti-design movement with other counter-cultural manifestations was reinforced by the use of a number of alternative strategies to encourage a movement towards liberation, or at least the will towards one. Gruppo 9999, for example, another of the Florence-based counter-design groups, worked on a number of different fronts, organizing a "happening" on the Ponte Vecchio, designing the interior of a discotheque in Florence in a fantastic, science-

fiction style and, with Superstudio, setting up the "Separate School for Expanded Conceptual Architecture".

In addition to the work of these three groups and of Sottsass, a number of other groups and individuals – among them Ugo La Pietra, Gianni Pettena, Riccardo Dalisi, Gaetano Pesce, the UFO group, Gruppo 65 and Gruppo Strum in Turin – also contributed, each evolving a particular means of demonstrating an essentially radical stance. Their common ground lay in their commitment to a humane use of technology and their shared desire for the abolition of object fetishism. All their efforts were characterized by an attempt to increase awareness of the damaging effects of the mainstream design movement, as well as to help create a mental environment in which change was possible. The result was the emergence of a debate that underpinned all architectural and design practice at this time in Italy – a unique phenomenon, since in no other country did architecture and design have the potential to influence cultural events and behaviour.

The impact of the ideas of the radical designers lasted into the early 1970s. After this their growing pessimism, coupled with the deepening economic recession, led many of them

Right: "Dream Beds" by Archizoom Associati, 1967. These were part of a series of prototype designs which employed a number of what were to become key strategies in the Italian counter-design movement. Included was the use of stylistic revivalism (in this case that of the 1930s), combined with references to kitsch and to contemporary Pop culture.

Far right: The Fourteenth Milan Triennale of 1968, which ended prematurely when students' and workers' protests forced it to close its doors. The events in the streets outside the Palazzo dell'Arte proved more significant to Italian culture than the exhibition inside; like many other areas of Italian life, mainstream design was at the time being widely criticized and challenged.

Left: Archizoom's "Centre for Eclectic Conspiracy", shown at the fated Milan Triennale of 1968, where it was one of the most radical designs among the majority of chic, mainstream exhibits.

into a period of inactivity during which some ceased to produce altogether while others caught their breath in preparation for a second burst of activity in the 1980s.

Two specialist magazines, *Casabella* (with Alessandro Mendini as editor from 1970 to 1976) and *IN* (run jointly by Pier Paolo Saporiti and Ugo La Pietra), promoted the radical cause. *Casabella* announced the formation of "Global Tools" in 1973. Nearly all the key individuals associated with the movement participated in this project, which aimed to extend radical ideas to a wider audience through education: it consisted of a set of laboratories available to young designers for free experimentation and discussion. While the impact of "Global Tools" on design practice was minimal it served, none the less, to demonstrate the high level of solidarity and shared idealism within the Italian radical design movement.

The early 1970s marked both the moment of consolidation and the end of the first phase of the radical design movement

as a strong cultural force in Italy. The period was punctuated by two major exhibitions: the first, held at the Museum of Modern Art in New York, was entitled *The New Domestic Landscape*; the second, which took place at the IDZ in Berlin, was called *Design als Postulat: am Beispeil Italien*. Both treated the radical design movement as a historical phenomenon more than an ongoing activity.

The New Domestic Landscape served as a stock-taking exercise for the Italian design movements of the previous decade. Emilio Ambasz, curator of the event, remarked in the introduction to the catalogue that the Italian design of those years fell into three categories: conformist, reformist and one associated with the idea of contestation. The work of the radical designers fell clearly into the last group and the exhibition not only included a number of individual objects, it also provided an opportunity for Superstudio, Pesce, Ugo La Pietra, Archizoom and Gruppo Strum to develop projects on the theme of environments for the future. Set alongside the more "conformist" work of Zanuso and Sapper, and the highly daring, yet actual, proposals of Sottsass, Rosselli, Colombo and Aulenti, these utopian projects, presented in the form of drawings and photomontages, seemed all the more radical by contrast. In a section of the catalogue dedicated to critical articles the art critic Germano Celant claimed that it was only by moving away from objects that architecture and design could become truly radical:

> a silence in performance, a non-realization of one's own ideas and projects – only this can lead architecture and design out of their institutionalized, commercial phase and give them a place in the true cultural revolution, based on ideas and actions intended to subvert the existing system.[9]

What Ambasz labelled "reformist" concurred with Celant's discussion about "realized design". This aspired to the status of "radical" but could never achieve it because of its alliance with industry and the market. A number of objects containing the radical message did in fact move into production and consumption, but this, according to Celant, rendered their subversive intentions totally impotent. The Zanotta company was particularly alert to the possibility of bringing the new radical ideas into production: the "Sacco", the "Blow" chair and "Joe Sofa" were all inspired by the same anti-formalism that underpinned the radical design movement. This reintegration of an anti-commercial philosophy into a commercial setting opened the radical movement to attack by critics who

considered it thus compromised, and Zanotta's pieces fell short of the political ideals outlined by the protagonists of anti-design. By the mid-1970s the counter-design movement had become largely ineffectual, either through the inactivity of its chief protagonists – an "authentic" strategy but one that rendered it excessively esoteric – or by moving into the market-place, thereby reinforcing object fetishism.

However, radical design had the longterm effect of re-introducing a level of debate into Italian design and of imbuing design with the power not merely to create culture but also to act as its own cultural critic. Although in this period its impact on society was minimal (it served as a mirror of dissatisfaction rather than as an agent of change), in the next decade it was to acquire a second wind and to succeed in making its message more effective at home and abroad.

Italian design was dominated in these years by the crisis engendered by a growing dissatisfaction with the dominance of industry on the one hand, and a growing association between design and consumerism on the other. The tension created by this new level of debate served to strengthen commitment to design as a whole, although at the same time, by the early 1970s, a cultural peak had been reached and a decline had set in. This was shown in the retrospective character of exhibitions and publications from this period – among them Paolo Fossati's book *Il Design in Italia* (1972), which looked back at the work of the major Italian designers from the 1940s onwards. Tomas Maldonado, Gillo Dorfles and Gui Bonsiepe also published books about design, providing testimonies to what was seen as the end of an era. The

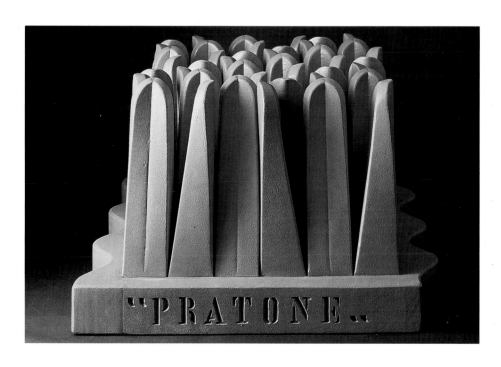

Left: "Big Meadow" mat by Gruppo Strum, 1971. Made of polyurethane foam, it looked solid but was in fact soft and flexible. One of the few examples of anti-design to leave the drawing board, its surrealistic sense of irony greatly appealed to the protagonists of the anti-design movement.

Left: "Joe Sofa", designed by Lomazzi, D'Urbino and De Pas and produced by Zanotta in 1971. Inspired by Claes Oldenburg's "soft" sculptures, this giant baseball glove seat was a classic item of mass-produced Italian Pop furniture from the early 1970s. It was made of polyurethane foam and covered in leather.

Right: "Aeo" chair designed by Paolo Deganello and manufactured by Cassina in the early 1970s. This highly original design by a member of the Archizoom group was one of the few examples of radical design put into mass production. Its novelty lay in its use of pastel colours and in the fact that it could be completely disassembled. With its slung canvas back it proposed an essentially "soft" form of seating, which stood in direct opposition to the more fixed, sculptural forms of mainstream design.

Left: "Blow" chair by Lomazzi, D'Urbino and De Pas for Zanotta, 1967. Made of transparent PVC, this inflatable chair epitomized the "anti-form" values of the radical design movement and established a vogue for similar projects in the late 1960s in both France and England. It was originally intended to be for use in a swimming pool, but became very popular in Pop interiors.

Right: "Sit Down" chair and ottoman designed by Gaetano Pesce and manufactured by Cassina in 1970. Inspired by the work of the American Pop sculptor Claes Oldenburg, Pesce rejected the idea of smooth contours. The anthropomorphic forms of his seating objects represented comfort rather than pure form and their lack of chic put them in opposition to the culture of conspicuous consumption so prevalent in Italian mainstream design.

recession had burst the bubble of both mainstream and alternative activity and it seemed, by 1975, as if the energy had gone out of both. The optimistic, progressive attitude of earlier years went sharply into decline.

The mid-1970s were years of profound insecurity – economically, socially and culturally – and it seemed as if the period of modern design development in Italy that had begun in 1945 had drawn to a natural close. In fact, resuscitation was near at hand and by the early 1980s the subject of Italian design, albeit now in a new guise, was once again on everyone's lips. This was a result of two factors: the re-emergence of Italian industry as a flexible structure capable of supporting much product innovation, and the second wave of Italian radical design which, in its new incarnation, allied itself more directly with the mass media and sought a wider audience. The combination of these two new developments led to a revitalization of Italian modern design as an important force in world trade and as a powerful symbol of the renewed strength of Italian society and culture.

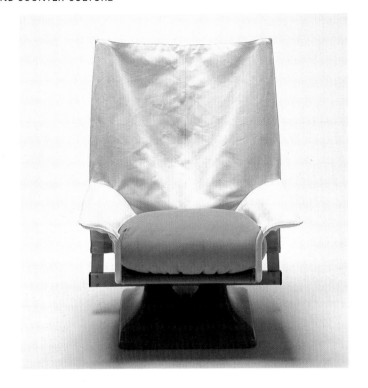

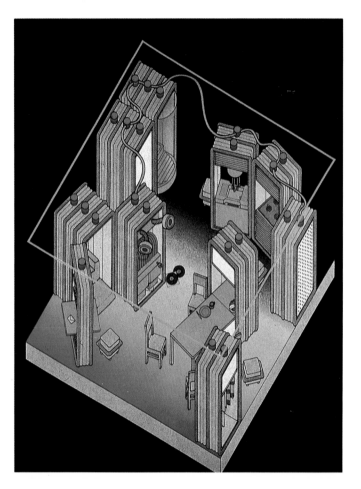

In 1972 an exhibition of Italian design was held at the Museum of Modern Art in New York, curated by Emilio Ambasz and entitled "Italy: The New Domestic Landscape–Achievements and Problems of Italian Design". It represented both mainstream work and anti-design of the 1960s. While most of its exhibits were production pieces it also commissioned a number of leading designers to present "micro-environments", providing the stimulus for some radical ideas about the domestic interior. Among them was Ettore Sottsass's proposal (this page) of a number of modules that could be arranged flexibly according to the wishes of the user. Each one contained a particular function, such as a

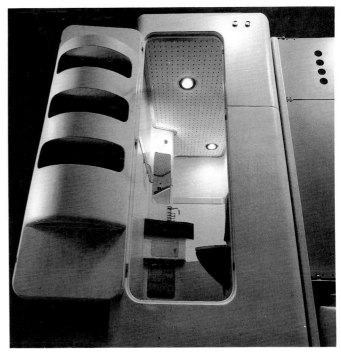

lavatory (above left). The aim was to encourage the use of an environment that did not totally condition the life of its inhabitants.

Mario Bellini's proposal for a "micro-environment" was the "Kar-a-Sutra", a cross between a car and a mobile home (right). Joe Colombo's design (above), described as a "Total Furnishing Unit", was a set of central "pods" containing many of their functions on the outer surface. Basing his idea on space research, he envisaged a set of pre-fabricated central units that would be placed in an open space in a number of flexible configurations. Some, such as the bathroom (above right) could be entered; others had necessities such as beds that could be pulled out.

CHAPTER

1976–1985
THE NEW DESIGN

The 1970s in Italy were years of unmitigated gloom, economically and culturally. Italian design continued to be well received abroad and moved into markets outside those of Europe but, generally speaking, it drew simply on tired continuations of the formula that had worked so well in the boom years of the 1960s. With only a few exceptions, it contained neither the energy nor the enthusiasm of that period. Traditional "status" materials – leather, wood and marble – largely replaced the innovative use of new materials, introducing a new conservatism into modern Italian furniture design. Anti-design went underground in the second half of the decade, weighed down by the pessimism that accompanied its utopian visions: it was disillusioned by its inability either to destroy or short-circuit the cycle of mass production, object and consumption that had displaced early post-war social idealism. The assassination in 1979 of the Prime Minister, Aldo Moro, acted as a confirmation of the nation's insecurity.

In spite of this prevailing mood, however, Italy had to export increasing amounts of goods in order to acquire new materials. The country's total dependence on the international economic system and the fact that it could no longer rely on being able to pay low wages to its workforce combined with the oil crisis to create a difficult situation. The USA and Japan, in addition to Europe, became important customers at this time and numerous efforts were made to obtain a high profile in these markets. As this could still not be achieved through technological sophistication, design continued to play an important role. The economic crises of the 1970s – inflation, devaluation and a severe credit squeeze – affected most adversely those firms that depended upon imports, while the exporters continued, relatively speaking, to flourish. Olivetti, however, went through severe economic

Left: "New York Sunrise" sofa, designed by Gaetano Pesce and manufactured by Cassina in 1980. Inspired by the vision of the sun rising over Manhattan, where Pesce lives for part of the year, this piece of anti-design, still dependent on ideas originated in Pop sculpture in the 1960s, was made of polyurethane foam fitted on to a plywood base.

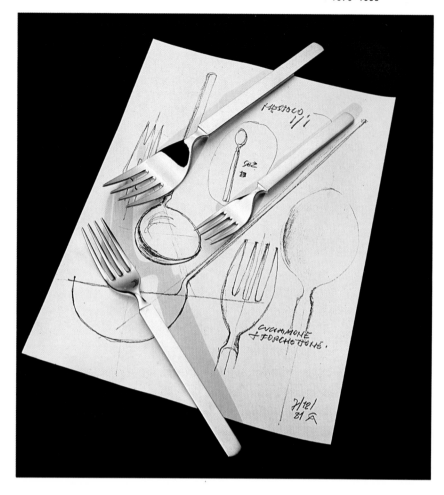

Left: "Dry" tableware, designed by Achille Castiglioni and manufactured by Alessi in 1982. These elegant pieces of flatware, available in silver or stainless steel, show Castiglioni's continuing concern to combine maximum utility with aesthetic integrity. They are highly sculptural and yet comfortable and efficient.

Right: Poster advertising Fiorucci "Baggy Line" jeans, 1977. During the 1970s the Fiorucci store opened a number of foreign outlets, disseminating the concept of Italian pop fashion internationally.

difficulties; of the large companies that had dominated the "economic miracle", only Fiat and Pirelli retained their former strength, and even the latter had to wait until 1980 to make its first profit for ten years.

THE SUBMERGED ECONOMY

It is difficult to generalize about the state of the Italian economy in the second half of the 1970s because of the growing importance of small-scale companies operating in the "black" or the "submerged" economy, whose profits did not appear in official figures. By the 1980s it had become clear that Italy's economic redemption lay almost entirely in the hands of these small but highly efficient firms:

> Between 1979 and 1981 Italy registered a higher rate of
> economic growth than any of its partners in the European
> Common Market. It displayed the most rapid growth in overall
> productivity, particularly in the manufacturing sector, and its
> balance of payments were at least as favorable as any in the
> Common Market. [1]

From 1979 onwards the graph of Italy's economic achievement turned upwards once again, and it became clear that, due to developments in the 1970s that went largely undocumented, the economy was not in the state of disarray indicated by the official figures. Instead there were numerous signs that, through its manufacturing ability alone, Italy was still a strong country.

Design continued to play a very strong role in this new economic picture. The policy of decentralization by large manufacturers who had experienced union problems from the late 1960s onwards encouraged the emergence of a "high technology cottage industry". This developed largely outside the industrial triangle, in the area that has become known as the "Third Italy" – Tuscany, Emilia Romagna and the Veneto. Organized on the principle of "flexible specialization" these small-scale concerns combined skilled labour with a use of highly flexible numerically controlled machines: as a result they produced high-quality products aimed not at local markets but at wealthy international ones. While many of these concerns had begun as subcontractors, supplying components and machine-tools to the large companies, many others, particularly those producing shoes, ceramics, leather goods, fashion, furniture and motor-bikes, designed and manufactured complete products. Because they operated flexibly and were intensely conscious of the worldwide increase in market differentiation and the concomitant need for product variation, their goods were often highly fashion-conscious and dependent, to a large degree, upon visual innovation and sophistication.

As we have seen, this tendency had a long tradition within the furniture industry which, in some ways, provided the model for this kind of specialized, flexible, small-scale manufacturing.

> Partly out of a fear of this dependence [on large firms], partly out of the desire to expand business, and even out of the fascination with new technologies, many small firms have broken the hammerlock of the large clients by developing and

marketing products of their own. Thus in the shoe industry, for example, the small enterprises produce for the high-fashion, high-quality sector of the industry where a premium is placed on distinctiveness and originality in design.[2]

Local designers visited European fashion shows and produced their own versions of the *haute couture* items that they saw there. These were subsequently sold through high-quality shops, mainly to order.

As had been the tradition through the 1960s, Italian products continued to sell internationally, by being a cut above mass-market products.[3] This was as true for motor-bikes as it was for furniture and shoes. The new small-scale manufacturers were ideally suited to the continuation of that approach, and their willingness to design new machines in order to create new goods produced an ideal situation for the promotion of design and designers.

THE FASHION PHENOMENON

Above: Salvatore Ferragamo with the lasts made for his famous clients in 1950. While a number of eminent Italians featured among his customers – Anna Magnani and Sophia Loren among them – Ferragamo's internationalism is demonstrated by the number of Hollywood stars and royalty who bought shoes from him.

Right: Fashion garments from Krizia, 1980s. Italian fashion is associated with simplicity, good cutting and visual elegance; it is expensive, and aimed at wealthy, sophisticated clients. The masculine, wide-shouldered look pioneered by Italian fashion houses has quickly become an international phenomenon.

Although its existence went back many years, and it had enjoyed a certain level of international success since the Second World War, the Italian fashion and fashion accessories industry came into a position of real prominence in these years, benefiting greatly from the new industrial structure. The shoe and leather goods industry had long been established on the basis of family concerns situated primarily in and around Florence. The Ferragamo shoe company, for example, was one of the most exclusive. Established on the return of Salvatore Ferragamo from the USA in 1927, it had utilized exclusively artisan labour up until the 1950s, when it was forced to introduce machinery to meet the growing demands of the export trade. Its stunningly original shoes, many of them, ironically, owing their innovative features to the result of material shortages during and after the Second World War, helped establish Italy as a leading country in shoe manufacture. Ferragamo himself was active in the 1950s in helping to promote the "Italian look" and in establishing Florence, with its network of small family-owned workshops, as the fashion accessory centre of Italy.

A few isolated individuals had established themselves before the war as leading figures in world fashion – Fortuny in Venice in the early part of the century, for example, and later Valentino – but Italian fashion did not have a high international profile until after the war. Then the high quality of Italian fabrics, style and craftsmanship were represented by such names as Nino Cerruti, the head of a firm that had dealt in woollen fabrics since 1881; Fabiani of Rome; Veneziana of Milan; and the Fontana sisters, originally from Parma, who set out to challenge the dominance of French *haute couture*. A school of elegant, highly exclusive and, above all, high-quality Italian clothing emerged, immediately acquiring an enthusiastic following.

It was with the advent of ready-to-wear clothing in the 1970s, however, rather than with *haute couture*, that Italian fashion finally made a breakthrough. It was associated then with names such as Krizia, Missoni, Versace, Armani and Ferré, but also manifested itself in the work of a number of other less well-known fashion houses which, operating without "named" designers, none the less produced high-quality, high-fashion, and above all, relatively inexpensive clothing.

The Italian fashion phenomenon, as it emerged in the 1970s, resulted from the coincidence of a handful of talented individuals, capable of exploiting the special strength of Italian manufacturing, with the expansion of a highly flexible, craft-based, small-scale industry that could produce goods to very high design and fabrication standards.

Among the first and the most sophisticated of the ready-to-wear designers was Mariuccia Mandelli, who in 1954 had gone into operation under the Krizia label. Frequently described as "the godmother of the new Milanese fashion" she established a number of the characteristics of this school, among them an emphasis on simple classic tailoring, originality and wearability. When Gianni Versace moved to Milan in 1972 (from a background in architecture) and Giorgio Armani launched his first collection in 1974 (from 1954 to 1960 he had been the menswear buyer for Rinascente), both designers were indebted to the pioneering work of Mandelli in establishing the particular high-quality idiom that became the hallmark of Milanese fashion. Armani, who included womenswear in his collection for the first time in 1975, became best known for his updating of such classic menswear items as the blazer and the simple cotton shirt as well as his elegant but eminently comfortable "unstructured" jacket. In a tradition within which tailoring played such an important role, Armani was able to experiment freely with classic shapes, adding details that, although small, completely transformed them.

The architectural training that underpinned so much of Italian design was also an important factor within fashion. Gian-Franco Ferré emerged from this particular background first into accessories design and later into ready-to-wear fashion. He launched his own label in 1974 and, by the early 1980s, had become one of Italy's leading fashion names.

However successful the top figures in the field, they were entirely dependent upon both the flexible, highly efficient structure of Italian manufacturing and the special nature of Italian retailing, which retained the role of the small specialized shop in selling fashion items right through the 1980s. Below the level of "named" designers there was another stratum that consisted, essentially, of merchant traders: among these were the houses of Fendi, Basile, MaxMara and Gucci (the last-named had been in existence since 1906, selling leather goods in Florence). All of them were committed to high standards of manufacture and design but sold under a brand name rather than a designer label, and all were family-owned firms striving for a place in domestic and world markets by producing ready-to-wear items which were eminently wearable. MaxMara set the pace in the late 1960s, innovating in design rather than simply copying existing fashionable styles, and a decade later Italian fashion on this level of the market had earned a strong reputation for quality.

One reason for the success of Italian fashion design lies in its acceptance within Italy. More than 50 per cent of all

Right: Knitwear by Missoni, winter 1980. Subtle toning shades and a strong sense of texture characterized the unique look created by the Missonis. Developed back in the 1950s they became, by the 1970s, one of the leading international knitwear houses aiming exclusive items at a wealthy clientele.

designer clothes made in Italy are sold in Italy and they can be found in relatively out-of-the-way places as well as in the main cosmopolitan centres. A high level of popular consciousness ensures that the industry has a ready market and provides it with a secure base from which it can extend into other areas.

The chic image of Italian fashion that came to be known internationally brought with it its own anti-design antidote in the form of the work of Elio Fiorucci, which owed more to British pop culture than to Milanese tailoring traditions. He set out in the early 1960s as a shoe salesman, selling, among other things, brightly coloured galoshes. In 1967 he opened his first clothes shop in Milan in which he sold designs by the leading young British designers of the day, among them Ossie Clark and Zandra Rhodes. In 1970 he launched his own production of jeans, fashion accessories and household items and established a unique niche for himself in the Italian market-place. New York and London outlets quickly followed, and by the middle of the decade Fiorucci had become internationally associated with young, cheap "pop fashion" and other lifestyle accessories. He proved that, just as two decades earlier, in spite of the need to import youth culture from the USA and Britain, Italy was able to provide a more stylish set of artefacts to accompany it than the countries that actually generated it.

The retail outlet of Benetton, which deals in cheap, stylish fashion separates aimed at a young market, grew up in the

Above: Shopping bags from Fiorucci. Inspired by British Pop culture in the 1960s, Elio Fiorucci became a major exporter of the Italian Pop style, which he created single-handedly. He has worked closely with designers such as Alessandro Mendini, who has provided him with striking features for his shop windows.

Above right: "Spaghetti" chair designed by G. Belotti and manufactured by Alias in 1979. This simple neo-Modernist design, consisting of plastic thread wound around a steel frame, was inspired by examples from the 1950s. It became an enormously popular chair, complementing the wide range of 1980s neo-Modernist interiors.

late 1970s and early 1980s, to become yet another massive Italian fashion success both at home and abroad. A typical product of the "Third Italy" (the company is run by two brothers and two sisters), it expanded enormously, selling off its stores on a franchise basis but managing to retain a very highly visible and unified corporate image for all its high street outlets.

FURNITURE

Hit by the worldwide recession, inflation and the high cost of raw materials, Italian furniture had to struggle to maintain its past reputation in the years after 1975. By the early 1980s the Arab countries had become important customers for a wide sector of the Italian furniture trade: this was demonstrated at the annual Milan furniture fairs by the acres of gilt and extravagant decoration that joined the more traditional modern image of luxury conveyed by chrome and black leather. The more progressive Italian companies, among them established firms such as Cassina, Poltronova, B and B Italia, Castelli, Zanotta, Tecno, Artemide, Poltrona Frau, as well as the more recent Driade, Casa-Nova, Skipper and Alias, stuck to their guns, however, producing innovatory new designs which were provided by a familiar cluster of "named" designers. The most significant development in the industry after 1975 was the huge increase in the number of small firms with fewer than fifty employees, coupled with rapid growth in investment in new production machinery. In keeping with the general tendency towards flexible specialization, this accounted for the continued high profile of design and the sustained commitment to high quality in the furniture industry, particularly where items aimed at export were concerned. Indeed, many new manufacturers were located outside the industrial triangle, in middle Italy. Brianza remained the centre for upholstered furniture, while 75 per cent of chair production now occurred in Friuli.

In the 1980s the home market for Italian furniture declined as a consequence of the worsening economic situation. One response to this was the growing concentration on what is called the "supplies" sector – furniture items aimed at the contract market for offices, hotels and public areas. Another was a developing interest in what the catalogue to the 1982 Milan Fair described as "flexibility, new proposals for ways of living, fantasy, multi-purpose furniture".[4] This was a response both to smaller living spaces and to the growing importance of the injection of "fashion" values into furniture, a strategy that was aimed at selling to the younger generation of consumers. A design by Gregotti for Casa-Nova from this

period, consisting of a sofa-bed with zip-on covers in bright colours, was one example. Increasingly, the fashionable styles and pastel colours associated with post-Modernism and the spare, industrial look of the "high tech" movement began to penetrate the furniture arena. The ability to introduce stylistic innovation so easily was entirely due to the flexibility and small-scale nature of the industry. Intended to give a boost to both the home and the export markets, it was coupled with more intensive marketing programmes to win back flagging markets. At this time the industry found itself competing increasingly with Third World countries where labour was much cheaper, so it had to intensify its concentration on design and high quality in order both to retain old markets and to win new ones.

By 1983 the Italian furniture industry had experienced its third successive year of decline. Exports showed a slight recovery, but the domestic market showed no signs of picking up and it seemed that the boom years were finally a thing of the past.

Right: Coffee-table for Poltronova designed by Gae Aulenti in the late 1970s. A glass surface mounted on giant castors, this highly innovative table was among the earliest "high-tech" objects to emerge in Italy. Its use of "ready-made" industrial components was reminiscent of the work of the Castiglioni brothers who were fascinated by the idea of "found" objects.

Below: "Sindbad" armchair designed by Vico Magistretti and manufactured by Cassina in 1981. After twenty years of innovative design for Cassina, Magistretti produced this new sofa concept based on the idea of a horse blanket thrown loosely over an upholstered base. His ideas remained simple, original and sophisticated.

THE "NEW" INDUSTRIES

The economic fate of the furniture industry was shared by other areas of manufacturing, among them automobiles, electrical and electronic goods. However, there were some signs of light at the end of the tunnel for a few of the large-scale companies. Olivetti, for instance, was taken over in the late 1970s by a professional manager, Carlo De Benedetti; as a result of his reorganizations, by 1983 the company had increased its revenue by 21 per cent and its profits by 40 per cent. This was achieved entirely by increasing expenditure on research and development, an area that had been badly neglected up until then. New initiatives included the manu-

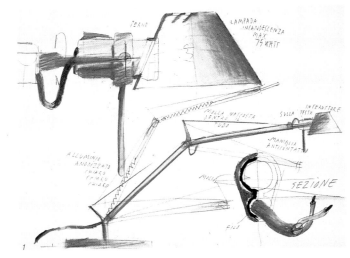

Right: Interior with "Maralunga" chair, designed by Vico Magistretti and manufactured by Cassina in 1979. This upholstered chair and ottoman reflected a continuous interest in sumptuous materials, simple form and comfort, which has characterized much Italian mainstream design in the 1980s. The light is by Achille Castiglioni and the mobile by Alexander Calder.

Above right: Sketch for a reading lamp by Michele De Lucchi, manufactured by Artemide in the early 1980s. A hinged light that could be angled in a number of different ways, its black, functional appearance was surprising from a leading member of the Memphis group.

facture of an electronic typewriter in 1978. An agreement between Olivetti and AT&T (American Telephone and Telegraph) in 1984 was also made with an eye to increased technological innovation and research.

Fiat's main initiative was the introduction of robots into its Mirafiori plant. This was done partly in response to union disruption: the late 1970s had been dominated by strikes and terrorist attacks. In 1979 the new managing director, Cesare Romiti, made the unprecedented decision to lay off twenty-three thousand workers and to install automated machinery in the factory. Within four years Fiat had begun to make profits once again, and by 1985 was "the sixth largest company in the world, and the biggest car producer in Europe with more than 12 per cent of sales. In Italy it has increased its share to 55.5 per cent of the market."[5]

As in the earlier period of Fiat's international success, design played an important part in this new achievement. In 1980 the company commissioned Giugiaro to design a new

compact car: the result was the Fiat "Panda" which quickly became a huge international success. Innovative both in the advances made in its production technology and in its strikingly spare look, appropriate to a period of worldwide recession, the little car re-established Fiat as a source of innovatory design. This was followed in 1983 with the launch of the "Uno", once again designed by Giugiaro, and voted car of the year by European car writers. It sold 325,000 units in that same year.

The 1980s in Italy were the decade of the car designer, who took over from the more traditional body-stylist as the image-maker for the automobile. The demand for economy cars meant that car design came to be as much about fuel consumption as stylish body curves, and the approach pioneered by Giugiaro and his company, Italdesign, proved the most appropriate one for the time. The simple box shape of the "Panda" emphasized its essentially utilitarian significance. The 1976 brief from Fiat had been a highly functional one, namely to "create a vehicle that weighed and cost the same as a Fiat 126 but which offered within these limits maximum comfort and performance."[6]

Other cars designed by Giugiaro included the Alfasud "Sprint" in 1978 and the Lancia "Delta" in 1979. He did not limit himself to car design, however, but turned his hand to a number of product designs as well, including a sewing machine for Necchi and a camera for the Japanese company, Nikon.

The motor-cycle was another example of Italian design excellence to come through the crisis of the 1970s. Because of trade agreements made between Fiat and the Japanese car manufacturers back in the 1950s, Italy had remained very faithful to home-made automobiles. This loyalty was equally evident in the areas of motor-scooters and motor-cycles and the 1980s witnessed as many "Vespas" and "MotoGuzzis" in the Italian environment as ever before.

The Guzzi company had survived by emphasizing quality, low price and styling. In contrast to the low-powered machines made by Japan, Guzzi concentrated on the high-powered models and managed, as a result, to retain its home market. In spite of a crisis in the mid-1960s the company was

Left: "Albero" plant stand by Achille Castiglioni, manufactured by Zanotta in 1983. In the 1980s Castiglioni designed a sequence of small household objects for Zanotta with a strong 1950s flavour. Available in pale blue or white, this little plant stand suited the post-Modernist mood of the day.

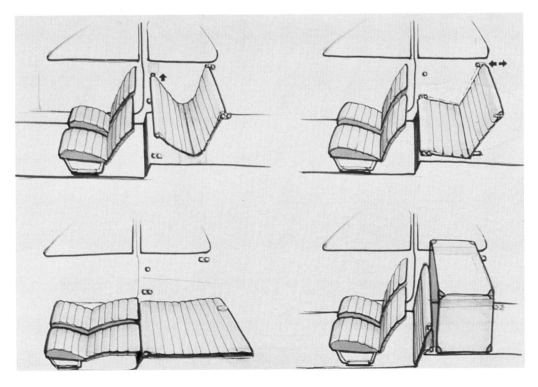

Above: Giorgio Giugiaro's Fiat "Panda" of 1980. Giugiaro's design studio, Italdesign, was approached by Fiat in 1976 to create a car that would repeat the success of the 500 and 600 models. The utilitarian little car that emerged concentrated on maximum roominess combined with a minimum of accessories. The simple back seat (sketch, left) was adjustable to accommodate extra luggage.

Above: Ferrari "Testarossa" sports car, designed by Pininfarina in 1986. In the wake of his "Dino" of two decades earlier, Pininfarina's design for this fantasy car took Italian styling to an extreme position. Every detail indicates speed and luxury and the dramatic impact of the whole evokes the continuation of a car culture associated exclusively with Italy. Subsequently Japanese manufacturers have perpetuated the tradition, often turning to Italy for inspiration.

Right: Giorgio Giugiaro's Fiat "Uno" of 1983. Giugiaro's design studio, Italdesign, created the "Uno" on the heels of their enormous success with the "Panda". Envisaged as a substitute for the earlier Fiat 127, it was available in three- and five-door versions. Although designed and developed very quickly, its cleanness of line has met with widespread international approval.

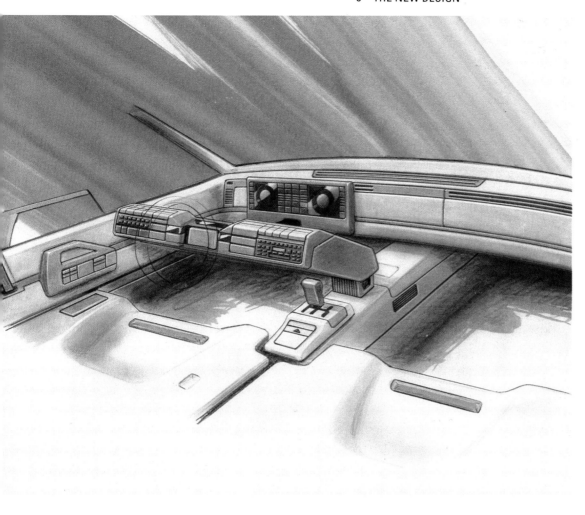

Left: Dashboard of the Alfa "Delfino", designed by the Bertone studio in 1983. The high-tech interior of this stylish car reflected the Bertone studio's continued interest in pushing the automobile to a technological extreme and providing a suitable "sci-fi" imagery, using very sleek forms and a minimum of excrescences.

flexible enough to be able to re-orientate its production and to move into new product lines that proved highly successful abroad.

In *elettrodomestici*, Zanussi continued to dominate the picture, managing to manufacture well-priced products that had the edge on the immediate competition where appearance and style were concerned. Based in Friuli, Zanussi expanded through the 1970s to become the biggest company of its kind in Italy and a European market leader. Its washing machines, fridges, cookers and freezers were produced on modern, mass production lines. In spite of this the company was experiencing enormous economic difficulties by the mid-1980s, the result of a temporary, and disastrous, sideways move into "brown" goods – stereos, televisions, etc. This crisis intensified the importance of design to the company, which used it as a means of making its products increasingly competitive. The responsibility of the company's product design lay with a Dutchman, Andries Van Onck, who was hired in the late 1970s to help give Zanussi a coherent image. Gino Valle remained in charge of corporate design while Massimo Vignelli designed the company's graphics.

One way in which Zanussi differentiated between the vast numbers of white cubes that came off its production lines (3.6 million fridges, freezers, washing machines, dish-washers and ovens in 1983, for example) was to break them down into different ranges destined for different markets. Three ranges were evolved – A, B and C – each of which was aimed at a very specific market.

The principal design challenge was to inject character into these otherwise anonymous products. Van Onck explained his personal approach towards this problem: "I like to create machines that have the feeling of being like a little household animal."[7] Touches of colour, brown and lime-green on the control panels, for instance, were used to add surface interest to the otherwise bland white boxes. Attention to such visual details as the composition of the control knobs demonstrated Van Onck's background as a European purist trained at the Ulm school, and played an important part in making Zanussi's products, although not the most expensive, among the most visually sophisticated on the European market.

Unlike the Italian approach to furniture production – which was to seek only the most exclusive outlets – the Zanussi company aimed its goods at a large mass market, thereby demonstrating one face of Italy's success in the 1980s. It was also the first company in this field to launch a post-Modernist product: its "Wizard" fridge, designed by Pezzetta, available in both metallic and marbled finishes and boasting a pointed roof complete with a small flag on the top. Indesit followed soon afterwards with its washing machine designed by the fashion designer Missoni, while Gruppi Borghi launched a range of fridges in rainbow colours, sounding the death knell for the idea of "white goods". By the second half of the 1980s this tendency had become fairly widespread in Italy, as indeed it was in Germany and Japan as well, and producers of small appliances – CGF with its hairdriers and irons, SIFAC with its mini-cookers and Faema with its coffee-machines, for instance – had all provided alternatives to the standardized white goods of yesteryear.

THE NEW RADICALISM

The possibility of a post-Modernist aesthetic emerged in Italy as one of the strongest design directions of the late 1970s and 1980s. While it came, eventually, to influence the highly conservative area of electrical appliances, it had, by the beginning of the 1980s, established itself as a viable alternative in the more innovatory context of furniture and small decorative items. A debate emerged that, in essence, carried on the discussions initiated by the counter-design movement of the late 1960s.

By now, however, the international cultural climate had become increasingly receptive to the ideas raised by Italian anti-design, seeing in them a valid alternative to what was being recognized internationally as the fading energies and growing irrelevance of the early twentieth-century Modern Movement. The changing economic, technological and industrial circumstances of the 1980s began a pendulum swing away from the neo-Modernist vision of the environment, in which the twin values of Rationalism and mechanized mass production had determined the norm, towards a much more fragmented vision within which cultural pluralism, multiple tastes, consumer choices and flexible mass production systems indicated a much less unified picture of the material world, and required a much less univalent design philosophy to accompany it.

One characteristic of Italian design in the late 1970s was the re-emergence of anti-design, which had seemed to fade out earlier in the decade. While some of the protagonists of the original movement had come to Milan to work in architectural practices, others had moved into architectural education and begun to influence a new generation of students. Adolfo Natalini, for example, a founder of the Superstudio group, was particularly influential in Florence, and young designers who worked with him, Michele De Lucchi among them, began to demonstrate their debt to the earlier ideas that had emanated from counter-design in the late 1960s and early 1970s. In 1973 De Lucchi set up a small group called Cavart, which worked within the by now familiar area of radical architecture, organizing seminars and producing films and documents. Ettore Sottsass continued to function on two fronts, heading an office for Olivetti and running his own private architectural and design practice. Young designers working for him in both contexts were strongly influenced by his sustained radicalism, and several of them began to reflect his philosophy in their own work.

The gentle hints of a second wave of energy in the area of anti-design began to surface in the second half of the 1970s. Although Milan was now the exclusive centre of progressive design there was also a strong feeling of internationalism in this second manifestation, as young designers from numerous other countries came in the 1970s and 1980s to what they regarded as the design mecca to work with the "great men" of Italian design and to try to absorb Italian culture.

The first attempt to harness these new energies and demonstrate the increased relevance of anti-design in the late 1970s was the emergence of Studio Alchymia, established in 1976 by the architect Alessandro Guerriero. He approached a group of designers, offering to exhibit their work in his gallery. The idea of an annual show was inspired by the increasingly important world of fashion design. Guerriero set out to exhibit three-dimensional design work in a similar way. The designers he approached in 1978 included Ettore Sottsass, Alessandro Mendini, Andrea Branzi, the UFO group, and Trix and Robert Haussmann, as well as representatives of a much younger generation, Daniele Puppa, Michele De Lucchi and Paola Navone. The shared commitment of these designers was to a philosophy of design that stood outside the mainstream, formalist, industry-linked phenomenon that the rest of the world still associated with Italy. They all allied themselves with "popular" rather than "high" culture. Thus themes already established in the late 1960s, such as stylistic revivalism, bad taste and the banal, dominated the vocabulary of the Studio Alchymia designers. The work that made up the first two collections – named, ironically, "Bau Haus" and "Bau Haus Side 2", and shown in 1979 and 1980 – was preoccupied with ideas of mass repro-

Left: Zanussi's "Wizard" range was designed by Roberto Pezzetta, head of Zanussi's industrial design team, in 1987. He broke new ground with this post-Modernist refrigerator – a rejection once and for all of the "white box". The "Wizard", complete with flag on top, was as much an item of furniture as an appliance; it is shown here in a company boardroom where it blends happily with a stack of televisions.

Right: Alessandro Mendini's "Infinite Furniture", designed for Studio Alchymia in 1981. This design is part of a series of furniture pieces with removable motifs applied to their surfaces. They are designed by a number of avant-garde Italian designers and fine artists. Mendini's idea was to remove the dominance of the individual designer and allow user participation in the arrangement of the decorations.

Below: Drawing for "Peter Pan" chair by Michele De Lucchi, 1982. A tubular steel frame covered by upholstery, this little "fun" chair could be dressed and undressed with layers of coloured and patterned cloth to create a range of different variations.

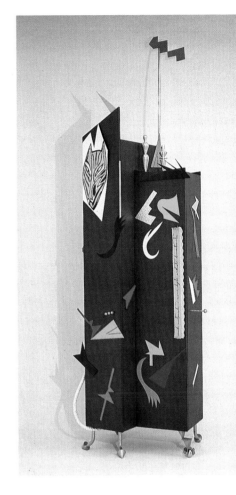

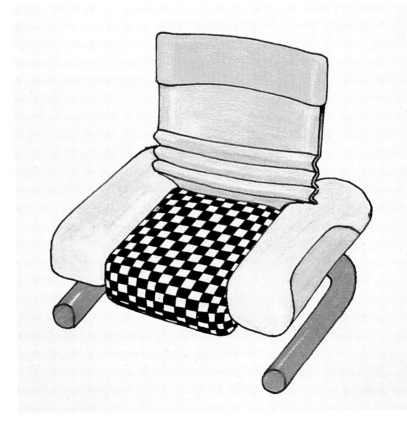

Right: "Vega" vase, designed by Marco Zanini and made for the third Memphis exhibition in 1982. Along with Sottsass, Zanini created a number of boldly shaped, brightly coloured, glass vessels which helped to redefine the role of objects made from traditional materials. Manufactured by a long-established Venetian firm, these items are none the less aggressively modern and have no formal traditional associations.

ducibility, the mass dissemination of fine art imagery and its inevitable transformation into "kitsch", and motifs culled from the 1950s (used not for their historical content but because they still influenced the banal environment of suburban Milan). The collections were, above all, a renewed attempt to reintegrate design with everyday life and culture: the 1950s, a time when design and culture had moved hand in hand, both of them committed to the same ideal of democracy and optimism, provided the inevitable model for much of the work.

Sottsass concentrated on the patterned surface, printed on to plastic laminate, which he described as "a material with no culture". All his patterns were inspired by such banal sources as the mosaic floors of suburban bars, the "wire netting of suburban fences" and the "spongy paper of government account books". They were, he explained, all "extracts from a figurative iconography found in spaces uncorrupted by the sophistication of the standard culture of private interior design."[8] This determination to find a new basis for the very language of design underpinned the entire project which, by the early 1980s, had earned the grandiose name of "The New Design".

Below: "Lido" sofa designed by Michele De Lucchi in 1982 and exhibited as part of the Memphis group's second exhibition in Milan. The bright colours and Sixties revival pattern on this sofa made it appear, typically, more like a child's toy than a serious piece of furniture. Its impact was enormous and it shocked all those used to traditional Milanese chic.

While Studio Alchymia acted as a catalyst, bringing together first- and second-generation counter-designers and pushing their work forward into a new context, it remained a highly intellectualized, elitist and, in the end, somewhat pessimistic project. Alessandro Mendini became the Studio's

key spokesman in the 1980s and he remained preoccupied with the ultimate inability of design to change society, or to do anything other than merely reflect its internal contradictions and inequalities. As he himself explained, "The avant-garde is fated to play an isolated, aristocratic, restricted and brief role: a kind of enervating programme of self-immolation consumes it and destroys it before it becomes widely acceptable."[9]

Alchymia allied itself closely with contemporary movements in Italian fine art that described themselves as "post-avant-garde", and it saw its continued role in the 1980s as, in Mendini's words, "problematic" rather than "affirmative". It wanted to pose questions rather than answer them. At the 1981 Milan Furniture Fair, Studio Alchymia presented its "infinite furniture", designed by Mendini with the assistance of a number of other designers and fine artists, such as Sandro Chia and Francesco Clemente, accompanied by an event from a group of performance artists. The ever-present themes of consumerism and the role of the mass media provided the essential problematic for Mendini and through the 1980s his work continued to wrestle with them in a number of different ways. From 1977 onwards he was the editor of *Modo*, a broadly based magazine formed to address problems of contemporary material culture; it became a major mouthpiece for the New Design movement as a whole through the late 1970s and 1980s.

A number of exhibitions and events also served to bring the work of the Italian radical designers to the notice of an international audience. Two shows in particular, the "Design Phenomene" exhibit presented by Studio Alchymia at "Forum Design", held in Linz in 1979, and "The Banal Object" displayed at the Venice Biennale of 1980, demonstrated the revival of energy in this area and showed that Italy was once again leading the way in progressive design, re-instating the need for debate and experimentation.

While Studio Alchymia remained locked within the ivory tower of intellectualism and unrealized possibilities, Ettore Sottsass, impatient with the circular arguments discussed there and the all-pervading pessimism, launched his own collection of radical objects in 1981. This he did in collaboration with a group of young designers who worked with him in various capacities, among them Michele De Lucchi, George J. Sowden, Marco Zanini, Aldo Cibic, Matheo Thun, Martine Bedin and Nathalie Du Pasquier, and with the assistance of a few international architects who were also personal friends – the Austrian Hans Hollein, the American Michael Graves, the Japanese Arata Isozaki and the Spaniard Javier Mariscal. The group christened itself "Memphis" because of

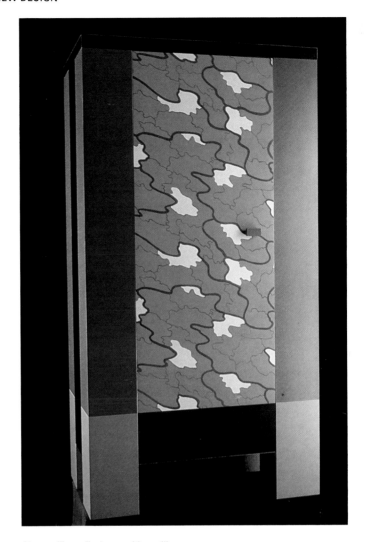

Above: "Luxor" closet with a silk-screened door, designed by George Sowden for the second Memphis group exhibition in 1982. A member of Sottsass's Olivetti office, the English-born Sowden became a key member of the Memphis group and has designed some of its most lasting objects. This wardrobe, with its rich pattern, helps turn a traditionally cumbersome piece of furniture into part of the general post-Modernist environment.

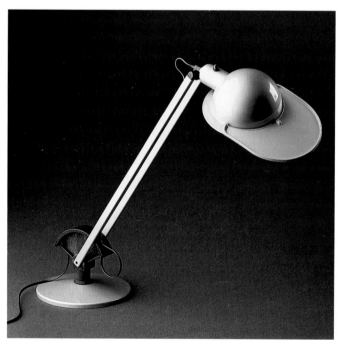

Top: "Icaro" wall light designed by Carlo Forcolini and manufactured by Artemide in 1985. Made of glass and perforated steel, it represents the neo-Modernist tendency characterizing one branch of Italian design in the 1980s. Forcolini's designs are elegant solutions to the technical, formal and practical problems of lighting.

Above: "Donald" desk lamp, designed by Perry King and Santiago Miranda, and manufactured by Arteluce in the early 1980s. The simple little metal light, with its movable head and additional eyeshade, earned its name from its resemblance to Disney's Donald Duck. King was one of the earliest English designers to settle and work in Milan.

Sottsass's continued commitment to the joint stimuli of contemporary pop culture and ancient cultures. Its members were both less selfconsciously intellectual in their statements and, above all, more optimistic in their proposals.

This was a deliberately internationally oriented proclamation about the need for design to reflect the cultural values implicit in an age when the mass media determine all levels of communication and all forms of social relationships. Thus pattern, colour, surface texture and fantastic form encouraged instant communication that functioned independently of the utility value of tables, chairs, lights, bookcases, and even televisions (utility value was not denied, of course; it simply took second place to the importance of image). The Memphis objects were not, like so many of the "classic" Italian objects, self-referential monuments acting as mediators of the values embraced by manufacturing industry. Instead, they related to the world of consumption and use, vying for attention with the vast number of other mass media-disseminated images that surround us. Although the pieces on display were hand-made prototypes, they were not conceived as "craft" objects. The industrial materials utilized – plastic laminate, steel and glass – were reminders that the Memphis designs were destined for manufacture in multiples, with the exact number and price being dependent upon the scale of demand.

THE DIFFUSION OF THE NEW DESIGN

While the Memphis experiment of 1981 started out as a modest, highly personal project it succeeded none the less in reopening the debate about the continued relevance or otherwise of Modernism, and in capturing the imagination of the world's design press. It was without doubt the most widely reported aspect of the Milan Furniture Fair of 1981. This was partly due to the absence of anything else of great interest at the main Fair site, but also because the Memphis pieces were so eminently photogenic and so ideally suited to representation by the mass media. Their overnight success was responsible for a renewed international interest in Italian design, now with a strong emphasis on its anti-design face rather than on the continued mainstream movement, which was producing only a handful of interesting objects. It became clear that, within the new international atmosphere of post-Modernistic attitudes towards architecture and design, Italy was playing a leading role as, indeed, it had already been doing for well over a decade. While in the USA and Great Britain, post-Modernism was associated with a strongly

Right: "Domestic Animals", designed by Andrea Branzi and produced by Zabro in 1985. Branzi, an ex-member of Archizoom and contributor to Studio Alchymia and Memphis, developed a range of prototype designs in the mid 1980s, destined for batch production. They investigated the way in which natural materials, such as bamboo and raw wood, have been used in the manufacture of furniture.

Below: "Apocalypse Now" by Carlo Forcolini, manufactured by Alias in 1984. A coffee table of "rusted" steel, with an adjustable light in its centre, it represents the interest in creating forms from industrial materials that has characterized much Italian design of the 1980s. Alias, set up to perpetuate the values of the European Modern Movement, has reproduced items by, among others, Van Doesburg and Pierre Chareau.

historicizing and somewhat reactionary tendency, in Italy it was formulated in much more forward-looking terms.

The Italian movement was well received and much emulated in the USA, Japan and Europe. Memphis itself spread its sphere of influence, with many of the individuals involved taking on commissions outside the country, but at home it continued to present an annual group show to coincide with the Furniture Fair. More people were brought into the group, particularly young unknown designers from abroad, and experimentation with different materials which lent themselves to textural exploration, such as marble and terrazzo, was encouraged. While the collection itself provided a kind of hot-house of Italian radicalism, to which visitors came from far and wide, there were broader and, in some ways, more significant spin-offs from the project. These were evident both in the mass-produced works commissioned from Memphis group members by companies in Italy and elsewhere, and in the proliferation of areas – fashion, graphics and advertising in particular – that began to be influenced by the Memphis style. While this would have devalued the high-minded intentions of the Modern Movement it served to confirm the role that the New Design played in the area of mass communications and mass culture. Sottsass's surface patterns were used extensively in the early 1980s and came to symbolize the New Design for a very wide audience. Memphis succeeded not only in suggesting a new philosophical base for design – "it is a widespread drive to attain renewal, a genetic and spontaneous mutation of the chromosomes of international design"[10] – but in providing a new iconography for it as well.

In its early manifestations Memphis functioned entirely outside the mainstream of Italian furniture manufacturing. But a number of companies, among them Zanotta, Driade, Bieffeplast and Artemide, were quick to realize the profound change in the international design mood and commissioned Sottsass and his colleagues to design pieces for them. Other manufacturers worked with other members of the anti-design school – Cassina with Paolo Deganello of Archizoom, for instance – and it soon became increasingly difficult to disentangle "mainstream" from "alternative". As the furniture industry took up the radical challenge and put it into production for the first time, the strong "anti-industry" message of the first generation of anti-designers was softened considerably and its ability to shock also lessened as a result.

Products other than furniture quickly responded to the same initiative. The Alessi company made a special contribution in metalwork by commissioning a number of international post-Modernist designers, among them Robert Venturi, Michael Graves, Charles Jencks, Aldo Rossi, Paolo Portoghesi, Alessandro Mendini and Richard Meier, to provide designs for its ambitious "Programme 6". Their eclectic proposals covered the entire international spectrum of post-Modernist themes and concerns, and established Alessi as a leading company in its field. Cult status was bestowed on Richard Sapper's "bollitore" kettle which whistled, when it boiled, like an American Am-trak train.

Even the most conservative area of domestic electrical appliances began to show signs of the new aesthetic tenden-

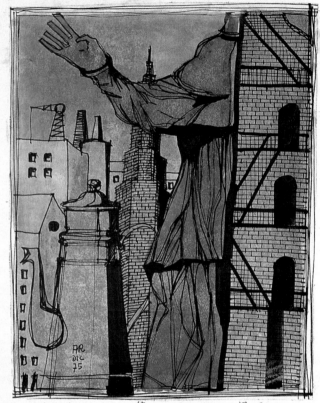

Above: Sketch by Aldo Rossi, 1975. It depicts a traditional Italian coffee-pot in an urban, architectural environment, expressing Rossi's view of products as architecture in miniature. This approach was clearly reflected in his design for the "Conica" coffee-pot for Alessi of 1980–83 (see below).

Below: A range of Alessi products from the late 1970s and 1980s. From left to right, they are: Richard Sapper's kettle (see page 224); Massimo Morozzi's pasta set; Oscar Tusquet's teapot; Aldo Rossi's "Conica" coffee-pot; Michael Graves's kettle, and Ettore Sottsass's oil and vinegar set.

Left and above: Oil and vinegar set designed by Achille Castiglioni and manufactured by Alessi in 1984. Along with many other leading Italian designers Castiglioni was approached by Alessi to provide small items in stainless steel. His oil and vinegar set, with tops that open as the bottles are tilted, demonstrates his continuing originality.

cies. Michele De Lucchi pioneered this with some designs for small appliances that he proposed to the Girmi company (although they never got past the prototype stage), and a blue-print for a "user-friendly" stereo-system, which looked more like a child's toy than an aggressive piece of sophisticated high technology. Gradually a number of production items began to bear signs of this "gentle" approach. Perhaps most radically of all, a few anti-designers took on board the problem of the most aggressive and most status-sensitive object of them all – the automobile. Sottsass imagined a car for his friend Elio Fiorucci which combined a grass-green floor with a sky-blue ceiling, in a fanciful attempt to lessen the gap between the worlds of advanced technology and of nature. The first post-Modernist car has, however, yet to be put into production.

By the mid-1980s Italy, or rather Milan in particular, was once again the home of design and was recognized as such by the entire industrialized world. The re-emergence of anti-design, and its new prominence internationally as the most progressive and relevant movement, renewed Italy's earlier reputation for producing visually sophisticated and culturally meaningful products. Above all, the renewal of the design debate showed that the intellectual base of Italian design practice was still thriving.

As the 1980s progressed, the strong, established internationalism resulted in a two-way exchange between Italy and a number of other countries. Italian companies such as Driade, Cassina and Tecno commissioned designs from abroad, in particular from the Frenchman Philippe Starck, the Japanese Tokiyuki Kita and the English architect Norman Foster. Italian designers, both mainstream and radical, among them Bellini, Giugiaro, Sottsass and Mendini, were all much in demand abroad, especially in Japan; Sottsass also worked for Knoll, the American-based furniture manufacturer. In the 1980s the two principal strengths of post-war Italian design, its flexible, progressive industry on the one hand and its highly creative and extremely versatile individual designers on the other, showed the rest of the world just how significant a cultural force design could be.

One branch of Italian radicalism became increasingly popular and consequently, in the eyes of some, "debased" as the 1980s progressed. The work of Mendini on the other hand, through what in 1983 became transformed into Zona Alchimia and, in 1984–5, into Nuova Alchimia, resisted commercialization and remained as a result somewhat esoteric and peripheral.

Andrea Branzi pursued his own interests in the relationship between social, cultural and industrial change in his "Domestic Animals" project. This was a series of designs for furniture items which, through their use of material such as untreated branches of trees, sought to reunite the worlds of nature and culture. A new design school, Domus Academy,

established in Milan in 1982, occupied much of his energy. Here he extended his ideas about "Primary Design" which stressed the "soft" qualities of the discipline, namely those relating to touch, smell, temperature, sound and the effects of lighting. Student projects, developing these themes, continued research that led further and further away from the "formal" object of the 1960s. With the help of Clino Trini Castelli, who had been working since the early 1970s on what he called "the reactive surface", and Massimo Morozzi, who was experimenting in the area of "soft design", the school functioned as a means of institutionalizing, academicizing and systematizing many of the enquiries that had inspired the early anti-designers in their search for alternatives to formalism.

Like all the other counter-design manifestations of this generation, however, the work of the Domus Academy became firmly international in orientation and increasingly conscious of the post-industrial, post-mass market context in which it operated. It confirmed that the contribution of Italian design was ultimately conceptual and philosophical in

Above far right: Salad servers in transparent plastic, designed by Anna Castelli Ferrieri and manufactured by Kartell in 1976. Their organic form is both pleasing to the eye and practical.

Far right: Tables, model no. 4310, designed by Anna Castelli Ferrieri for Kartell in the 1980s. Bright colours and a high-quality finish represent Kartell's continuing interest in plastic objects, which compete in Italy with luxury objects in a range of other materials.

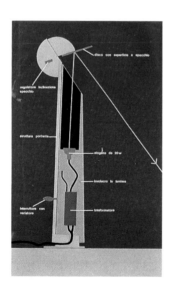

Above and right: "Gibigiana" reading lamp, designed by Achille Castiglioni and manufactured by Flos in 1981. As with so many of Castiglioni's ingenious lighting designs, the basic form of this little desk lamp is dictated by its function. The light source is reflected downwards by a mirror and the stem has been given a metal "skirt". The ultimate appearance, however, is bird-like – a strong image that removes the design from the level of mere utility.

nature, and that it drew its energies from being oppositional and by integrating itself with the contemporary cultural debate.

By the mid-1980s, in spite of the new wave of energy which had characterized the early years of that decade, the anti-design movement was becoming increasingly integrated into mainstream activity: it was losing its bite and becoming just another fashionable gesture. The impact of the shock tactics employed by Memphis in 1981 began to fade from view, caught in the trap of incessantly repeating what were, by definition, only short-lived statements. On one level Italian design seemed to be simply pandering to a style-hungry international market.

On the other hand, however, the move towards integration with the growing cultural pluralism of the mid-1980s can be seen as the final emergence of a real alternative to the Modern Movement that had held sway right up to the 1970s, and the culmination of sustained post-war Italian attempts to establish a post-Functionalist design movement. By the middle of the 1980s this had become a reality and the Italians were showing the way ahead to the rest of the world.

ETTORE SOTTSASS

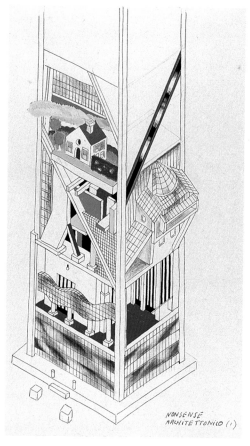

The career of Ettore Sottsass began in Milan in the immediate post-war years but he first reached prominence with his work for Olivetti and for his anti-design experiments in the 1960s. In the 1980s he re-emerged as the leading figure within what came to be called the "New Design" movement, although he drew on work that he had been doing as far back as the 1950s. He has remained committed to a radical approach towards design – suspicious of the absolute control of the manufacturing industry, of the dominance of "good taste" and of the emphasis on materialism and consumerism – and he has drawn on the twin forces of Pop and primitive cultures in an attempt to sidestep such tendencies. The Memphis project, initiated in 1981, brought him into the limelight again but he also continued to work outside this context on a range of radical designs, which were developments of his own personal themes and obsessions. His work from the 1970s and 1980s includes a range of glass designed for a Memphis exhibition in 1986 (above left); the "Beidermeier sofa", designed for an exhibition in Milan in 1982 (above); a sideboard entitled "That Hotel Downtown New York" (right) and bookshelf, "Lemon Sherbert" (left), both designed for the Blum Helman gallery, New York, in 1987, and a design for a piece of "nonsense" architecture from the late 1970s (far left).

CONCLUSION

After a few centuries, Italy finally has become, in 1987, one of Europe's greatest success stories.

W. Scobie, 1987[1]

In the second half of the 1980s Italian society, particularly that part of it located in the north, is enjoying a standard of living at least on a level with that of Britain and France. The concept of "Il Sorpasso", the idea that Italy has, in fact, surpassed the wealth of those European countries, is much discussed, and encourages Italy to go from strength to strength. Statistics show, for example, that Italians own more cars per head than Britons (360 per 1,000 to Britain's 312), and that, with the underground economy taken into account, the Italian per capita gross domestic product is well ahead of its British and French equivalents.

This unmitigated success has been achieved through the efforts of Italian industry and of Italy's leading industrialists as well as, of course, through the country's continued ability to sell style to foreign customers. In an article about Italy written for the *Observer* newspaper in 1987, William Scobie pinpointed "the worldwide hunger and willingness to pay for Italian style, from Breda-built subway cars for the Washington metro to Pininfarina-designed Cadillac bodies".[2] It is a phenomenon that shows no signs of abating.

The individuals who are still the leading names in the world of Italian design – Pininfarina, Giugiaro, Armani, Versace, Zanuso, Castiglioni, Magistretti, Bellini, Pesce and even Sottsass – are no longer young men, however, and

Left: Whistling kettle designed by Richard Sapper for Alessi in 1984. Made of stainless steel with a coxcomb, plastic handle, it made the sound of an American Am-trak train when it boiled. Uniting a traditional kitchen item with an aggressively modern form, it became a cult object in the 1980s, more looked at and photographed than actually used.

Far right: Masanori Umeda's "Tawaraya" ring, designed and made for the first Memphis group exhibition in 1981, in which several foreign architects were invited to participate. Ettore Sottsass, acknowledged leader of the group, is on the right; he is surrounded by its original members: from the left, Aldo Cibic, Andrea Branzi, Michele De Lucchi, Marco Zanini, Nathalie Du Pasquier, George J. Sowden, Matteo Thun and Martine Bedin.

Right: Computer terminal in the control room of RAI, the Italian broadcasting corporation, in Rome, designed by Maurizio Morgantini. This high-technology interior has been described as a "telematic spaceship" set within a 1930s building. It was designed with an emphasis on the sensorial interface between man and machine and represents one of the new directions of post-Formalist Italian design.

their unfaltering abilities are ones that derive from maturity and experience rather than the spontaneity of youth. With only a few exceptions (among them the talented young designers who have surfaced with the success of Memphis), this older generation of Italian designers has not been succeeded by a younger one, able to carry on where they leave off.

Even the chic forms of Italian fashion, the youngest of the Italian design disciplines, are clearly aimed at the older woman: "Milan fashion designers gave us power dressing because they know that the power still resides with women. The Italians have not sold out to the idea of youth in the way that the British have."[3] The same applies to the highly styled Italian automobiles which, on the basis of their prices alone, are not young people's playthings.

Where furniture and other domestic products are concerned, Italy still manages to lead the way, but today's mood is different from that of only five years ago when rebellion and debate were in the air. Exceptional designs such as Alberto Meda's carbon fibre chair for Alias, and Gaetano Pesce's felt chairs for Cassina, both launched at the Milan Furniture Fair in 1987, prove that Italian ingenuity and flair are as strong as ever but, in general, the formula has become a little tired.

Even the shocking proposals put forward by Memphis and Studio Alchymia in the early part of the decade have lost their power to surprise and have become an acceptable genre providing an alternative strand to that of the traditional modern mainstream.

If Italian design has become middle-aged, however, the international enthusiasm for the "modern style" has, for its part, been replaced by a growing interest in nostalgia and revivalism. This applies even to the classics of the Modern Movement which have been resuscitated, in particular by Cassina and Zanotta, adding fuel to the fire of the historicist tendency by an increasingly revisionist attitude towards modern design.

The vital role for modern design in the years of reconstruction after the Second World War, and through the ensuing crises of the subsequent four decades, seems to have burned itself out. It is being replaced by a new interest in advanced technology (computerized industry is, without doubt, an important part of Italy's future), mass marketing and mass retailing. While Fiat, Zanussi and Benetton continue to sell Italian style to the whole world, their real skills lie in their ability to reach the right markets, to direct the right product to the right customer.

In many ways these developments can be seen as a natural extension of the industrial design process, and of the expansion of mass manufacturing in a capitalist economic system. They represent a need to move beyond product appearance to the more abstract aspects of making and selling consumer goods in large numbers. Increased competition has also meant that Italy had to develop much more sophisticated marketing strategies than the ones it used in the early days when it was out on its own. What is missing from this new emphasis, however, is the level of cultural and philosophical debate that characterized the heroic years of Italian design

Above: Stainless steel fruit bowl designed by George J. Sowden for the Swiss company, Bodum, in 1987. Many members of the original Memphis team have been approached by manufacturers in different countries for designs, often allowing them to take the Memphis imagery into the area of "quality" goods.

Right: "Antonio" side table, designed by Marco Zanuso Jnr for the Memphis group show in 1987. The elegant form of this little table in wood, metal and glass shows that Memphis no longer needs to shock, but can concentrate on renewing the language of design in an increasingly sophisticated way.

and gave it its uniqueness and its strength. Also missing is the input of the creative individual who was all-important in the early years. While designers' names are used increasingly in product advertising and the mass media, and the "designer object" plays a highly significant role in 1980s culture worldwide, this tendency has replaced the simpler notion of the designer and industry working together, as they did in Italy through the 1950s and 1960s. The widespread commodification of design and the designer has meant that a true appreciation of the creative role of the individual has perhaps been lost for ever. In many ways this is the result of the link between design and conspicuous consumption that was forged in Italy during the years of the economic miracle, and that has been so influential.

While Italy paved the way for the absorption of design and the designer into the ideology of big business, it also, it must be remembered, established an antidote to this tendency in the form of the anti-design movement of the late 1960s. More than any other design manifestation of the second half of the twentieth century, this served to re-establish, in theory at least, the essential links between design and society without the intervention of the mass manufacturing industry. Even more important was the tension created by the simultaneous and contradictory existence of both mainstream and alternative design practice.

Ironically, now that Italy is finally enjoying economic security and international prestige, there is a growing feeling that some of the means by which it has achieved its position have reached the end of their natural lifespan. The Piaggio company's decision to cease production of D'Ascanio's "Vespa" reflects the end of an era — one that was characterized by multiple crises and that in turn engendered a number of strong cultural movements, among them modern industrial design.

Left: Armchair designed by Massimo Iosa-Ghini for the Memphis group show in 1987. Innovative in form, its use of neo-Modernist materials elaborates on all the possibilities open to a designer working in a post-Functionalist era.

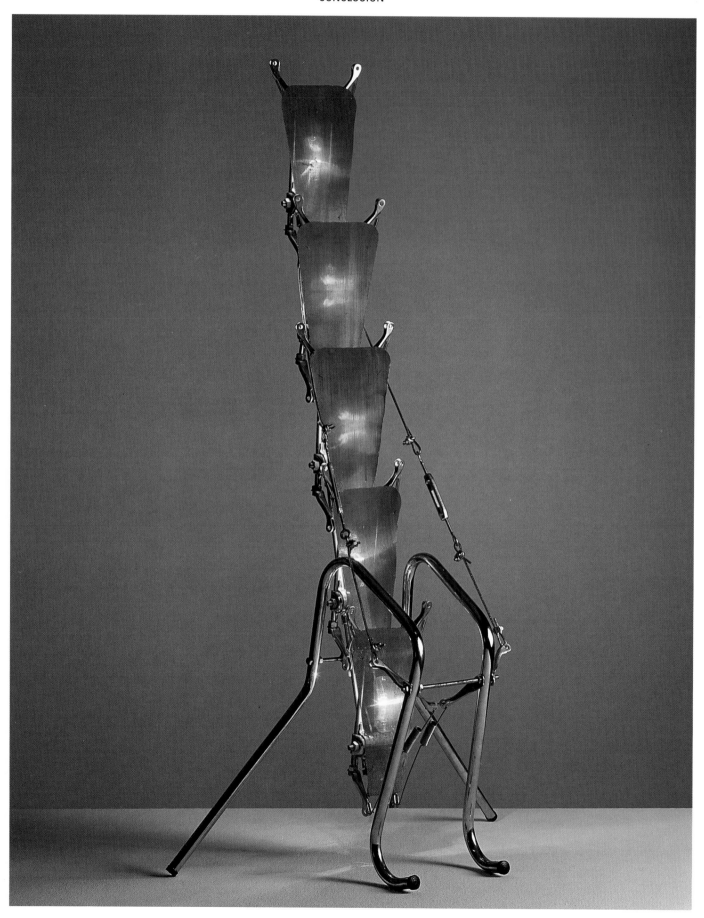

Italian style is still, of course, highly desirable, and its products are of a quality unrivalled elsewhere. It is, however, a somewhat conservative force, containing few of the youthful and ebullient qualities displayed by much of the design emerging from countries relatively new to this area, such as France and Spain. With the forty-year period since 1945 drawing to a close in Italy, the international spotlight has today been turned on Spain, in particular, as the hoped-for home of the new modern design movement. There are striking parallels with the situation in Italy at the end of the Second World War: a new democracy emerging from an age of Fascist rule; a few large-scale companies that are expanding rapidly, combined with a strong, unspoilt artisanal tradition ready to adapt to modern requirements; an optimistic attitude towards the future; a burning need to export goods to Europe; the emergence of a consumer society; and the presence of a small group of talented designers ready to respond to the challenge. Will the same formula be as successful again?

Left: Light designed by Laura Agnoletti and Marzio Rusconi Clerici for Amoroso Immago in 1987. This expressive light, made from "found" electrical, mechanical and industrial materials, is a sign that Italian design in the late 1980s is functioning within an increasingly international context. This kind of complex aesthetic, expressing a highly ambivalent approach towards the world of high technology, represents concerns that are being articulated in many different contexts and are not confined to the Italian design debate.

Below: The Fiorucci store in New York, 1976, the first foreign branch of the Milan-based fashion company. The use of Fifties revival style was characteristic of its owner's interest in popular culture and "kitsch".

NOTES

Introduction

1. Umberto Eco, "Phenomena of this sort must also be included", *Italian Re-Evolution: Design in Italian Society in the Eighties*, ed. P. Sartago, La Jolla Museum of Contemporary Art: California, 1982, p. 129.
2. "Design and the Critics", ed. P. Scarzella, *Ottagono* 81, June 1986, Milan, p. 78.

2 1915–1939 "Proto-Design": Tradition and Modernity

1. G. D. H. Cole, *Practical Economics*, Allen Lane: Harmondsworth, 1937, p. 100.
2. Martin Clark, *Modern Italy 1871–1982*, Longman History of Italy Vol. 7, Longman: Essex, 1984, p. 191.
3. Quoted in D. Merlin, *Pininfarina 1930–1983: Prestige and Tradition*, Edita: Lausanne, 1980, p. 22.
4. Quoted in R. Moss, "The Anatomy of an Image", *Industrial Design*, November 1961, New York, p. 54.
5. Pier Carlo Santini, *The Years of Italian Design: a Portrait of Cesare Cassina*, Electa: Milan, 1981, p. 9.
6. Ibid., p. 13.

3 1940–1955 "The Form of the Useful": Reconstruction and Design

1. W. D. Teague, "An Italian Shopping Trip", *Interiors*, November 1950, New York, p. 57.
2. Leopold Schreiber, "Contrasts in Current Italian Design", *Design*, July 1949, London, p. 10.
3. Ernesto N. Rogers, editorial, *Domus*, January 1946, Milan, p. 3.
4. Pier Bottoni, "The Eighth Triennale", *Domus*, July 1947, Milan, p. 32.
5. Gio Ponti, "Italy's Bid on the World Market", *Interiors*, 1953, New York, p. 79.
6. F. H. K. Henrion, "Italian Journey", *Design*, January 1949, London, p. 10.
7. J. Dunbar, "Letter from the Tenth Triennale", *Industrial Design*, October 1954, New York, p. 26.
8. Gio Ponti, "Italy's Bid on the World Market", p. 78.
9. Andrea Branzi and Michele De Lucchi, *Il Design Italiano Degli Anni '50*, IGIS: Milan, 1981, p. 29.
10. F. H. K. Henrion, "Italian Journey", p. 9.
11. Andrea Branzi and Michele De Lucchi, *Il Design Italiano*, p. 27.
12. "Design and the Critics", ed. P. Scarzella, *Ottagono* 81, June 1986, Milan, p. 79.

4 1956–1965 "The Good Life": Designing the Italian Miracle

1. Gregotti, "Italian Design 1945–1971", *Italy: The New Domestic Landscape – Achievements and Problems of Italian Design*, ed. E. Ambasz, The Museum of Modern Art: New York, 1972, p. 339.
2. Max Bill, "Forma, Funzione, Bellezza", *Stile Industria*, January 1954, Milan, p. 3.
3. Alberto Rosselli, "Industrial Design Teaching and Productive Realities", *Stile Industria*, 21, 1959, Milan, p. 1.
4. Ibid.
5. Daniele Baroni, Introduction to Tecno catalogue, 1978, p. 4.
6. Roberto Olivetti, *Stile Industria* 37, 1962, Milan, p. 21.
7. Ettore Sottsass, "How to Survive in a Company. Perhaps", unpublished lecture, 1979.

8. A term used by a number of Italian design critics in the 1960s to describe the philosophy underpinning the work of designers such as the Castiglioni brothers and Marco Zanuso, who took a particularly technological approach towards the problem of finding rational, modern forms for their objects.
9. Ettore Sottsass, "Experience with Ceramics", *Domus*, 1970, Milan, p. 7.
10. Penny Sparke, *Ettore Sottsass Jnr*, Design Council: London, 1982, p. 46.

5 1966–1975 Consumerism and Counter-Culture

1. James A. Michener, *A Michener Miscellany*, Corgi: New York, 1975, p. 325.
2. Martin Clark, *Modern Italy 1871–1982*, Longman History of Italy, Vol. 7, Longman: Essex, 1984, p. 353.
3. Ibid.
4. G. Castelli, *Kartell News* 10, September 1983, Milan, p. 1.
5. G. C. Argan, "Ideological Development in the Thought and Imagery of Italian Design", *Italy: The New Domestic Landscape*, p. 359.
6. Umberto Eco, "Phenomena of this sort must also be included", *Italian Re-Evolution: Design in Italian Society in the Eighties*, ed. P. Sartago, La Jolla Museum of Modern Art: California, 1982, p. 130.
7. Mildred S. Friedman, Introduction to *Design Quarterly* 89, 1973, Minneapolis, p. 3.
8. Ibid., p. 18.
9. Germano Celant, "Radical Architecture", *Italy: The New Domestic Landscape*, p. 282.

6 1976–1985 The New Design

1. M. J. Piore and C. F. Sabel, "Italian Small Business Development: Lessons for U.S. Industrial Policy", *American Industry in International Competition*, ed. J. Zysman and L. Tyson, New York, 1983, p. 394.
2. Ibid., p. 396.
3. Ibid., p. 399.
4. Taken from press information provided by the Organizing Committee of the Salon of Italian Furniture (COSMIT) at the 1982 International Furniture Exhibition in Milan.
5. John Haycraft, *Italian Labyrinth: an Authentic and Revealing Portrait of Italy in the 1980s*, Penguin: Harmondsworth, 1987, p. 11.
6. *Design Giugiaro: la Forma dell'Automobile*, ed. C. Gardini and M. Bugli, Automobilia: Milan, 1980, p. 126.
7. Deyan Sudjic, "The Man in the White Box", *Blueprint* 9, July–August 1984, London, p. 13.
8. Ettore Sottsass, Introduction to *Catalogue for Decorative Furniture in Modern Style 1978–1980*, Milan, 1980, pp. 1, 2.
9. Alessandro Mendini, Editorial in *Modo* 26, January–February 1980, Milan, p. 9.
10. *Memphis: the New International Style*, ed. B. Radice, Electa: Milan, 1981, p. 5.

Conclusion

1. William Scobie, "La Dolce Italia", *Observer*, Sunday 15 November, 1987, London, p. 65.
2. Ibid., p. 66.
3. Colin McDowell, "Praising the Female Form", "La Dolce Italia", p. 67.

FURTHER READING

Social, Economic and Political Background

Bagnasco, A., *Le Tre Italie*, Il Mulino: Bologna, 1977.

Barzini, L., *The Italians*, Hamish Hamilton: London, 1971.

Berger, S. and Piore, M., *Dualism and Discontinuity in Industrial Societies*, Cambridge University Press: New York, 1980.

Brusco, S., "The Emilian Model: Productive Decentralisation and Social Integration", *Cambridge Journal of Economics*, Cambridge, vol. 6, no. 2, 1982.

Buxton, J., "A Nation of Small Firms", *Design*, London, October 1983.

Cassels, A., *Fascist Italy*, The Forum Press: London, 1985.

Castronovo, V., *Economica e societa in Piemonte dall'Unita al 1914*, Mondadori: Milan, 1969.

Castronovo, V., *Giovanni Agnelli*, Einaudi: Turin, 1972.

Castronovo, V., *L'Industria italiana dall'Ottocento a oggi,*, Mondadori: Milan, 1980.

Chabod, F., *A History of Italian Fascism*, Weidenfeld and Nicolson: London, 1963.

Clark, M., *Modern Italy 1871–1982*, Longmans: London, 1984.

Clough, S. B., *The Economic History of Modern Italy*, Harper and Row: New York, 1964.

Cohn, J. "Financing industrialisation in Italy 1894–1914", *Journal of Economic History*, Cambridge, no. XXVII, 1967.

Corbini, E., *Limiti e scelta della Ricostruzione economica*, Scritti e Discorsi: Rome, 1946.

Daneo, C., *La Politica economica della Ricostruzione*, Einaudi: Turin, 1975.

D'Antonio, M., *Sviluppo e crisi del capitolismo italiano 1951–1972*, De Donato: Bari, 1973.

Graziani, A. (ed.), *L'Economica italiana: 1945–1970*, Il Mulino: Bologna, 1971.

Gringrod, M., *The Rebuilding of Italy: Politics and Economics 1945–1955*, Greenwood Press: London and New York, 1955.

Haycraft, J., *Italian Labyrinth: An Authentic and Revealing Portrait of Italy in the 1980s*, Penguin: Harmondsworth, 1987.

Hughes, H. S., *The U.S. and Italy* (3rd edition), Harvard University Press: Cambridge, Mass., 1980.

Mack Smith, D., *Italy: A Modern History*, University of Michigan Press: Ann Arbor, 1959.

Mammarella, G., *Italy after Fascism – a Political History, 1943–65*, University of Notre Dame Press: Indiana, 1966.

Melograni, P., *Fascismo e grande industria 1919–1940*, Electa: Milan, 1978.

Podbielski, G., *Italy: Development and Crisis in the Postwar Economy*, Clarendon Press: Oxford, 1974.

Piore, M. J. and Sabel, C. F., "Italian Small Business Development: Lessons for U.S. Industrial Policy", J. Zysman and L. Tyson (eds.), *American Industry in International Competition*, Cornell University Press: Ithaca, 1983.

Sabel, C. F., *Work and Politics: The Division of Labor in Industry*, Cambridge University Press: New York, 1982.

Saladino, S., *Italy from Unification to 1919: Growth and Decay of a Liberal Regime*, The Forum Press: London, 1985.

Salvati, M., *Il Sistema economico italiano: analisi di una crisi*, Il Mulino: Bologna, 1975.

Sassoon, D., *Contemporary Italy: Politics, Economy and Society since 1945*, Longmans: London and New York, 1986.

Seton Watson, C., *Italy from Liberalism to Fascism*, Methuen: London, 1967.

Tannenbaum, E. R., *Fascism in Italy*, Allen Lane: London, 1973.

Valli, V., *L'Economica e la politica economica italiana (1945–1979)*, Etas Libri: Milan, 1979.

Vivarelli, R., "Revolution and Reaction in Italy", *Journal of Italian History*, London, no. 1, 1978.

Woolf, S. J. (ed.), *The Rebirth of Italy*, Longman: London, 1972.

Twentieth-Century Design

Alfieri, B., "1939–1959: Appunti per una storia del disegno industriale in Italia", *Stile Industria*, May 1960.

Allen, B., "Italy's New Idiom", *Industrial Design*, New York, October, 1967.

Ambasz, E. (ed.), *Italy: The New Domestic Landscape*, Museum of Modern Art: New York, 1972.

Anselmi, A. T., "L'Industrial design alla Triennale", *Civiltà delle Macchine*, vol. 5, nos. 5–6, November 1957.

Anselmi, A. T. "XI Triennale dell'industrial design", *Stile Industria*, vol. 4, no. 14, October 1952.

Ballo, G., "Designers Italiens", *Ideal Standard*, vol. 7, April–May 1964.

Ballo, G., "Oggi il design: la situazione in Italia", *Rassegna – Modi di abitare oggi*, Milan, nos. 11–12, September 1970.

Branzi, A., *The Hot House: Italian New Wave Design*, Thames and Hudson: London, 1984.

Compasso d'Oro 1954–1984: Trent'anni di design italiano, Electa: Milan, 1985.

Crispolti, E., "Premesse storiche dell'industrial design", *Civiltà delle Macchine*, vol. 7, no. 2, March–April 1958.

Dunbar, J., "Letter from the Triennale", *Industrial Design*, New York, October 1954.

Edilizia Moderna, no. 85, 1964.

Fossati, P., *Il Design in Italia 1945–1972*, Einaudi: Turin, 1972.

Frateili, E., *Il Disegno industriale italiano 1928–1981 (Quasi una storia ideologica)*, Celid: Turin, 1982.

Grassi, A. and Pansera, A., *Atlante del design italiano 1940–1980*, Fabbri: Milan, 1980.

Gregotti, V., *Il Disegno del prodotto industriale: Italia 1860–1980*, Electa: Milan, 1982.

Gregotti, V., *New Directions in Italian Architecture*, New York: Braziller, 1968.

Gregotti, V., "Per una storia del design Italiano", *Ottagono*, nos. 32, 33, 34, 1974–75.

Henrion, J. F. K., "Italian Journey", *Design*, London, January 1949.

Hiesinger, K. B. and Marcius, G. H., *Design since 1945*, Thames and Hudson: London, 1983.

"Italy's Bid on the World Market", by "O.G.", *Interiors*, New York, April 1953.

Michener, J. A., "Italian Designers", *A Michener Miscellany*, Corgi: New York, 1975.

Modern Italian Design, Manchester: Manchester City Art Gallery, 1956.

Pansera, A., *Storia e cronaca della Triennale*, Longanesi: Milan, 1978.

Pica, A., *Forme nuove in Italia*, Bestetti: Milan and Rome, 1957 and 1962.

Pica, A., *Storia della Triennale 1918–1957*, Il Milione: Milan, 1957.

Premio Compasso d'Oro ADI 1970, Sisar: Milan, 1971.

Sartago, P., *Italian Re-Evolution: Design in Italian Society in the Eighties*, Museum of Contemporary Art: La Jolla, California, 1982.

Schreiber, L., "Contrasts in Current Italian Design", *Design*, London, July 1949.

Taborelli, G. and Fagone, V. (eds.), *Disegno italiano*, Silvana: Milan, 1979.

Teague, W. D., "An Italian Shopping Trip", *Interiors*, New York, November 1950.

Manufacturing Industries

Arflex '51 '81, Lucini: Milan, 1981.

Allen, D., "Olivetti of Ivrea", *Interiors*, New York, December 1952.

Banham, R., "Fiat: the Phantom of Order", *New Society*, London, 18 April 1985.

Burckhardt, F. (ed.), *Cibi e Riti*, Alessi: Crusanallo, 1981.

Casciani, S., *Mobili come architettura: il disegno della produzione Zanotta*, Arcadia: Milan, 1985.

Colombini, G., "Casalinghi Kartell", *Stile Industria*, no. 19, 1958.

Design Process: Olivetti 1908–1983, Olivetti: Milan, 1983.

Mastropietro, M. (ed.), *An Industry for Design: the Research, Designers and Corporate Image of B & B Italia*, Edizione Lybra Immagire: Milan, 1986.

Mendini, A., *Paesaggio casalingo: la produzione Alessi nell'industria dei casalinghi dal 1921 al 1980*, Editoriale Domus: Milan, 1979.

Moss, R., "The Anatomy of an Image", *Industrial Design*, New York, November 1961.

Santini, P. C., *The Years of Italian Design: a Portrait of Cesare Cassina*, Electa: Milan, 1981.

Scarzella, P., *Il Bel metallo: storia dei casalinghi nobili Alessi*, Arcadia: Milan, 1985.

Sudjic, D., "Man in a White Box", *Blueprint*, London, July–August 1984.

Thomas, M. H., "Design Policy begins at the Top", *Design*, London, February 1950.

Individual Designers

Alfieri, B. and Ferruccio, B., *Pininfarina*, La Rinascente: Milan, 1958.

Celant, G., *Marcello Nizzoli*, Comunita: Milan, 1968.

Di Castro, F. (ed.), *Sottsass's Scrapbook*, Documenti di Casabella: Milan, 1976.

Dorfles, G., *Marco Zanuso*, Editalia: Rome, 1971.

Ferrari, P., *Achille Castiglioni*, Electa: Milan, 1984.

Gardini, G. and Bugli, M. (eds.), *Design Giugiaro: la forma dell'automobile*, Automobilia: Milan, 1980.

Labro, M., *Gio Ponti*, La Rinascente: Milan, 1958.

McCarty, C., *Mario Bellini: Designer*, Museum of Modern Art: New York, 1987.

Merlin, D., *Pininfarina 1900–1930: Prestige and Tradition*, Edita: Lausanne, 1980.

Piva, A., *BBPR a Milano*, Electa: Milan, 1982.

Radice, B. (ed.), *Ettore Sottsass: Design Metaphors*, Idea Books: Milan, 1987.

Santini, P. C., "Introduzione ad Ettore Sottsass", *Zodiac*, Milan, no. 11, 1963.

Santini, P. C., "Marcello Nizzoli: Designer", *Notizie Olivetti*, no. 71, April 1961.

Sparke, P., "A Peasant Genius", *Design*, London, June 1981.

Sparke, P., *Ettore Sottsass Jnr*, Design Council: London, 1982.

Sparke, P., "In Praise of the Banal", *Design*, London, July 1981.

Sudjic, D., "Sottsass and Co", *Crafts*, London, November–December 1987.

Tanchis, A., *Bruno Munari: from Futurism to Post-Industrial Design*, Lund Humphries: London, 1987.

Tomasso, T., "Enzo Mari", *Domus*, no. 458, January 1968.

Zevi, B. (ed.), *Giuseppe Terragni*, Zanichelli: Bologna, 1980.

Writings by Designers

Albini, F., "Dibattito sulla tradizione in architettura", *Casabella*, 206, 1955.

Archigram Associati, "La distruzione degli oggetti", *IN: Argomenti e immagini del design*, vol. 2, nos. 2–3, March–June 1971.

Archigram Associati, "Le stanze vuote i gazebi", *Domus*, no. 462, May 1968.

Bellini, M., "Superfici e tensione costante discorso sulla topologia delle membrane elastiche", *Lineastrutture*, vol. 1, no. 1, 1966.

Branzi, A., *Domestic Animals: the Neoprimitive Style*, Thames and Hudson: London, 1987.

Branzi, A., *Moderno, Postmoderno, Millenario: scritti teorica 1972–80*, Studio Forma: Milan, 1980.

Castiglioni, A., "Le dessin industriel italien", *Architecture d'aujourd'hui*, Paris, no. 48, 1963.

Castiglioni, A., "Analisi e guidizi sul design", *Edilizia Moderna*, no. 85, 1965.

Castiglioni, L., "Radio e TV: due storie parallele", *Stile Industria*, no. 11, April 1957.

Castiglioni, R. (ed.), *Ettore Sottsass: esercizio formale*, Alessi: Crusanallo, 1979.

De Angeles, A., "Design Note", *IN: Argomenti e immagini del design*, no. 12, January 1974.

Mari, E., *Funzione della ricerca estetica*, Comunita: Milan, 1970.

Mendini, A., "Le avanguardia del design italiano", *Modo*, no. 28, April 1980.

Mendini, A., "Radical design", *Casabella*, no. 267, 1972.

Mendini, A., "Storia dell'industrial design", *Gatto Selvatico*, Rome, 1962.

Munari, B., *Design e comunicazione visuale: contributo a una metodologia didattica*, Laterza: Bari, 1968.

Munari, B., "Design in plastica", *Mobilia*, Copenhagen, November 1970.

Onck, A. Van, "Didattica del design e design della didattica", *Casabella*, vol. 24, nos. 350–51, July–August 1970.

Rossi, A., *La conica ed altre caffettiere*, Alessi: Crusanallo, 1984.

Sottsass, E., "Automazione e design", *Stile Industria*, vol. 9, no. 37, March 1962.

Sottsass, E., *Catalogue for Decorating Furniture in Modern Style 1979–80*, Studio Forma: Milan, 1980.

Sottsass, E., "Conversations with Designers", *Design*, London, January 1974.

Sottsass, E., "Could Anything be More Ridiculous?", *Design*, London, no. 262, 1970.

Sottsass, E., "Experience with Ceramics", *Domus*, no. 489, Milan, 1970.

Sottsass, E., "Memoires di panna montana", *Domus*, no. 445, December 1966, and no. 472, March 1969.

Zanuso, M., *1971 Dunhill Industrial Design Lectures*, Trevor Wilson: Melbourne, 1971.

Design Theory

Argan, C. G., "Arte, artigianato, industrial", *Comunita*, vol. 3, no. 5, September–October 1949.

Argan, C. G., "Disegno industriale", *Notizie Olivetti*, Ivrea, no. 71, April 1961.

Argan, C. G., "Industrial design come fattore dello integrazione sociale", *Aut–aut*, no. 24, 1954.

Argan, C. G., "Planning e design", *Civiltà delle Macchine*, vol. 2, no. 6, November 1954.

Bill, M., "Forma, funzione, bellezza", *Stile Industria*, no. 3, 1954.

Bonsiepe, G., "Panorama del disegno industriale", *Lineastrutture*, no. 21, May 1971.

Bonsiepe, G., *Teoria e pratica del disegno industriale*, Feltrinelli: Milan, 1975.

Castelli, C. T., *Il Lingotto primario*, Arcadia: Milan, 1985.

Cetica, T., *La Funzione sociale dell'industrial design*, Fiorentina: Florence, 1983.

Ciribini, G., "Per una didattica dell'industrial design", *Superfici*, vol. 1, nos. 2–3, May–September 1961.

Colombo, F., "Consumi, comfort e idola nella societa opulenta: la casa della middle class", *Casabella continuata*, vol. 27, no. 281, November 1963.

Della Volpe, G., *Critica del gusto*, Feltrinelli: Milan, 1960.

Dorfles, G., "Evoluzione del concetti di industrial design", *Stile Industria*, vol. 3, no. 7, January 1956.

Dorfles, G., *Il Disegno industriale e la sua estetica*, Cappelli: Bologna, 1965.

Dorfles, G., "Il futuro del disegno industriale", *Ideal Standard*, vol. 7, April–May 1964.

Dorfles, G., "La professione del designer", *Design Italia*, no. 2, 1966.

Dorfles, G., *Le Oscillazione del gusto*, Lerici: Milan, 1958.

Dorfles, G., *Simboli, comunicazione, consumo*, Einaudi: Turin, 1962.

Eco, U., "Cultura di massa ed evoluzione della cultura", *De Homine*, Rome, vol. 2, nos. 5–6, June 1963.

Eco, U., "Dal cucchiaio alla città", *L'Espresso*, no. 23, 1972.

Eco, U., *Opera aperta*, Editalia: Rome, 1971.

Frateili, E., "Fortuna e crisi del design italiano", *Zodiac*, no. 20, December 1970.

Frateili, E., "La produzione d'arte e l'industrial design", *Comunita*, vol. 11, no. 53, October 1957.

Frateili, E., "Lo sviluppo della capacità creative nelle scuole di 'design'", *Stile Industria*, no. 19, 1958.

Maldonado, T., *Avanguardia e razionalità*, Einaudi: Turin, 1974.

Maldonado, T., *Disegno industriale: un riesame*, Feltrinelli: Milan, 1976.

Maldonado, T., "Il disegno industriale come professione e come problema educativo", *Superfici*, vol. 1, no. 4, November–December 1961.

Maldonado, T., "La nuova funzione dell'industrial design", *Casabella*, vol. 30, no. 303, March 1966.

Maldonado, T., *La Speranza progettuale: ambiente e società*, Einaudi: Turin, 1970.

Marcolli, A., "Disegno industriale", *Superfici*, no. 1–2, 1961.

Menna, F. (ed.), *Industrial design (quarderni di "Arte oggi")*, Villar: Rome, 1962.

Paci, E., "Quantità e qualità", *Civiltà delle Macchine*, vol. 1, no. 6, November 1953.

Radice, B., *Elogia del banale*, Studio Forma: Milan, 1980.

Rogers, E. N., "Programma: Domus, la casa dell'uomo", *Domus*, vol. 19, no. 205, January 1946.

Rosselli, A., "Industrial Design Teaching and Productive Realities", *Stile Industria*, no. 21, 1959.

Spadolini, P. L., *Design e società*, Le Monnier: Florence, 1969.

Tedeschi, P., *Il Disegno industriale*, Calderini: Bologna, 1965.

Tintori, S., *Cultura del design: un profilo dell'arte e della tecnica nella storia della civiltà*, Tamburini: Milan, 1964.

Period Styles and Design Movements

Assunto, R., "La crisi del design", *Lo Botte e il Violino*, vol. 2, no. 2, March 1968.

Baacke, R. P., Brandes, U. and Erlhoff, M., *Design als Gegenstand: der Neue Glanz der Dinge*, Frolich und Kaufmann: Berlin, 1983.

Branzi, A. and De Lucchi, M., *Il Design italiano degli anni '50*, IGIS: Milan, 1981.

Dansi, S. and Patetta, L., *Rationalisme et architecture en Italie*, Electa: Milan, 1976.

De Seta, C., *La Cultura architettonica in Italia fra le due guerre*, Laterza: Milan, 1978.

"Dibattito sulla Triennale", *Casabella*, no. 333, February 1969.

Gardiner, S., "Coffee bars", *Architectural Review*, London, September 1955.

Gregotti, V., "1918–1940: Novecento, razionalismo e la produzione industriale", *Ottagono*, no. 36, 1975.

Jencks, C., "The New International Style", *Domus*, no. 623, December 1981.

Jencks, C., "The Supersensualists", *Architectural Design*, London, June 1971 and January 1972.

Michail, M. C. T., "Da 'Stile' a 'Stile Industria': la cultura dell'oggetti negli anni Quaranta", *Ottagono*, no. 66.

Navone, P. and Orlandini, B., *Architettura "Radicale"*, Documenti di Casabella: Milan, 1974.

Radice, B., *Memphis: Research, Experience, Result, Failures and Successes of New Design*, Rizzoli: New York, 1985.

Radice, B., *Memphis: the New International Style*, Electa: Milan, 1981.

Raggi, F., "Radical Story", *Casabella*, no. 382, October 1973.

Rogers, M. R., *Italy at Work: her Renaissance in Design Today*, Compagnia Nazionale Artigiana: Rome, 1950.

Sparke, P., "The New Avant-garde in Italian Furniture", *Mobilia*, Copenhagen, no. 303, 1981.

Vercelloni, I., *1970–1980 Dal Design al Post-Design*, Casa Vogue: Milan, 1980.

Veronesi, G., *Stile 1925: Ascesa e caduta delle arti deco*, Vallecchi: Florence, 1978.

Woudhuysen, J. and Sudjic, D., "The New International Style", *Design*, London, November 1981.

Materials and Design

Baroni, D., "La plastica; una rivoluzione incompiuta", *Ottagono*, no. 55, 1979.

Dorfles, G. "Estetica del mobile metallico", *Civiltà delle Macchine*, no. 5, 1955.

The Materials of Design, Rassegna: June, 1983.

Plastiche e Design, Arcadia: Milan, 1985.

Zanuso, M., Piano, R. and Lucci, R., *Elementi di tecnologia dei materiale come introduzione allo studio del design*, Tamburini: Milan, 1967.

Design Media

Furniture and Interior Design

Aloi, R., *L'arredamento moderno*, Hoepli: Milan, 1955.

Aloi, R., *Esempi di arredamenti moderni*, Hoepli: Milan, 1957.

Aloi, R., *Mobili tipo*, Hoepli: Milan, 1956.

Bangert, A., *Italienisches Möbeldesign: Klassiker von 1945 bis 1985*, CIP: Munich, 1985.

Baroni, D., *L'oggetti lampada: forma e funzione*, Electa: Milan, 1981.

Bossaglia, R., *Il Mobile Liberty*, Instituto Geografico de Agostina: Novara, 1971.

Forma e colore nell'arredamento moderno, Gorlich: Milan, 1967.

"Il disegno del mobili razionale in Italia 1928–48", *Rassegna*, 4 October 1980.

Leonardi, S., *Produzione e consumo dei mobili per abitazione in Italia*, Feltrinelli: Milan, 1959.

Massoni, L., *Made in Italy: Mobili, illuminazione, complementi di arredamento*, Mondadori: Milan, 1986.

Transport

Anselmi, A. T. (ed.), *Carrozzeria Italiana: Advancing the Art and Science of Automobile Design*, Automobilia: Milan, 1980.

Fusi, L., *Le vetture Alfa Romeo dall 1910*, Electa: Milan, 1966.

Haslam, M., Garner, P., Harvey, M. and Conway, H., *The Amazing Bugattis*, Royal College of Art: London, 1979.

Hebdige, D., "Object as Image: The Italian Scooter Cycle", *Block*, London, no. 5, 1981.

Stevans, J., "The Romance of the Scooter", *Scooter World*, London, February 1972.

Fashion

Italian Fashion: The Origins of High Fashion and Knitwear, vol. I; *From Anti-fashion to Stylism*, vol. II, Electa: Milan 1987.

Malossi, G., *Liberti tutti: 20 anni di moda spettacola*, Mondadori: Milan, 1987.

Mulassano, A., *Il Mass Modo–Fatti e personaggi dell'Italian look*, Electa: Milan, 1979.

Phillips, K., *Italian Footwear Through the Ages*, ANCI: Milan, 1979.

Ceramics

Mostra della ceramica italiana 1920–1940, Turin: Palazzo Nervi, 1982.

Products

Prina, A. M. (ed.), *Cucina e cultura*, Idea Books: Milan, 1984.

Periodicals

Abitare, Milan, from 1962
Casabella, Milan, from 1929
Casa Vogue, Milan, from 1968
Civiltà delle Macchine, Turin, from 1953
Comunità, Milan, from 1966
Domus, Milan, from 1928
Edilizia Moderna, Milan, from 1950
Ideal Standard, Milan, from 1959
Il Mobile Italiano, Milan, 1957–60
IN: Argomenti e immagini del design, Milan, 1971–74
Interni, Milan, from 1954
La Casa, Rome, 1955–61
Lo Stile, Milan, 1941–47
Modo, Milan, from 1977
Ottagono, Milan, from 1966
Pirelli, Milan, 1948–72
Rassegna, Milan, from 1966
Stile Industria, Milan, 1954–63
Zodiac, Milan, from 1959

MAJOR EXHIBITIONS

Modern Italian Design
City Art Gallery, Manchester, 1956.

Italy: The New Domestic Landscape
Museum of Modern Art, New York, 1972.

Ettore Sottsass Jnr, de l'Objet Fini à la Fin de l'Objet
Centre de Création Industrielle, Paris, 1976.

Ettore Sottsass Jnr
The Israel Museum, Jerusalem, 1978.

Memphis
The Boilerhouse Project, London, 1981–82.

Gli Anni Trenta: Arte e Cultura in Italia
Palazzo Reale, Milan, 1982.

Mostra della Ceramica Italiana 1920–1940
Palazzo Nervi, Turin, 1982.

INDEX

Numbers in **Bold** refer to main entries.
Numbers in *Italics* refer to picture captions.

237